Albert Kenrick Fisher

Report on the Ornithology of the Death Valley Expedition of 1891

Albert Kenrick Fisher

Report on the Ornithology of the Death Valley Expedition of 1891

ISBN/EAN: 9783744670234

Printed in Europe, USA, Canada, Australia, Japan

Cover: Foto ©Andreas Hilbeck / pixelio.de

More available books at **www.hansebooks.com**

REPORT ON THE ORNITHOLOGY OF THE DEATH VALLEY EXPEDITION OF 1891, COMPRISING NOTES ON THE BIRDS OBSERVED IN SOUTHERN CALIFORNIA, SOUTHERN NEVADA, AND PARTS OF ARIZONA AND UTAH.

By A. K. FISHER, M. D.

The present report includes an enumeration of all the birds observed throughout the region traversed by the different members of the expedition. It was considered advisable to unite all the observations in one general report rather than attempt to treat of the avifauna of special localities in a number of separate papers. At the same time a few local lists may be found under particular areas in Part I.

A number of side trips were made to special localities by small parties, which not only materially increased the observations on the birds already met with, but also added a number of species to the list. Among these trips may be mentioned one made by Dr. Merriam and Mr. Bailey, who extended their observations as far east as St. George, Utah. They were thereby enabled to add valuable notes on several of the birds of the Great Basin not seen elsewhere. After the main party had disbanded in the fall, a trip was made by Mr. Nelson along the coast from San Simeon to Carpenteria, and one to Monterey by Mr. Bailey, which resulted in partially filling up a wide gap among the water birds.

Owing to the unusual interest shown in matters relating to Death Valley, and to the entire absence of reliable information concerning the species inhabiting this area, it seemed best to append a special list of the birds observed there, with brief annotations. This list is believed to be reasonably complete, since the valley was visited by one or more members of the expedition every month except May, from January to June inclusive. A list of the species found in Owens Valley is added for comparison. (See pp. 150–158.)

The known ranges of a number of species were much extended by the expedition, notably in the cases of *Oreortyx pictus plumiferus*, *Dryobates scalaris bairdi*, *Chordeiles texensis*, *Pyrocephalus rubineus mexicanus*, *Calypte costæ*, *Icterus parisorum*, *Leucosticte tephrocotis*, *Junco hyemalis thurberi*, *Spizella atrigularis*, *Peucæa cassini*, *Harporhynchus lecontei*, and a few others; and the distribution of many better-known species was more definitely determined.

The known range of the plumed quail (*Oreortyx pictus plumiferus*) was carried eastward from the eastern slope of the Sierra Nevada to Mount Magruder, Nevada, and to all the desert ranges of southern California west of Death Valley. This valley apparently limits the distribution of this bird on the east, as the species was nowhere seen in the Grapevine or Charleston mountains, although both ranges are well timbered and bear brush which might afford suitable food and shelter.

Baird's woodpecker (*Dryobates scalaris bairdi*) was quite common among the tree yuccas on the Mohave Desert at Hesperia, and its range was extended northward to Vegas Valley, Nevada, and the valley of the Santa Clara, in southwestern Utah, by Dr. Merriam. The vermilion flycatcher also was secured in the same valley, though previously unknown north of Fort Mohave, Ariz. The Texas nighthawk (*Chordeiles texensis*) was found to be a common summer resident in all the valleys east of the Sierra Nevada from Owens Valley, California, to St. George, Utah, where Dr. Merriam secured the eggs. It was taken also in the San Joaquin Valley, California, near Bakersfield. Scott's oriole (*Icterus parisorum*) is another species whose range was carried northward from a short distance above our southern border in California to about latitude 38°, where it was common in places among the tree yuccas, and also on the slopes of some of the desert ranges as high as the junipers and piñons. Along the northern line of distribution it was found in Nevada at the Queen mine in the White Mountains, at Mount Magruder, and in the Juniper Mountains, and in Utah in the Beaverdam Mountains. Costa's humming bird (*Calypte costæ*) was very common wherever water occurred throughout the desert region, ranging northward nearly to latitude 38°, and eastward to the Beaverdam Mountains, Utah. Its nest was frequently found in the low bushes and cactuses on the hillsides near springs and streams.

The discovery that the gray-crowned finch (*Leucosticte tephrocotis*) breeds in the southern Sierra and in the White Mountains is especially interesting both because its breeding range was previously unknown, and because no species of the genus had been recorded from the Sierra Nevada south of about latitude 40°, while the present species was common nearly to the 36th parallel.

Most satisfactory results were accomplished in working out the distribution of Thurber's junco (*Junco hyemalis thurberi*), a recently described race whose range was not definitely known. In the Sierra Nevada it was common from the Yosemite Valley, the most northern point visited by any member of the expedition, to the southern end of the range, and in the desert ranges eastward to the Grapevine and Charleston mountains, where its place was occupied, in winter at least, by its more eastern representative, Shufeldt's junco. The little black-chinned sparrow (*Spizella atrigularis*) was found to be not an uncommon summer resident on the slopes of several of the desert ranges and also on the east slope of the Sierra Nevada as far north as Independence Creek in Kearsarge Pass. This was a great surprise, as heretofore the species has been recorded within our limits only along the southern border, and its presence was not suspected until a specimen was taken in the Panamint Mountains in April.

LeConte's thrasher (*Harporhynchus lecontei*), contrary to our expectations, was a common resident throughout the principal desert valleys from Owens Valley at the east foot of the Sierra Nevada across southern California and Nevada to southwestern Utah, where it was found nearly to the summit of the Beaverdam Mountains. Northward it was observed in Owens Valley almost to Benton, a short distance south of the 38th parallel. It was also taken by Mr. Nelson in the southern part of the San Joaquin Valley, California, about Buena Vista Lake.

The bird life of a region is materially affected by various agencies, such as changes in the character of the country brought about by the destruction of forests, the drying up of springs and water courses, and other causes. But in the High Sierra the sheep industry is doing more than anything else to make that region uninhabitable for certain species of birds and also for other forms of life, as long since pointed out by Mr. Henshaw (Appendix JJ, Annual Report of the Chief of Engineers for 1876, p. 225). During the summer the sheep almost totally destroy all the smaller plants and shrubs which, except in the wet meadows, do not grow again until the following spring. The writer has walked for miles along the hillsides where these animals had recently grazed without seeing a plant of any description save the larger woody shrubs. That the destruction of vegetation by sheep in this region is a potent cause of the scarcity of ground-inhabiting birds is evident by contrast to anyone visiting the national parks where no sheep are allowed to graze and where the vegetation is consequently uninjured and many species of birds abundant.

One member of the expedition, Mr. Vernon Bailey, traversed the Virgin Valley in southwestern Utah and eastern Nevada and the Detrital and Sacramento valleys, Arizona, during the winter of 1888–'89. His notes on several of the birds observed are incorporated in the present report.

With few exceptions it was thought better not to include matter from published reports partially covering the same region, since most of this material has been republished already in Mr. Belding's Land Birds of the Pacific Coast District.

In the following report 290 species and subspecies of birds are dwelt upon at greater or less length. The nomenclature adopted is that of the American Ornithologists' Union.

The writer wishes to extend his sincere thanks to all members of the expedition who assisted in collecting specimens or information for the present report. He wishes also to acknowledge the kindness of Mr. L. Belding, who furnished data on certain birds observed by him during a short trip to the Yosemite National Park in June, 1891. In all important instances credit is given to the observer under the head of each species.

Without this substantial help, so freely given, little more than a fragmentary report would have been possible.

LIST OF BIRDS.

1. Æchmophorus occidentalis.
2. Colymbus nigricollis californicus.
3. Podilymbus podiceps.
4. Urinator imber.
5. Urinator pacificus.
6. Urinator lumme.
7. Uria troile californica.
8. Larus glaucescens.
9. Larus californicus.
10. Larus delawarensis.
11. Larus heermanni.
12. Larus philadelphia.
13. Sterna maxima.
14. Phalacrocorax dilophus albociliatus.
15. Phalacrocorax penicillatus.
16. Phalacrocorax pelagicus resplendens.
17. Pelecanus erythrorhynchos.
18. Pelecanus californicus.
19. Merganser americanus.
20. Merganser serrator.
21. Anas boschas.
22. Anas strepera.
23. Anas americana.
24. Anas carolinensis.
25. Anas discors.
26. Anas cyanoptera.
27. Spatula clypeata.
28. Dafila acuta.
29. Aythya americana.
30. Aythya vallisneria.
31. Aythya collaris.
32. Glaucionetta clangula americana.
33. Charitonetta albeola.
34. Histrionicus histrionicus.
35. Oidemia americana.
36. Oidemia perspicillata.
37. Erismatura rubida.
38. Chen hyperborea.
39. Anser albifrons gambeli.
40. Branta canadensis hutchinsii.
41. Branta canadensis occidentalis.
42. Dendrocygna fulva.
43. Plegadis guarauna.
44. Botaurus lentiginosus.
45. Ardea herodias.
46. Ardea egretta.
47. Ardea virescens.
48. Nycticorax nycticorax nævius.
49. Grus canadensis.
50. Rallus virginianus.
51. Porzana carolina.
52. Fulica americana.
53. Phalaropus tricolor.
54. Recurvirostra americana.
55. Himantopus mexicanus.
56. Gallinago delicata.
57. Tringa minutilla.
58. Ereunetes occidentalis.
59. Calidris arenaria.
60. Limosa fedoa.
61. Totanus melanoleucus.
62. Symphemia semipalmata inornata.
63. Heteractitis incanus.
64. Actitis macularia.
65. Numenius longirostris.
66. Numenius hudsonicus.
67. Charadrius squatarola.
68. Ægialitis vocifera.
69. Ægialitis nivosa.
70. Ægialitis montana.
71. Oreortyx pictus plumiferus.
72. Callipepla californica.
73. Callipepla californica vallicola.
74. Callipepla gambeli.
75. Dendragapus obscurus fuliginosus.
76. Centrocercus urophasianus.
77. Columba fasciata.
78. Zenaidura macroura.
79. Pseudogryphus californianus.
80. Cathartes aura.
81. Elanus leucurus.
82. Circus hudsonius.
83. Accipiter velox.
84. Accipiter cooperi.
85. Accipiter atricapillus striatulus.
86. Buteo borealis calurus.
87. Buteo lineatus elegans.
88. Buteo swainsoni.
89. Archibuteo ferrugineus.
90. Aquila chrysaëtos.
91. Haliæetus leucocephalus.
92. Falco mexicanus.
93. Falco peregrinus anatum.
94. Falco columbarius.
95. Falco sparverius deserticolus.
96. Pandion haliaëtus carolinensis.
97. Strix pratincola.
98. Asio wilsonianus.
99. Asio accipitrinus.
100. Syrnium occidentale.

LIST OF BIRDS—Continued.

101. *Megascops asio bendirei.*
102. *Bubo virginianus subarcticus.*
103. *Speotyto cunicularia hypogæa.*
104. *Geococcyx californianus.*
105. *Coccyzus americanus occidentalis.*
106. *Ceryle alcyon.*
107. *Dryobates villosus hyloscopus.*
108. *Dryobates pubescens gairdnerii.*
109. *Dryobates scalaris bairdi.*
110. *Dryobates nuttallii.*
111. *Xenopicus albolarvatus.*
112. *Sphyrapicus varius nuchalis.*
113. *Sphyrapicus ruber.*
114. *Sphyrapicus thyroideus.*
115. *Ceophlœus pileatus.*
116. *Melanerpes formicivorous bairdi.*
117. *Melanerpes torquatus.*
118. *Melanerpes uropygialis.*
119. *Colaptes cafer.*
120. *Phalænoptilus nuttalli.*
121. *Phalænoptilus nuttalli californicus.*
122. *Chordeiles virginianus henryi.*
123. *Chordeiles texensis.*
124. *Cypseloides niger.*
125. *Chætura vauxi.*
126. *Aëronautes melanoleucus.*
127. *Trochilus alexandri.*
128. *Calypte costæ.*
129. *Calypte anna.*
130. *Selasphorus platycercus.*
131. *Selasphorus rufus.*
132. *Stellula calliope.*
133. *Tyrannus tyrannus.*
134. *Tyrannus verticalis.*
135. *Tyrannus vociferans.*
136. *Myiarchus cinerascens.*
137. *Sayornis saya.*
138. *Sayornis nigricans.*
139. *Contopus borealis.*
140. *Contopus richardsonii.*
141. *Empidonax difficilis.*
142. *Empidonax pusillus.*
143. *Empidonax hammondi.*
144. *Empidonax wrightii.*
145. *Pyrocephalus rubineus mexicanus.*
146. *Otocoris alpestris arenicola.*
147. *Otocoris alpestris chrysolæma.*
148. *Pica pica hudsonica.*
149. *Pica nuttalli.*
150. *Cyanocitta stelleri.*
151. *Cyanocitta stelleri frontalis.*
152. *Aphelocoma woodhousei.*
153. *Aphelocoma californica.*
154. *Corvus corax sinuatus.*
155. *Corvus americanus.*
156. *Picicorvus columbianus.*
157. *Cyanocephalus cyanocephalus.*
158. *Molothrus ater.*
159. *Xanthocephalus xanthocephalus.*
160. *Agelaius phœniceus.*
161. *Agelaius gubernator.*
162. *Sturnella magna neglecta.*
163. *Icterus parisorum.*
164. *Icterus bullocki.*
165. *Scolecophagus cyanocephalus.*
166. *Coccothraustes vespertinus.*
167. *Pinicola enucleator.*
168. *Carpodacus purpureus californicus.*
169. *Carpodacus cassini.*
170. *Carpodacus mexicanus frontalis.*
171. *Loxia curvirostra stricklandi.*
172. *Leucosticte tephrocotis.*
173. *Leucosticte atrata.*
174. *Spinus tristis.*
175. *Spinus psaltria.*
176. *Spinus psaltria arizonæ.*
177. *Spinus lawrencei.*
178. *Spinus pinus.*
179. *Poocætes gramineus confinis.*
180. *Ammodramus sandwichensis alaudinus.*
181. *Ammodramus sandwichensis bryanti.*
182. *Chondestes grammacus strigatus.*
183. *Zonotrichia leucophrys.*
184. *Zonotrichia leucophrys intermedia.*
185. *Zonotrichia leucophrys gambeli.*
186. *Zonotrichia coronata.*
187. *Zonotrichia albicollis.*
188. *Spizella monticola ochracea.*
189. *Spizella socialis arizonæ.*
190. *Spizella breweri.*
191. *Spizella atrigularis.*
192. *Junco hyemalis.*
193. *Junco hyemalis shufeldti.*
194. *Junco hyemalis thurberi.*
195. *Junco pinosus.*
196. *Amphispiza bilineata.*
197. *Amphispiza belli.*
198. *Amphispiza belli nevadensis.*
199. *Peucæa cassini.*
200. *Peucæa ruficeps.*
201. *Melospiza fasciata fallax.*
202. *Melospiza fasciata montana.*
203. *Melospiza fasciata heermanni.*
204. *Melospiza fasciata guttata.*
205. *Melospiza fasciata rufina.*
206. *Melospiza fasciata graminea.*
207. *Melospiza lincolni.*
208. **Passerella iliaca unalaschcensis.**

LIST OF BIRDS—Continued.

209. *Passerella iliaca megarhyncha.*
210. *Passerella iliaca schistacea.*
211. *Pipilo maculatus megalonyx.*
212. *Pipilo maculatus oregonus.*
213. *Pipilo chlorurus.*
214. *Pipilo fuscus mesoleucus.*
215. *Pipilo fuscus crissalis.*
216. *Pipilo aberti.*
217. *Habia melanocephala.*
218. *Guiraca cærulea eurhyncha.*
219. *Passerina amœna.*
220. *Calamospiza melanocorys.*
221. *Piranga ludoviciana.*
222. *Piranga hepatica.*
223. *Progne subis hesperia.*
224. *Petrochelidon lunifrons.*
225. *Chelidon erythrogaster.*
226. *Tachycineta bicolor.*
227. *Tachycineta thalassina.*
228. *Clivicola riparia.*
229. *Stelgidopteryx serripennis.*
230. *Ampelis cedrorum.*
231. *Phainopepla nitens.*
232. *Lanius ludovicianus excubitorides.*
233. *Vireo gilvus swainsoni.*
234. *Vireo solitarius cassini.*
235. *Vireo solitarius plumbeus.*
236. *Vireo bellii pusillus.*
237. *Vireo vicinior.*
238. *Helminthophila luciæ.*
239. *Helminthophila ruficapilla gutturalis.*
240. *Helminthophila celata lutescens.*
241. *Dendroica æstiva.*
242. *Dendroica auduboni.*
243. *Dendroica nigrescens.*
244. *Dendroica townsendi.*
245. *Dendroica occidentalis.*
246. *Siurus noveboracensis notabilis.*
247. *Geothlypis macgillivrayi.*
248. *Geothlypis trichas occidentalis.*
249. *Icteria virens longicauda.*
250. *Sylvania pusilla pileolata.*
251. *Anthus pennsylvanicus.*
252. *Cinclus mexicanus.*
253. *Oroscoptes montanus.*
254. *Mimus polyglottos.*
255. *Harporhynchus redivivus.*
256. *Harporhynchus lecontei.*
257. *Harporhynchus crissalis.*
258. *Helcodytes brunneicapillus.*
259. *Salpinctes obsoletus.*
260. *Catherpes mexicanus conspersus.*
261. *Thryothorus bewickii spilurus.*
262. *Thryothorus bewickii bairdi.*
263. *Troglodytes aëdon aztecus.*
264. *Cistothorus palustris paludicola.*
265. *Certhia familiaris occidentalis.*
266. *Sitta carolinensis aculeata.*
267. *Sitta canadensis.*
268. *Sitta pygmæa.*
269. *Parus inornatus.*
270. *Parus inornatus griseus.*
271. *Parus gambeli.*
272. *Parus rufescens neglectus.*
273. *Chamæa fasciata henshawi.*
274. *Psaltriparus minimus californicus.*
275. *Psaltriparus plumbeus.*
276. *Auriparus flaviceps.*
277. *Regulus satrapa olivaceus.*
278. *Regulus calendula.*
279. *Polioptila cærulea obscura.*
280. *Polioptila plumbea.*
281. *Polioptila californica.*
282. *Myadestes townsendii.*
283. *Turdus ustulatus.*
284. *Turdus ustulatus swainsonii.*
285. *Turdus aonalaschkæ.*
286. *Turdus aonalaschkæ auduboni.*
287. *Merula migratoria propinqua.*
288. *Hesperocichla nævia.*
289. *Sialia mexicana.*
290. *Sialia arctica.*

Æchmophorus occidentalis. Western Grebe.

The western grebe was seen only in the San Joaquin Valley, where Mr. Nelson observed a few at Buena Vista Lake, in October.

Colymbus nigricollis californicus. Eared Grebe.

The eared grebe was found in most of the larger ponds or lakes throughout the region visited by the expedition. At Owens Lake, Calif., large flocks were seen as late as the middle of June. Hundreds of dead ones were observed along the shore, where they were drifted by the wind. The writer counted the bodies found within the limits of a given distance, and estimated the total for the entire lake shore

as 35,000. One of two causes, or both combined, must account for the death of so many. Either the water, which is saturated with salt and soda, is in some way injurious to them, or remaining to search for proper food, which does not exist in the lake, they become so weak from innutrition as to be unable to fly and die of starvation.

The mortality observed is not unusual, but seems to be of regular occurrence. Mr. Nelson, while camped at Keeler, in December, 1890, reported large numbers of dead grebes along the shore, and further stated that a light wind, blowing in shore, brought in half a dozen or more recently dead and excessively emaciated birds.

A specimen was secured on the reservoir at Furnace Creek, Death Valley, by Mr. Bailey April 11, and another on Pahranagat Lake, where many others were seen, May 24. Mr. Nelson saw a single individual in a glacier lake at the head of San Joaquin River, which was more likely the horned grebe; Mr. Stephens found several at Little Owens Lake, May 6-11; and Mr. Palmer observed eight or ten pairs, in full breeding plumage, on Elizabeth Lake July 2, and several on Crane Lake, near Gorman Station, Calif., June 28. Mr. Nelson saw the species at Buena Vista Lake, in the San Joaquin Valley, in October, and found it common along the coast south of San Simeon in November.

The horned grebe (*Colymbus auritus*) may have been associated with the present species in some localities, but it was not identified.

Record of specimens collected of Colymbus nigricollis californicus.

Collect-or's No.	Sex.	Locality.	Date.	Collector.	Remarks.
....	♂	Death Valley, California	Apr. 11, 1891	V. Bailey	Furnace Creek.
....	♂	Keeler, Inyo Co., Calif.	June 2, 1891	T. S. Palmer	

Podilymbus podiceps. Pied-billed Grebe.

A few dabchicks were seen by Mr. Nelson along the coast between San Simeon and Carpenteria, in November.

Urinator sp.——?

Mr. Nelson reported loons as common along the coast south of San Simeon in November. No adults were observed, all the birds being in immature plumage and remarkably unsuspicious. It is probable that the above note includes two and possibly three species, namely, the Pacific, red-throated, and common loons.

Uria troile californica. California Murre.

The California murre was found by Mr. Bailey to be common along the shore at Monterey, Calif., where a female was secured October 5.

Larus glaucescens. Glaucous-winged Gull.

Mr. Nelson found this species common along the coast of California south of San Simeon in November.

Larus californicus. California Gull.

Mr. Nelson saw three gulls of this species flying up Owens River, California, opposite Lone Pine, in December, 1890. Along the shores of Owens Lake from one to half a dozen were seen almost every day through December. A specimen shot on December 28 had its craw full of duck meat and feathers, and from the actions of its associates when a duck was shot it was evident that they prey upon such game, since the lake affords little other food.

The same observer saw a number of gulls of this species at Buena Vista Lake, in the San Joaquin Valley, in October, and found it common along the coast from San Simeon to Carpenteria, November 4 to December 18, 1891.

Larus delawarensis. Ring-billed Gull.

Mr. Nelson observed the ring-billed gull a few times at Owens Lake, and secured two specimens at a pond abounding in small fish near Lone Pine, in December, 1890. He found it rather common along the coast from San Simeon to Carpenteria, November 4 to December 18, 1891.

Larus heermanni. Heermann's Gull.

Common along the coast from San Simeon to Carpenteria, November 4 to December 18, 1891.

Larus philadelphia. Bonaparte's Gull.

Mr. Nelson saw one immature bird on a small lake near Lone Pine the last of December, 1890, and found a few along the coast from San Simeon to Carpenteria, November 4 to December 18, 1891.

Sterna maxima. Royal Tern.

A large tern, which Mr. Nelson reported as this species, was very common about the bays and inlets along the coast south of San Simeon.

Phalacrocorax dilophus albociliatus. Farallone Cormorant.

Mr. Nelson reported this cormorant as common along the coast from San Simeon to Carpenteria, November 4 to December 18.

Phalacrocorax penicillatus. Brandt's Cormorant.

Common in the same place.

Phalacrocorax pelagicus resplendens. Baird's Cormorant.

Noted by Mr. Nelson at Santa Barbara.

Pelecanus erythrorhynchos. White Pelican.

Mr. Stephens saw a flock of white pelicans sailing high in the air, midway between Haway Meadows and Olancha, at the southern end of Owens Lake, May 15. Mr. Palmer found the wings and shoulder girdle of one of these birds at Crane Lake, near Old Fort Tejon, July 2, and saw an individual on a small lake at Lone Pine, August 23.

Mr. Nelson saw the species at Buena Vista Lake, in the San Joaquin Valley, in October, and observed a large flock on Morro Bay in November.

Pelecanus californicus. California Brown Pelican.

Brown pelicans were common about San Francisco Bay and outside of the Golden Gate during the latter part of September. Mr. Bailey found them numerous at Monterey, September 28 to October 9, and Mr.

Larus californicus "These birds are often seen walking awkwardly along the furrow after the plow securing the worms that are brought to the surface. A small flock were seen feeding on the carcass of a steer" (McLean Field Notes, Sur, Mch 2-6, 12-14 1894).

Nelson found them abundant all along the coast from San Simeon to Carpenteria, November 4 to December 18.

Merganser americanus. Merganser.

A flock of a dozen or more sheldrakes was seen at Soda Springs (locally known as Kern River Lakes), in the Sierra Nevada the first week in September, and a specimen shot there by Mr. Bailey August 15, belongs to this species.

Merganser serrator. Red-breasted Merganser.

A few red-breasted mergansers, according to Mr. Nelson, were living in the lakes near Lone Pine in December, 1890, and the remains of one were found on the shore of Owens Lake in June. Dr. Merriam shot an adult male in a small pond in Vegas Wash, Nevada, May 2, saw a pair at the Bend of the Colorado, May 3, and noted three females at the mouth of Beaverdam Creek, Arizona, May 9 and 10.

Anas boschas. Mallard.

The first mallard seen was a fine adult male, which was secured as it arose from one of the irrigating ditches in the alfalfa field at Furnace Creek, in Death Valley, January 23. Mr. Nelson noted several small flocks at Saratoga Springs, at the south end of the valley, early in February, and a few in Vegas Wash, Nevada, March 3–6. At Ash Meadows, Nevada, this duck was not uncommon, and a number were secured for the mess during the first three weeks in March. Dr. Merriam saw a pair of mallards and several single birds in Pahranagat Valley, Nevada, May 22–26, and Mr. Stephens noted a few in Oasis Valley, Nevada, March 15–19. In Owens Valley, California, Mr. Nelson found it sparingly about the lakes at Lone Pine in December, 1890; Mr. Stephens saw males and females at Little Owens Lake, May 6–11, and was confident that it bred in the meadows about Olancha, at the foot of Owens Lake, May 16–23. Dr. Merriam shot two and saw others in a small tule pond in Kern Valley, California, June 22, and the writer saw several at the same place July 13. At Walker Basin, California, several females were seen with their broods of young. A specimen of the latter in the down, secured July 13, had its stomach distended with grasshoppers, which insects were abundant everywhere in the neighborhood of the sloughs.

At Bakersfield, in the San Joaquin Valley, a flock of nearly full-grown birds was flushed from one of the old water ditches on July 19. At a small pond near Trout Meadows, in the Sierra Nevada, Mr. Bailey saw a flock of ten individuals about the middle of August, and on September 7 he and the writer saw a flock containing six birds at the same place. Mr. Nelson saw the species at Buena Vista Lake in October, and along the route from San Simeon to Carpenteria, in November and December.

Anas strepera. Gadwall.

The gadwall did not begin to arrive at Ash Meadows, Nevada, until about March 8, from which time until March 21, when the party left the vicinity, it increased gradually in numbers and furnished, together with many of the other ducks, an agreeable change in the fare. Mr. Nelson found the species in small numbers in the bays and creeks between San Simeon and Carpenteria, Calif., in November and December.

Anas americana. Baldpate; Widgeon.

The spring flight of widgeons began at Ash Meadows, Nevada, about March 8, where they soon became common in the small ponds and sloughs. This was the only locality where the species was at all common.

Mr. Nelson reported two or three seen and one killed at Saratoga Springs, Death Valley, California, early in February; a single bird killed in Pahrump Valley, Nevada, the middle of the same month, and one seen in Vegas Wash, Nevada, about the middle of March. Dr. Merriam mentioned one shot at Furnace Creek in Death Valley, April 8. Mr. Nelson noted a few widgeons in the bays and creeks between San Simeon and Carpenteria, Calif., in November and December.

Anas carolinensis. Green-winged Teal.

Small flocks of green-winged teal were seen at Furnace Creek, Death Valley, January 23 to February 4. They were found either at the reservoir or in the irrigating ditches which flow through the alfalfa field. At Ash Meadows, Nevada, the species was very common, occurring in flocks which varied in size from a few individuals to several hundred birds.

Mr. Nelson found it common at Saratoga Springs, in the southern end of Death Valley, early in February, at Pahrump Ranch, Nevada, February 12–28; and saw small flocks about the large springs in Pahrump and Vegas valleys, March 3–16.

At Hot Springs, Panamint Valley, the writer saw a wing of this species April 20, and Mr. Nelson saw a specimen at the same place in January. The latter observer found it common at Buena Vista Lake in the San Joaquin Valley, California, in October, and between San Simeon and Carpenteria in November and December.

Anas discors. Blue-winged Teal.

The blue-winged teal was met with in two localities only. Mr. Stephens recorded seeing a small flock at Little Owens Lake, May 6–11; and the writer shot an individual out of a mixed flock of cinnamon and green-winged teal at Ash Meadows, Nevada, March 20.

Anas cyanoptera. Cinnamon Teal.

The cinnamon teal is a common species in suitable localities throughout the desert regions of the southern part of the Great Basin. It was first observed at Ash Meadows, Nevada, March 18, at which date a few were found in mixed flocks, and a little later considerable numbers came in, both in flocks by themselves and associated with other ducks. Mr. Nelson observed a female near Jackass Spring, in Cottonwood

Cañon, Panamint Range, June 1. Mr. Stephens saw several about the ponds at Grapevine Spring, California, April 1–4, and one was secured at Hot Spring, Panamint Valley, April 17. On the last trip to Death Valley Mr. Bailey secured a female in the reservoir at Furnace Creek, June 19. It was undoubtedly a pensioner, as its ovaries were undeveloped. During the spring and early summer Dr. Merriam found this duck breeding at numerous warm springs and alkali ponds throughout the districts visited in the Lower Sonoran zone in southern Nevada and southwestern Utah, and at Little Owens Lake, California. A female was killed in a patch of fine watercress in Upper Cottonwood Spring at the east base of the Charleston Mountains, Nevada, April 30; a flock of twenty-two was seen at Vegas Spring, Nevada, May 1, and many were noted in Vegas Wash, May 2. It was seen also in the lower Santa Clara Valley, Utah, May 11–15, and was common throughout Pahranagat Valley, Nevada, May 22–26, where it was breeding in the marshes.

Record of specimens collected of Anas cyanoptera.

Collector's No.	Sex.	Locality.	Date.	Collector.	Remarks.
134	♂ ad ♀	Ash Meadows, Nevada.......... Death Valley, California........	Mar. 20, 1891 June 19, 1891	A. K. Fisher...... V. Bailey..........	Furnace Creek.

Spatula clypeata. Shoveller.

At Lone Pine and Owens Lake, California, Mr. Nelson reported the shoveller as a common species, and at the latter place found it feeding extensively on the larvæ and pupæ of a small fly (*Ephydra hians*) which abounds in the lake. The remains of a large number of these birds were seen about the lake in June. A flock of four was seen on the reservoir at Furnace Creek, in Death Valley, the latter part of January, and the species was common at Ash Meadows, Nevada, where a number were killed early in March. Mr. Palmer found a pair breeding in a pond near Gorman Station, the last of June.

Dafila acuta. Pintail.

The sprigtail was common at Ash Meadows, Nevada, during the first two weeks in March, and many were killed for the mess. Mr. Nelson reported a number seen and some killed at Saratoga Springs, at the south end of Death Valley, February 1, and several seen in Vegas Wash, Nevada, March 3–10.

Aythya americana. Redhead.

The redhead was common at Ash Meadows, Nevada, during the first half of March, and together with the mallard, pintail, widgeon, and gadwall furnished considerable food for the party.

Mr. Nelson saw one in Vegas Valley, Nevada, in March, and Mr. Stephens another at Little Owens Lake, California, early in May.

Aythya vallisneria. Canvasback.

Ash Meadows, Nevada, was the only place where canvasback ducks were met with; a few were killed there early in March.

Aythya collaris. Ring-necked Duck.

The ring-necked duck was found only at Ash Meadows, Nevada, in March, where several in fine adult plumage were shot.

Glaucionetta clangula americana. Golden-eye.

Mr. Nelson saw a few whistlers on the lakes at Lone Pine in December, 1890, the only individuals of this species seen.

Charitonetta albeola. Bufflehead.

Mr. Nelson reported a few buffle headed ducks about the ponds at Lone Pine, California, in December, 1890.

Histrionicus histrionicus. Harlequin Duck.

None of our party saw this species. Mr. Belding, who has been so fortunate as to see a few each year, saw a pair in May, near Crockers, which is about 20 miles northwest of the Yosemite Valley.

Oidemia americana. Scoter.

Mr. Nelson found this scoter not very common at Morro Bay, California, in November.

Oidemia perspicillata. Surf Scoter.

The surf scoter was very common at Morro Bay, California, where Mr. Nelson found mainly immature birds.

Erismatura rubida. Ruddy Duck.

The ruddy duck was first met with at Ash Meadows, Nevada, where a few were killed about the middle of March. Three were seen and secured in the reservoir at Furnace Creek, Death Valley, March 22. Mr. Stephens saw it about the ponds at the ranch at Grapevine Spring, California, April 1-4: and Dr. Merriam observed it in Pahranagat Valley, Nevada, May 22-26. Near the western border of the Mohave Desert in California Mr. Palmer found several in bright plumage on Elizabeth Lake, July 2; one on a pond near Gorman Station on the same day; and several on Castac Lake, July 10. It was probably breeding at all three of these places.

Chen hyperborea. Lesser Snow Goose.

A flock of snow geese was seen by Mr. Nelson about Morro Bay in November, 1891. Mr. Bailey found this species common in flocks in Virgin Valley, where it was first observed near Bunkerville, Nev., January 23, 1889. They frequented the shores of Virgin River, where they fed on the bleached stems and tender roots of a small club-rush. The gullets of two individuals secured contained nothing except the remains of this plant.

Anser albifrons gambeli. White-fronted Goose.

A white-fronted goose remained several days in company with four Canada geese during the latter part of March in the alfalfa field at Furnace Creek, Death Valley, California.

Branta canadensis hutchinsii. Hutchin's Goose.

Very few geese were heard or seen during the time the expedition was in the field. Mr. Nelson reported hearing a flock which passed over the camp at Lone Pine, in Owens Valley, late one evening in December, 1890, and another on the east slope of the Charleston Mountains, Nevada, March 3-16, 1891. At Furnace Creek ranch, Death Valley, four Canada geese and one white-fronted goose remained in the alfalfa field for several days during the latter part of March. The above records may apply to the white-cheeked goose (*Branta c. occidentalis*). Mr. Nelson saw a few Hutchin's geese at Buena Vista Lake, in the San Joaquin Valley, California, in October, and shot a pair near San Simeon. Others were seen at different points along the coast, although nowhere common.

Dendrocygna fulva. Fulvous Tree Duck.

Owens Valley, California, was the only locality where this species was observed. Mr. Stephens found it quite common and unsuspicious at Little Owens Lake, where he secured a pair, May 8. He also saw a flock of a dozen or more at Ash Creek, near the southern end of Owens Lake, June 1.

Record of specimens collected of Dendrocygna fulva.

Collector's No.	Sex.	Locality.	Date.	Collector.	Remarks.
54	♀	Little Owens Lake, California.	May 8, 1891	F. Stephens	
55	♂	......do.........	...do.....	...do...........	

Plegadis guarauna. White-faced Glossy Ibis.

Mr. Stephens saw a small flock of the glossy ibis at Little Owens Lake, May 6-11, and observed one at a springy place at Haway Meadows May 12-14. At Furnace Creek, Death Valley, the wings and tail of a specimen which had been killed near a ditch in the alfalfa field were seen at the ranch.

Botaurus lentiginosus. Bittern.

The bittern was not uncommon at Ash Meadows, Nevada, during the first three weeks in March, where it was seen in the marshes along the irrigating ditches or by the larger springs, in which places small fish were abundant. Dr. Merriam saw several in Pahranagat Valley, Nevada, May 22-26, where it undoubtedly bred. In Owens Valley Mr. Stephens found it at Alvord June 26-28; at Bishop, June 30, and Mr. Nelson shot one near Lone Pine in December, 1890. The latter observer saw the species at the head of Morro Bay, California, and at a small lake near San Luis Obispo in November of the following year.

Ardea herodias. Great Blue Heron.

In California, great blue herons were not uncommon at Bakersfield, in the San Joaquin Valley, where they were seen flying back and forth from the river to their resting grounds, July 17-20. At the following places single individuals were seen: At a small lake near Lone Pine, December, 1890; at Tejon ranch, near the mouth of the Pass, July 13; at Little Owens Lake, June 20; at Kernville, July 12, and at Soda Springs, September 7. Mr. Nelson found the species common in the San Joaquin Valley wherever the streams or lakes furnish it proper surroundings. He reported it common on the coast between San Simeon and Carpenteria, and saw a few near San Luis Obispo and between Carpenteria and Santa Paula in November and December.

Ardea egretta. Egret.

A white egret was seen by Dr. Merriam at a little pool of muddy water between the south end of Panamint Valley and Lone Willow Spring, California, April 24; and another at the Great Bend of the Colorado, May 4. The latter was on the Arizona or east side of the river, opposite the mouth of Vegas Wash. Mr. Nelson saw several about Morro Bay, California, in November.

Ardea virescens. Green Heron.

The green heron was not uncommon along the river, sloughs, and old ditches near Bakersfield, in the San Joaquin Valley, California, July 17–20; one was seen at Elk Bayou, near Tulare, in the same valley, July 22; and Mr. Stephens saw one at Little Owens Lake, California, May 6–11.

Nycticorax nycticorax nævius. Black-crowned Night Heron.

As a matter of course, night herons were rare in a region where streams and lakes containing fish were almost absent. Dr. Merriam saw an adult April 7, resting on a rock near the road in Windy Gap, between Panamint and Death valleys. Several were seen by him on a small alkaline pond at the west end of the Mohave Desert (Antelope Valley), June 28, and one in northwestern Arizona (where Beaverdam Creek joins the Virgin), May 9. Mr. Stephens saw several at Little Owens Lake May 6–11, and Mr. Palmer saw one at Crane Lake, at the west end of the Mohave Desert, June 28, and again July 2. Mr. Bailey shot an immature specimen near the reservoir at Furnace Creek, Death Valley, June 19. Its stomach contained two carp about 5 inches long. At Keeler, in Owens Valley, one was observed near a small fresh-water pond not far from the lake, June 26. At Walker Basin several were seen flying over toward their feeding grounds, and one was observed at the edge of a slough July 13–16.

At Bakersfield, in the San Joaquin Valley, the species was common July 17–20, and at Morro Bay, on the coast, in November.

Grus canadensis. Little Brown Crane.

A little brown crane was seen for several days around the fields and marshes at Ash Meadows, Nevada, and finally was secured March 10. It was a female, and proved to be very good eating. The stomach contained small bulbous rootlets, foliage of young plants, and a quantity of barley, which it had picked up from the place where the horses had been fed.

NOTE.—Mr. Nelson saw four birds at Lone Pine, in Owens Valley, December, 1890, which he thought were whooping cranes, and saw a flock of seventeen sand-hill cranes at the Bend of the Colorado in March. In both cases the birds were too far off for positive identification, and as the region is out of the known range of the former species, it is probable that some other large bird was mistaken for it.

Rallus virginianus. Virginia Rail.

Mr. Nelson reported the species as common at Saratoga Springs in Death Valley, where Mr. Bailey caught a specimen in a trap February 3. One was seen at Ash Meadows, Nevada, about the middle of March, and the species was not uncommon at Lone Pine in Owens Valley, where two were secured June 7–10. Mr. Nelson saw one at the head of Morro Bay, Calif., in November. Dr. Merriam frequently heard a rail among the tules and reeds in Pahranagat Valley, Nevada, May 26, but was unable to say whether it was this species or the sora.

Record of specimens collected of Rallus virginianus.

Collector's No.	Sex.	Locality.	Date.	Collector.	Remarks.
	♀	Death Valley, Calif.	Feb. 3, 1891	V. Bailey	Saratoga Springs.
310	♂ juv.	Owens Valley, Calif.	June 7, 1891	A. K. Fisher	Lone Pine.
326	♂ juv.	do	June 10, 1891	do	Do.

Porzana carolina. Sora.

A sora rail was seen at Ash Meadows, Nevada, March 10; one at Grapevine Spring, California, the first part of April; and another at Little Owens Lake, early in May. No others were seen.

Fulica americana. Coot.

Coots were common at a number of places where tule marshes occurred. A number were seen in the Mohave Desert, along the edge of the Mohave River at Victor, early in January. In Death Valley it was found common at Saratoga Springs about February 1, and again in the latter part of April. At Ash Meadows, Nevada, it was common during the first three weeks in March, and a few were seen in Vegas Wash, early in the month. In Owens Valley, Mr. Stephens found it common at Little Owens Lake, May 6–11, and at Ash Creek, on the southwestern side of Owens Lake, the first of June. At Lone Pine it was common on the lakes in December, 1890, and at a lake south of the same place, August 23, 1891. A pair with their young was seen in a small pond, June 5. In Nevada, Dr. Merriam observed the species in the marshes in Vegas Wash, May 2; in the valley of the Muddy, May 6; and in Pahranagat Valley, May 24. At the west end of the Mohave Desert, in California, Mr. Palmer found coots common on Elizabeth Lake, July 2, and saw several on Crane Lake and on ponds near Gorman Station,

June 29. Mr. Bailey found it numerous in fresh-water ponds at Monterey.

Several were seen at Soda Springs or Kern River Lakes, in the Sierra Nevada, September 7. Mr. Nelson found it abundant in the lakes and along the streams in the San Joaquin Valley, October 5-27, and along the coast. At San Simeon, he saw a group sunning themselves on a strip of sandy beach just above the reach of the incoming rollers.

Phalaropus tricolor. Wilson's Phalarope.

Mr. Bailey shot an adult male near the overflow of a ditch in the alfalfa field at Furnace Creek ranch, Death Valley, June 19, and Mr. Stephens secured two at Alvord, in Owens Valley, June 27.

Record of specimens collected of Phalaropus tricolor.

Collector's No.	Sex.	Locality.	Date.	Collector.	Remarks.
122	♂	Death Valley, Calif.	June 19, 1891	V. Bailey	Furnace Creek.
123	♂	Owens Valley, Calif.	June 27, 1891	F. Stephens	Alvord.
	♂	...do...	...do...	...do...	Do.

Recurvirostra americana. Avocet.

Avocets were found in a few places both east and west of the Sierra Nevada. A flock of eighteen was seen at Ash Meadows, Nevada, March 15, and most of them secured. Mr. Stephens saw a small flock at Little Owens Lake, California, May 6-11, and the writer saw seven standing at the edge of a bar in Kern River, below Kernville, Calif., July 13. Mr. Nelson found it sparingly about the lakes at Lone Pine, in December, 1890; at Buena Vista Lake, in the San Joaquin Valley, in October; saw one individual at the head of Owens Valley in July; and a few at Morro Bay in November. Dr. Merriam saw a dozen or more at the northwestern end of Owens Lake, June 19.

Himantopus mexicanus. Black-necked Stilt.

Near the west end of the Mohave Desert, in California, Mr. Palmer saw sixteen black-necked stilts at Elizabeth Lake, July 2, and three at Castac Lake, July 10. No others were seen during the entire season.

Gallinago delicata. Wilson's Snipe.

Wilson's snipe were seen in a few localities, both in California and Nevada.

Mr. Nelson saw several in marshy spots near Owens River at Lone Pine, Calif., until the latter part of December, 1890, when a fall in temperature drove them away. Mr. Stephens saw one at Grapevine Spring, California, April 1; a number at Little Owens Lake, May 6-11; and one at Furnace Creek, Death Valley, April 11.

Mr. Bailey flushed one at Resting Springs, California, February 16, and Mr. Nelson saw several near Cottonwood Spring at the east foot of the Charleston Mountains early in March. At Ash Meadows, Nevada, a number were seen and one killed March 16. Mr. Nelson saw one at the head of the Cañada de las Uvas and another at Buena Vista Lake, California, in October, and found the species not common, but generally distributed along the coast marshes between San Simeon and Carpenteria in November and December.

Tringa **minutilla.** Least Sandpiper.

Least sandpipers were seen in a few places only. Mr. Nelson reported the species as common on the shores of Owens Lake in December, 1890, and along the coast from San Simeon to Carpenteria the following autumn. Two small flocks were seen about an alkaline pond at Hot Springs in Panamint Valley, and a specimen was secured April 22. Near Bakersfield one was flushed from an old irrigating ditch July 19, and Mr. Nelson saw several near a small pond on the east side of Mount Piños, in the latter part of October.

Ereunetes occidentalis. Western Sandpiper.

The western sandpiper was seen in a few localities only. Dr. Merriam shot a specimen out of a flock of four in the Virgin Valley, Nevada, just below the mouth of the Muddy, May 6, and Mr. Stephens found the species rather common along the shore of Little Owens Lake, California, May 6–11. The writer found several in company with snowy plovers, at Keeler, on the shore of Owens Lake the 1st of June. Mr. Nelson reported it as common along the shores of Morro Bay in November.

Calidris arenaria. Sanderling.

Mr. Bailey secured a specimen of this wader at Monterey, Calif., October 3.

Limosa fedoa. Marbled Godwit.

Mr. Nelson reported this godwit as common at Morro Bay, on the coast of California, in November.

Totanus melanoleucus. Greater Yellow-legs.

Mr. Nelson reported several small parties of greater yellow-legs about the ponds at Lone Pine, Calif., in December, 1890, and found the species common at Morro Bay the following November.

Symphemia semipalmata inornata. Western Willet.

Mr. Nelson found the willet common at Morro Bay, Calif., in November.

Heteractitis incanus. Wandering Tattler.

The wandering tattler was common at Monterey, where Mr. Bailey secured a specimen October 3.

Actitis macularia. Spotted Sandpiper.

This species was not rare near the permanent streams. Dr. Merriam found it along several of the water courses in the southern part of the Great Basin, where two were found at the Great Bend of the Colorado

River in Nevada, May 4; several along Beaverdam Creek, northwestern Arizona, May 10; many in Pahranagat Valley, Nevada (where the species was breeding), May 24; and one in Oasis Valley, Nevada, June 1.

Mr. Nelson saw a single individual on Willow Creek Cañon, in the Panamint Mountains, May 22; and observed the species at the head of Owens River and on the western slope of the Sierra Nevada, but found it nowhere common. Mr. Belding saw it at Mirror Lake, in the Yosemite Valley. The writer saw it along Kern River, near Kernville, July 11–12, and at Soda Springs or Kern River Lakes September 5. Mr. Bailey found it common around the fresh-water pools at Monterey early in October.

Numenius longirostris. Long-billed Curlew.

Mr. Nelson saw four sickle-billed curlews on the shore of Owens Lake December 27, and subsequently Mr. Bailey saw a flock of about a dozen. Mr. Stephens observed one near Ash Creek, on the same lake, the last of May.

Numenius hudsonicus. Hudsonian Curlew.

In California Mr. Nelson found the hudsonian curlew at Buena Vista Lake in the San Joaquin Valley in October, and found it common at Morro Bay in November.

Charadrius squatarola. Black-bellied Plover.

The only record of the black-bellied plover was a male secured by Mr. Bailey at Monterey, Calif., October 3.

Ægialitis vocifera. Killdeer Plover.

The killdeer plover is the commonest wader in the desert regions and occurs wherever there is water enough to form marshy places in the vicinity of streams or springs. Dr. Merriam found it particularly abundant at Hot Springs, in Panamint Valley, Calif., April 20–25; at the junction of Beaverdam Creek with the Virgin River, Arizona, May 9; along the Santa Clara River near its junction with the same river, in southwestern Utah, May 11–15; at Willow Spring, in the western part of the Mohave Desert, June 26; at Owens Lake, June 19, and in Kern Valley, California, June 22. In Nevada he found it also, though in less abundance, at Vegas Spring, May 1; at the Bend of the Colorado River, May 4; at Bunkerville, in the Virgin Valley, May 8; in Pahranagat Valley and at Pahranagat Lake, May 22–26;

The writer first observed it at Furnace Creek ranch, Death Valley, in the latter part of January, where it was noisy on moonlight nights; Dr. Merriam observed it at the same place about the middle of April; and Mr. Bailey and the writer found it not uncommon on their last trip to the Valley, June 19–22. One was seen by the latter observer at Resting Springs, California, February 16, and a number at Ash Meadows, Nevada, during the first three weeks of March. Mr. Nelson saw a few solitary individuals about the ranch in Pahrump Valley,

February 12-28; also at the ranch in Vegas Valley, and thence down the Vegas Wash as far as water occurred, March 3-16. In Owens Valley the same observer found it sparingly distributed along Owens River and on the shore of Owens Lake in December, 1890, and the writer found it not uncommon in the same valley, both at Keeler and Lone Pine, June 3-15. In other parts of the valley Mr. Stephens found it at Little Owens Lake, May 6-11; Haway Meadows, May 12-14; Olancha, May 16-23; Ash Creek, May 30 to June 3; Alvord, June 26-28; Bishop, June 30 to July 1; Morans, July 4-7; and at Benton, July 9-10. He also found it rather common in Oasis Valley, Nevada, March 15-19; and at Grapevine Spring, California, April 1-4. In the Sierra Nevada Mr. Nelson found the killdeer at the head of Owens River up to an altitude of 2,440 meters (8,000 feet), and on the western slope from the San Joaquin Valley up into the Yosemite as high as 1,220 meters (4,000 feet); Mr. Stephens found it common at Menache Meadows, May 24-26; and Mr. Dutcher saw one on Big Cottonwood Creek about half a mile below his meteorological camp, September 11. Near the west end of the Mohave Desert Mr. Palmer saw the species at Elizabeth Lake, July 2, and near Crane Lake, June 29. The writer saw killdeers on the eastern slope of Walker Pass, July 1, and Mr. Bailey on the western slope the following day. Several were seen at the South Fork of Kern River, July 3-10; at Kernville, July 11-13; at Walker Basin, July 13-16; and at Bakersfield, in the San Joaquin Valley, July 17-20. At Three Rivers, California, in the western foothills of the Sierra, the killdeer plover was common July 25-30, and on the return trip September 14-17.

Mr. Bailey found it common at Monterey, Calif., September 28 to October 9; and Mr. Nelson reported it as common and generally distributed in the San Joaquin Valley, about San Luis Obispo, and along the coast from San Simeon to Carpenteria and Santa Paula, in November and December.

Record of specimens collected of Ægialitis vocifera.

Collector's No.	Sex.	Locality.	Date.	Collector.	Remarks.
122	♀	Ash Meadows, Nev	Mar. 10, 1890	A. K. Fisher	
	♂	Death Valley, Calif	June 19, 1891	V. Bailey	Furnace Creek.

Ægialitis nivosa. Snowy Plover.

This handsome little plover was observed by the writer on the shores of Owens Lake, near Keeler, May 30 to June 4, where it was common in small flocks of five or ten on the alkaline flats which border the lake. Like most other birds in the vicinity, it fed extensively, if not exclusively, on a species of small fly (*Ephydra hians* Say), which was found in immense masses near the edge of the lake. Many of these swarms of flies were four or five layers deep and covered an area of 15 or 20 square feet. Some idea can be formed of the inexhaustible supply of food which this insect furnishes for birds when it is known that colonies of equal size occurred at close intervals in suitable localities all around the lake, which has a shore line of between 40 and 50 miles.

The species was evidently breeding at the time, but no eggs or young were found. The birds were tame and unsuspicious, and allowed a person to approach within a few yards before taking wing, and if not too closely pressed would run along ahead of the observer. As Mr. Nelson found the species at this same place December 27, 1890, it is undoubtedly a resident in Owens Valley.

Mr. Bailey found this plover numerous on the beach at Monterey, Calif., September 28 to October 9.

Record of specimens collected of Ægialitis nivosa.

Collector's No.	Sex.	Locality.	Date.	Collector.	Remarks.
276	♂	Keeler, Inyo County, Calif.	June 1, 1891	A. K. Fisher	
277	♂	...do...	...do...	...do...	
278	♂	...do...	...do...	...do...	

Ægialitis montana. Mountain Plover.

According to Mr. Nelson, mountain plovers were common in flocks in October at several places on the open grassy plains in the San Joaquin Valley, Calif.

Oreortyx pictus plumiferus. Plumed Quail.

The known range of the mountain quail was considerably extended by the fieldwork of the expedition. In Cajon Pass, in the San Bernardino Mountains, a small band was seen and an individual secured January 2. In the Panamint Mountains a feather was found in Johnson Cañon, and a pair or so of the birds seen April 6. The Indians, as well as some of the inhabitants of Panamint, knew the bird well, and stated that it was common in many parts of the mountains. Dr. Merriam and Mr. Bailey saw it among the junipers on the north slope of Telescope Peak, April 17–19, and Mr. Nelson found it a common breeding species among the piñons on Willow Creek, Mill Creek, and in Cottonwood Cañon, in the more northern part of the range. Death Valley, with the barren, treeless range immediately to the east, prevents the extension of the species in that direction as effectually as it does the valley quail. In the Argus Range the plumed quail was common. Mr. W. C. Burnett saw a pair at the summit of Shepherd Cañon, and above Maturango Spring the males were heard throughout the day uttering their not unpleasant call notes. At Searl's garden, which is near the southern end of this range, Mr. Stephens heard that they came down into the garden in summer. In the Coso Mountains the species was still more common among the piñons, where several specimens were secured during the latter half of May. In the Inyo Range it was reported as not uncommon

Oreortyx   "Mountain quail are reported as occurring back of the range a few miles from Jamesburg (McMillan Fieldnote Feb 16-23/94

at Cerro Gordo, and Mr. Nelson found it common among the nut pines along Waucoba Creek the last of June. On Mount Magruder, Nevada, Dr. Merriam found it common and breeding June 4-9. On this mountain the plumed quails were distributed in pairs, a pair occupying the chaparral on each hillside among the piñons.

In the Sierra Nevada Mr. Stephens heard them west of Little Owens Lake, May 6-11; at Menache Meadows at an altitude of 3,050 meters (10,000 feet), May 24-26; at Independence Creek, where young were seen near the mouth of the cañon, June 18-23; and at Bishop Creek August 4-10. Mr. Nelson found the mountain quail common at the head of Owens River and on the headwaters of the San Joaquin River on the opposite slope. On the western slope of Walker Pass we found it common among the chaparral in the cañons, where it was associated more or less with the valley quail, which was abundant there. At Walker Basin a flock was seen on the hillside above the valley on July 14. In the Sierra Liebre Dr. Merriam saw one near Alamo ranch June 30, and Mr. Palmer found it common on Frazier Mountain, where half-grown young were found July 9. In the southern Sierra Nevada it was common in the Sequoia National Park, and especially near the openings, and coveys of half-grown young were seen every day during the first week in August. It was common also at Horse Corral Meadows August 9-13. A flock was seen at Big Cottonwood Meadows August 26, and another at Round Valley, 12 miles south of Mount Whitney, August 28. At the latter place birds were running about among the bare rocks above timber line. At Soda Springs, or Kern River Lakes, small flocks were seen and several individuals taken September 3. A number were observed around Mineral King the first part of August, and again in September. In the coast ranges Mr. Nelson found the plumed quail common near La Panza the last of October, and in the mountains back of San Simeon in November.

Record of specimens collected of Oreortyx pictus plumiferus.

Collector's No.	Sex.	Locality.	Date.	Collector.	Remarks.
17	♂ ad.	Cajon Pass, Calif.	Jan. 2, 1891.	A. K. Fisher.	
	♀	Panamint Mountains, Calif.	May 13, 1891.	E. W. Nelson.	
	♂	........do........	May 17, 1891.	Do.	
	♂	........do........	May 21, 1891.	Do.	
234	♂	Argus Range, Calif.	May 13, 1891.	A. K. Fisher.	
247	♂	Coso Mountains, Calif.	May 23, 1891.	Do.	
265	♂	........do........	May 27, 1891.	Do.	
266	♀	........do........	....do......	Do.	
361	♂ juv.	Walker Pass, Calif.	July 3, 1891.	Do.	
362	♂ juv.	........do........	....do......	Do.	
		Soda Springs, Kern River, Calif.	Aug. 12, 1891.	V. Bailey.	

Callipepla californica. California Quail.

The only places from which the typical California quail was recorded are Monterey and Boulder Creek on the coast of California, where Mr. Bailey found it common during the first part of October.

Callipepla californica vallicola. Valley Quail.

The valley quail was found abundantly in many places, and its eastern range in southern California was carefully and definitely mapped. As might be expected, it was found at every point west of the Sierra Nevada visited by members of the expedition. To the east of this range, and the ranges forming its southern continuation, the species was common out to the edge of the Mohave Desert and Salt Wells Valley, and all through Owens Valley as far north at least as Benton, where both Mr. Nelson and Mr. Stephens found it. It was common along the western base of the White Mountains and in the Inyo, Coso, Argus, and Panamint mountains. In the latter range its eastern distribution ends—Death Valley, with the barren, treeless mountains beyond forming a complete barrier to its further extension. The valley quail was not found in the Grapevine Mountains, in Panamint or Saline valleys, or in the Mohave Desert proper, though around the edges of this desert it was seen on the south at the summit of Cajon Pass, on the north at Lone Willow and Leach Point springs, and on the west at Willow Spring and Antelope Valley. The easternmost limits of its range are the San Bernardino Mountains on the south side of the Mohave Desert, and Leach Point Spring on the north side. The latter locality is only a short distance west of the extreme south end of Death Valley. Here Dr. Merriam shot specimens April 25.

In the Panamint range it was common in Johnson and Surprise Cañons, and Mr. Nelson found it in Cottonwood, Mill Creek, and Willow Creek cañons.

In the Argus Range this quail was common in Shepherd Cañon, at Maturango Spring and at other places visited. In the Coso Mountains it was found to range from the lowest part of the valley up through the cañons to the tops of the high peaks, where it was quite closely associated with the mountain quail (*Oreortyx*) during the breeding season. In the Inyo Mountains, Mr. Nelson found it on the east slope at Hunter's arastra and Waucoba Creek, and along the west slope up to the piñons. At Lone Pine, in Owens Valley, young, just able to fly, were seen June 4–15, and at Walker Pass, flocks containing a hundred or more on July 1–2. These flocks were composed of several families, as they contained from ten to fifteen adults and young that varied in size from those just hatched up to half-grown birds. At the west slope of Walker Pass, the valley quail was again found ranging above the lower limit of the mountain quail. At Three Rivers, in the western foothills of the Sierra Nevada, these quails, both adult and young, were found in the oaks feeding on the young acorns July 25–30.

Throughout the San Joaquin Valley, Mr. Nelson found it common about ranches, along water courses or near springs. It was excessively abundant at some of the springs in the hills about the Temploa Mountains and Carrizo Plain. In the week following the expiration of the close season, two men, pot-hunting for the market, were reported to have killed 8,400 quail at a solitary spring in the Temploa Mountains. The men built a brush blind near the spring, which was the only water within a distance of 20 miles, and as evening approached the quails came to it by thousands. One of Mr. Nelson's informants who saw the birds at this place stated that the ground all about the water was covered by a compact body of quails, so that the hunters mowed them down by the score at every discharge. The species was common along the coast from San Simeon to Carpenteria and Santa Paula, in November and December.

Record of specimens collected of Callipepla californica vallicola.

Collector's No.	Sex.	Locality.	Date.	Collector.	Remarks.
16	♂ ad.	Cajon Pass, Calif	Jan. 1, 1891	A. K. Fisher	
65	♀	Lone Willow Spring, Calif	Jan. 16, 1891	...do	
	♀	...do	Jan. 17, 1891	E. W. Nelson	
140	♀	Panamint Mountains, Calif	Mar. 26, 1891	A. K. Fisher	Johnson Cañon.
	♀	...do	Apr. 19, 1891	E. W. Nelson	Surprise Cañon.
	♂	...do	...do	...do	Do.
	♀ juv.	...do	June 13, 1891	...do	
	♂	Argus Range, Calif	Jan. 2, 1891	V. Bailey	Shepherd Cañon.
	♀	...do	...do	...do	Do.
185	♂	...do	Apr. 27, 1891	A. K. Fisher	Do.
244	♂	Coso Mountains, Calif	May 24, 1891	...do	
245	♀	...do	...do	...do	
	juv.	Inyo Mountains, Calif	July 1, 1891	E. W. Nelson	
72	♀ juv.	Owens Lake, Calif	June 3, 1891	F. Stephens	
357	♂ juv.	Walker Pass, Calif	July 1, 1891	A. K. Fisher	
358	♀ juv.	...do	...do	...do	
359	♂ juv.	...do	...do	...do	
376	♀ juv.	Kern River, Calif	July 5, 1891	...do	South Fork.
377	♂ juv.	...do	...do	...do	
404	♂ im.	Three Rivers, Calif	July 28, 1891	...do	

Callipepla gambeli. Gambel's Quail.

Gambel's quail is essentially a desert bird, though rarely found at any great distance from water. It was first observed in winter by our party at Furnace Creek, in Death Valley, where it was reported to have been introduced by the Borax Company from Resting Springs. A few young were seen here June 19-21 by Mr. Bailey and the writer, and a female shot for a specimen had an egg in the lower part of the oviduct. At Resting Springs, California, which is in the Amargosa Valley, it was excessively abundant in February and furnished considerable food for the party. It was so common among the mesquite and other brush that steel traps set for diurnal mammals were often sprung by it, and in a few instances quail were found in traps set in pouched gopher holes. A few were seen at Ash Meadows, Nevada, in March. At the ranch in Pahrump Valley, Nevada, it was fully as abundant as at Resting Springs and was considered a great nuisance by the proprietor of the place, owing to the damage it does to the crops. Mr. Nelson, who was alone in camp for several days in this locality, gives the following notes on its habits: "I noticed that when a flock of quail came to feed on grain left by the horses, an old male usually mounted the top of a tall bush close by and remained on guard for ten or fifteen minutes, then, if everything was quiet, he would fly down among his companions. At the first alarm the flock would take to the bushes, running swiftly, or flying when hard pressed. They roosted in the dense bunches of willows and cottonwoods growing along the ditches. As a rule the birds walked under the roosting place and flew up one or two at a time into the tree or bush, though sometimes they flew into the tree from a distance. When feeding they have a series of low clucking and cooing notes which are kept up almost continually."

Dr. Merriam found Gambel's quail abundant below Mountain Spring, in the southern part of the Charleston Mountains, Nevada, April 29-30, and shot several at Upper Cottonwood Springs, at the east base of the same mountains, April 30. He contributes the following notes concerning its presence in eastern Nevada, northwestern Arizona, and southwestern Utah: In Nevada it was common at the Great Bend of the Colorado, May 4, where several sprung traps set for small mammals; in the Valley of the Virgin and Lower Muddy it was not only abundant but so unwary that it ran along in front of the horses in considerable numbers, early in May; it was tolerably common in the southern part of Pahranagat Valley, May 22-26, but shy and difficult of approach. At the mouth of Beaverdam Creek, northwestern Arizona, and thence up over the Beaverdam Mountains, Utah, it was exceedingly abundant as it was also in the Santa Clara Valley, Utah, May 11-15, and a few were found as far north as the Upper Santa Clara Crossing. The species is said to reach Shoal Creek at the south end of the Escalante Desert occasionally, but is rare there.

Record of specimens collected of Callipepla gambeli.

Collector's No.	Sex.	Locality.	Date.	Collector.	Remarks.
72	♂	Death Valley, Calif.	Jan. 24, 1891	A. K. Fisher	Furnace Creek.
73	♂	...do	...do	...do	Do.
74	♀	...do	...do	...do	Do.
75	♀	...do	...do	...do	Do.
	♂	...do	June 19, 1891	V. Bailey	Do.
	♀	...do	...do	...do	Do.
102	♂ ad.	Resting Springs, Calif.	Feb. 8, 1891	A. K. Fisher	
104	♂ ad.	...do	...do	...do	
	♂	Pahrump Valley, Nev	Feb. 15, 1891	T. S. Palmer	
28	♂	Ash Meadows, Nev	Mar. 4, 1891	F. Stephens	

Dendragapus obscurus fuliginosus. Sooty Grouse.

The Sooty Grouse was nowhere common, and the only ones seen outside of the Sierra Nevada were one by Mr. Nelson in the upper part of the White Mountains, in July, and a pair by Mr. Stephens at the Queen mill, Nevada, in the same mountains, July 11-16.

On the eastern slope of the Sierra, one was seen by Mr. Stephens at Menache Meadows, the latter part of May; another on Independence Creek about the same time; one adult and two broods, at Bishop Creek, August 4-10; and it was found sparingly at the head of

Columba fasciata   At Jamesburgh "a beautiful grove of live oaks at the head of a stream is used by a band of about three hundred wild pigeons." That they Xxx reluctantly on the grain that has been sown in the fields at this particular swarm, is shown by the distended crops of the birds shot" (McLellan Field Notes Mch 16-23, 1894).

Owens River, in the latter part of July. In the Sequoia National Park a few were seen both at the saw mill and at Halsted Meadows. At Horse Corral Meadows a flock of ten or fifteen was seen and two secured, August 11. Several were seen in Kings River Cañon about the meadows, August 13-16; at Big Cottonwood Meadows throughout the summer; and grouse were not uncommon near timber line, at Mineral King and vicinity, during August and first half of September. Mr. Nelson found a few about the summit of Mount Piños in October.

Record of specimens collected of Dendragapus obscurus fuliginosus.

Collector's No.	Sex.	Locality.	Date.	Collector.	Remarks.
146	♀ juv.	Sierra Nevada Calif	Aug. 7, 1891	F. Stephens	Bishop Creek.
147	♀ juv.	do	do	do	Do.
150	♀ im.	do	Aug. 9, 1891	do	Do.
151	♀ ad.	do	do	do	Do.
160	♂ ad.	do	Aug. 23, 1891	do	Olancha Peak.
10	♂ ad.	do	July 6, 1891	B. H. Dutcher	Big Cottonwood Meadows.

Centrocercus urophasianus. Sage Grouse.

On Mount Magruder, on the Nevada side of the boundary line between California and Nevada, many piles of sage hens' excrement were found among sage brush on the main peak, by Dr. Merriam and Mr. Bailey. They were told by a prospector that sage hens used to be common on the mountain, but are very scarce now, having been killed off a few winters ago by unusually deep snow. At the head of Owens River, on the eastern slope of the Sierra Nevada, Mr. Nelson found this bird ranging in among the lower border of the pines (*Pinus jeffreyi*,) where he saw numerous tracks. Near Mammoth Pass also he found it common among the sage brush at about 2,450 meters (8,000 feet) altitude. The same observer stated that the sage hen was a common species in the northern half of the White Mountains up to 3,050 meters (10,000 feet) altitude, where he killed a half-grown bird from a large covey. Mr. Stephens learned from the miners at the Queen mine, Nevada, that this grouse occurred in the gulches around the mines.

Columba fasciata. Band-tailed Pigeon.

At Three Rivers, in the western foothills of the Sierra Nevada, California, Mr. Palmer saw three band-tailed pigeons among the oaks the last of July, and the species was reported to be quite common in the barley stubble of a neighboring ranch. Mr. Nelson found it common among the oaks in the Tehachapi and Temploa mountains, and saw a few about San Luis Obispo during the last of October. Along the route from San Simeon to Carpenteria it was abundant among the oaks in November. Flocks of from 10 to a 100 were feeding on the berries of *Arbutus menziesii* as well as upon acorns. He saw a few flocks between Carpenteria and Santa Paula during the last part of December.

Zenaidura macroura. Mourning Dove.

After the spring migration set in, the mourning dove was a common species all through the desert region wherever water occurred. There was no bird that indicated the close proximity of water with more certainty than the dove, and wherever it was found congregated in any numbers water was confidently looked for. The three following records are the only ones which indicate its presence in the region during the winter: Two were seen drinking from a stream at San Bernardino, Calif., December 28, 1890; one was seen near the roadside at Lone Pine in the same month, and a single individual was found at Furnace Creek in Death Valley, the latter part of January. Migrants were first observed at the last-mentioned place April 9–12, and at Hot Springs, in Panamint Valley, April 21. At Lone Willow Spring Dr. Merriam saw several April 24, and at Leach Point Spring he observed large numbers as they came to the water to drink, and fifteen were secured for food the evening of April 25. In Amargosa Cañon and at Resting Springs they were seen April 27. Mr. Nelson found it exceedingly abundant in the vicinity of springs and streams in the Panamint and Grapevine mountains, where it ranged well up among the piñons. He found them more sparingly at the head of Owens River, in the Sierra Nevada, on both slopes of the Inyo Mountains, and up to the piñons in the White Mountains. They were nesting in various situations, some on the ground sheltered by a bush, others on horizontal branches of cottonwoods, willows, or piñons, and one he found in a small cup-shaped depression on the top of a tall granite boulder 6 feet from the ground. Doves were very common in the Argus Range in Shepherd Cañon and at Maturango Spring, where they filled in very nicely the shortcomings of the mess. In the Coso Mountains the species was just as abundant and occurred up through the cañons to the summit of the range.

Dr. Merriam contributes the following records for eastern Nevada, northwest Arizona, and southwest Utah: In the Charleston Mountains, Nevada, it was seen both at Mountain Spring, and at the Upper Cottonwood Springs at the east foot of the mountains, April 30; at Vegas ranch, May 1; abundant in Vegas Wash and at the Bend of the Colorado, May 2–4; in the valley of the Muddy and Virgin it was common May 7–8; in the Juniper Mountains dozens came to Sheep Spring to drink, the evening of May 18; at Pahroc Spring it was very abundant May 20–22; in Pahranagat Valley it was common and unusually tame May 22–26; at Quartz Spring, on the western slope of the Desert Mountains, it fairly swarmed on the evening of May 22, there being no other water for many miles in any direction; in Oasis Valley it was abundant June 1, feeding on seeds of the bunch grass (*Oryzopsis cuspidata*), and was common on Mount Magruder June 4–9. At the mouth of Beaverdam Creek in northwestern Arizona doves were excessively abundant May 9–10, and were common throughout the juniper belt of the Beaverdam Mountains, Utah, May 10–11. In the Santa Clara Valley, Utah, they were likewise abundant May 11–15.

California Vulture in the San Gabriel Range, California Sept 25 1893. One was shot at but not killed. R.H.Lawrence. (Auk. XI Jan. 1894, pp. 76-77)

A California Vulture.

THE following letter from Archibald Campbell to San Diego (Cal.) *Sun*, from Laguna, on the border of the desert, seems to refer to the California vulture, of which lately we are hearing more and more. The letter is dated Aug. 1, and says among other things:

"To-day as Henry E. Clark was riding near the laguna he noticed a large bird among some carrion crows, eating at a steer which had died from a rattlesnake bite. It flew up into a tree, where he shot it with a rifle, and the shot broke its thigh. It then flew away among some rocks, when he threw his riata over it and caught it, and it tried to get away and it nearly unhorsed him. He gave it another shot through the wing and disabled it. He brought it home and it measured 9ft. 3in. across the wings and 4ft. 4½in. long from the beak to the end of its tail. Valentine, the captain of the Indians, says it is a female and not near so large as the males. The males have the under part snow white, while this is pretty dark. I think it is the California vulture, which approaches the condor in size and has wings even longer in proportion. Last Sunday, as a party of us were out on the high peaks overlooking the desert, three of the birds kept circling around overhead, and now and again by far the biggest of the birds would swoop down suddenly toward us and make such ugly demonstrations that the ladies got scared and we all left on that account. I think their young were in the cliffs above us and they wanted to scare us away. The biggest was whiter underneath than the other two, and I think that it was one of the smaller birds that was shot. Mrs. Wiegar from San Diego, who was up here on a visit, skinned the bird, and on her return will take it with her and put it on exhibiton at the Chamber of Commerce. They are very rare here now. Valentine says they used to be very numerous here when he was young. Two years ago we used to see a solitary vulture every now and again, but he disappeared, and now these three are to be seen near the same place. This one, I think, could have easily carried off a spotted fawn, a young calf or a baby."

In the report on the ornithology of the Death Valley expedition for 1891, Dr. A. K. Fisher reported this bird as moderately abundant in certain localities west of the Sierra Nevadas in California. Dr. Palmer reported it from Frazier Mountain and near the Tejor ranch, Dr. Fisher and Mr. Bailey saw one near Walker's Basin in the San Joaquin Valley and at San Emiglio, and near there Mr. Nelson found it quite common in October. The same gentleman found it common along the coast near San Simeon and in the Santa Yñez Mountains.

It is said that not long ago a Mr. W. A. Burris killed one of these birds near Sargent's, San Benito county, California, with a charge of No. 9 shot. The specimen, which weighed 25lbs. and measured 9¼ft. in extent of wings, was preserved, and is now in the collection of the California Academy of Sciences.

Forest & Stream Vol. 41, No. 12, Sept 23, 1893, p.250

Pseudogryphus: A dead body of a california vulture was seen lying in a field near Sur Post office. It had been killed some months before (McLean Fieldnotes Mch. 2-6 1894).

Mr. F. Stephens saw 26 California Vultures in Walker Basin, Oct 1894 Auk, XII, 1895, 81.

In Owens Valley, California, the species was abundant from one end to the other. At Lone Pine, during the first part of June, quantities of nests, one of which contained three young, were found in the willow and cottonwood groves. During the last trip to Death Valley, Mr. Bailey and the writer found it common in the Panamint Mountains, and saw four at Furnace Creek June 19–21.

In the Sierra Nevada doves were common in Walker Pass July 1–3; along the valley of Kern River, July 3–13; at Walker Basin, July 13–16; at Bakersfield, in the San Joaquin Valley, July 17–20; at Three Rivers in the western foothills, and along the Kaweah below the pines, the last of July. In the High Sierra Mr. Palmer saw a pair in Kings River Cañon, August 14; Mr. Dutcher shot one and saw others at Big Cottonwood Meadows early in September; and it was seen at Soda Springs and Trout Meadows about the same time. In the Cañada de las Uvas, California, it was abundant at Old Fort Tejon in June and July, and Mr. Stephens found it rather common at Reche Cañon, near San Bernardino, September 22–26. Mr. Nelson reported it as common in the San Joaquin Valley in October, and saw a few along the coast from San Simeon to Carpenteria, and at Santa Paula, in November and December.

Mourning doves furnish a large amount of food to the Indians during the spring and summer. Before migration commences the Indians build rude huts of brush, grass, and weeds, in which to secrete themselves, near the springs and streams. Loopholes are made on the sides toward the water, through which arrows are shot at the birds as they alight to drink.

Record of specimens collected of Zenaidura macroura.

Collector's No.	Sex.	Locality.	Date.	Collector.	Remarks.
299	♀ juv.	Owens Valley, Calif.	June 6, 1891.	A. K. Fisher	Lone Pine.
300	♀ juv.	......do............	...do......	...do......	Do.

Pseudogryphus californianus. California Vulture.

It was with considerable surprise and pleasure that we found the California vulture still tolerably common in certain localities west of the Sierra Nevada, in California. Mr. Palmer reported seeing one flying above Frazier Mountain July 9, and while on his way to Tejon ranch, July 11, saw three others soaring overhead in company with turkey buzzards, and stated that it was an easy matter to distinguish the two species.

On July 16, about 3 miles from Walker Basin, on the road leading to Bakersfield, in the San Joaquin Valley, Mr. Bailey and the writer saw one of these vultures in company with the turkey buzzards flying about the carcass of a cow. The white on the underside of its wings was plainly visible.

At San Emigdio and the adjacent foothills Mr. Nelson found it quite common in October, and was told that it became very numerous there in winter. He also found it common along the coast near San Simeon, and in the Santa Ynez Mountains. In all these places it was shy and difficult of approach. On the pass at the head of Owens River, July 24, and on the trail above Lone Pine, August 27, Mr. Nelson saw solitary birds which he thought belonged to this species.

Cathartes aura. Turkey Vulture.

The turkey buzzard was seen in various localities, both in the desert and in the mountain regions, but was nowhere common. It was first met with in Death Valley, where a few were seen during the latter part of March. Dr. Merriam saw a number sailing over the Mohave Desert March 29 and 30, and saw several congregated about a dead horse at Furnace Creek, Death Valley, April 11. He saw one in Emigrant Cañon in the Panamint Mountains about the middle of April, and another at Hot Springs, in Panamint Valley, April 20. Mr. Nelson saw a few over Mesquite Valley, and in the Grapevine Mountains in May; found it sparingly in the Inyo Mountains, from the valley to the summit, in the latter part of June, and in the White Mountains in July.

In the Argus Range the writer saw it in Shepherd Cañon and at Maturango Spring, in the latter part of April and first part of May; a few were found at Coso the latter part of May, and around Owens Lake and Lone Pine in June. The species was noted all through Owens Valley, from the southern part to the upper end, and at the base of the White Mountains. On the last trip to Death Valley some were seen at Furnace Creek, June 19-21.

In the Sierra Nevada it was seen at Kernville, along the valley of the Kern River, and in Walker Basin in July; and in the High Sierra at Horse Corral, Big Cottonwood, and Whitney meadows, in August.

It was seen at Old Fort Tejon, and in Tehachapi Valley, California, in June, by Dr. Merriam and Mr. Palmer. In the San Joaquin Valley it was seen at various places from Bakersfield to Visalia and Three Rivers. Mr. Bailey saw it at Monterey the last of September; and Mr. Stephens at Reche Cañon, near San Bernardino, about the same date. In Nevada Dr. Merriam saw it in Vegas Wash, May 3; in the Virgin Valley, May 8; Pahranagat Valley, May 22-26; Ash Meadows, May 30; and a few on Mount Magruder, June 4-8. In the Santa Clara Valley, Utah, it was rather common, May 11-15.

Mr. Nelson found it common in the San Joaquin Valley, in the Tehachapi Mountains, and along the route from San Simeon to Carpenteria about the end of the year.

Elanus leucurus. White-tailed Kite.

Mr. Nelson found the white-tailed kite rather uncommon about San Luis Obispo, where he shot a specimen and saw others in November The species was not seen elsewhere.

An adult ♀ Vulture was killed near Julian San Diego Co. June 2 1888 it measured 3 ft 7 10/10 in. long and 9 ft. 2 7/10 in. extent weighed 21 lbs. (Avifauna Vol I No.2 P.18 Oct 1895)

A male was killed April 21 1895 7 miles NE of Santa Monica Calif. — extent 9 ft 8 in. weight 27 lbs. (Ibid)

A California vulture was seen by John Van Denburgh sitting on a fence near the road between Big Pine & Bishop Creek Owens Valley July 19, 1893 (Proc. Acad. Nat. Sci. Phila. Apr 1898 p.28)

Circus hudsonius. Marsh Hawk.

Wherever there was sufficient water to form considerable areas of marsh land, the marsh hawk was pretty certain to be observed. An adult male was secured at Furnace Creek in Death Valley, January 29; several were seen at Resting Springs in February; and the species was not uncommon at Ash Meadows, Nevada, in March.

In Nevada Mr. Nelson found it common in Pahrump and Vegas valleys in February and March, especially about the ranch in the former place, and Mr. Stephens reported an unusual preponderance of birds in the blue plumage in Oasis Valley about the middle of March. Dr. Merriam saw one in Oasis Valley, June 1; both blue and red birds at Ash Meadows, May 30, and in Pahranagat Valley May 22-26; he shot a male in Meadow Creek Valley May 19, and saw several in the Lower Muddy and Virgin valleys May 6-8.

In California marsh hawks were common in a number of places throughout Owens Valley in winter as well as during the breeding season, and were doubtless attracted by the vast number of meadow mice (*Arvicolæ*) which swarm through the wet meadows and marshes.

Marsh hawks were common along the South Fork of Kern River, where they were seen often through the day skimming over the alfalfa fields and marshes, and in the High Sierra a few were seen at Whitney and Big Cottonwood meadows. At the west end of the Mohave Desert Dr. Merriam saw one near Gorman ranch, June 28; Mr. Bailey found it at Monterey in September, and Mr. Nelson reported it as common in the San Joaquin Valley and around Carpenteria later in the fall.

Accipiter velox. Sharp-shinned Hawk.

We found this species nowhere as common as it is in most of the Eastern States; the total number seen by members of the party, both during migration and in the breeding season, being less than could be seen in southern New York on any day in early September.

The writer saw two at the ranch at Furnace Creek, Death Valley, in the latter part of January; Mr. Nelson observed one at Bennett Wells in the same valley about the same time; and Dr. Merriam saw two at the former place, April 11. The species was seen at Resting Springs, California, the first week in February. In Nevada it was observed at Ash Meadows early in March; Mr. Nelson saw several and killed one at the ranch in Pahrump Valley February 12-28; and saw it among the mesquite thickets on his route from Ash Meadows to the Bend of the Colorado, March 3-16. Dr. Merriam saw one at Vegas Wash May 2; one at the Bend of the Colorado River, Nevada, May 4; one at the west side of the Beaverdam Mountains, Utah, May 10.

In California he saw one in Owens Valley about the middle of June, and one in Kern Valley, June 22. At Hot Springs, in Panamint Valley, Mr. Nelson shot a specimen early in January, and Dr. Merriam saw two during his stay, April 19-24; one in Emigrant Cañon, in the

Panamint Mountains, April 14; and another on the north side of Telescope Peak, April 18; and the writer saw one in Surprise Cañon, April 20.

Mr. Nelson saw the species once or twice in the piñon belt along Waucoba Creek, in the Inyo Mountains, in the latter part of June; and a few in the foothills on the west slope of the Sierra Nevada, in August. Mr. Bailey and the writer observed two or three on the western slope of Walker Pass in the same range July 2-3; one was observed in Kings River Cañon, August 15; and another at Three Rivers in the western foothills, September 13. Mr. Koch secured a pair near their camp in Cottonwood Meadows July 30; Mr. Palmer reported seeing two at Old Fort Tejon; and Mr. Bailey found it not uncommon at Whitney Meadows and at Soda Springs, in August.

Mr. Stephens saw one at Grapevine Spring, California, the first week in April; one at Olancha, at the southern end of Owens Lake, the third week in May, and one at Bishop Creek, early in August. Mr. Bailey saw several at Monterey, during the first week of October. Mr. Nelson found it common in the San Joaquin Valley between Bakersfield and San Emigdio in October, and saw a few along the coast from San Simeon to Carpenteria and Santa Paula in November and December.

Record of specimens collected of Accipiter velox.

Collector's No.	Sex.	Locality.	Date.	Collector.	Remarks.
22	♂ ad.	Sierra Nevada, Calif	July 30, 1891	B. H. Dutcher	Big Cottonwood Meadows.
23	♀ ad.	......do......	......do......	......do......	Do.

Accipiter cooperi. Cooper's Hawk.

This hawk was even more rare than the sharp-shinned, as scarcely two dozen were seen during the time the expedition was in the field. In Cajon Pass in the San Bernardino Mountains, on January 2, the writer decoyed one by imitating the squealing of a mouse; one was seen at Hesperia on the Mohave Desert, January 4; one or two at the ranch at Furnace Creek, Death Valley, the latter part of the same month, and a few were seen at Ash Meadows, Nevada, during the first half of March. Mr. Stephens saw one which had been killed at Scarf's garden, on Borax Flat, April 23-26, and one at Bishop Creek, in Owens Valley, the first week in August.

In the Sierra Nevada Mr. Nelson noted the species on the divide between the Merced and San Joaquin rivers; Mr. Bailey saw one on the Kaweah River; two at Whitney Meadows; the writer saw one at the latter place September 2, and secured a specimen at Three Rivers, in the western foothills, July 28. Its stomach contained the remains of a Beechey's spermophile.

Mr. Nelson found a few among the oaks in the lower part of the Tehachapi and Temploa mountains in October, and along the route between San Simeon and Carpenteria in November.

Accipiter atricapillus striatulus. Goshawk.

No specimens of this handsome and daring hawk were taken by any member of the expedition. Mr. Nelson stated that a hawk flew over his camp at Lone Pine, Owens Valley, in December, 1890, which he thought belonged to this species, and Mr. Bailey is quite certain he saw an individual among the sequoias on Kaweah River, and another at Soda Springs, or Kern River Lakes.

Buteo borealis calurus. Western Red-tail.

The western red-tail was observed at most localities visited by members of the expedition in California, Nevada, and Utah. It was seen on the Mohave Desert near Victor, early in January, several were observed in Death Valley between Bennett Wells and Saratoga Springs about the 1st of February, and one at the former place in Death Valley, on June 21.

At Resting Springs, California, a fine specimen was secured, and others seen early in February. In Nevada it was noted at Ash Meadows, in Pahrump Valley, in Vegas Wash, at the Bend of the Colorado, at Pahroc Spring, in Pahranagat Valley, in Oasis Valley, at Mount Magruder, and on the Charleston and Grapevine mountains. On Mount Magruder one was shot by Dr. Merriam as it swooped to pick up a wounded dove, June 7, and another at the mouth of Beaverdam Creek, Arizona, May 9. The stomach of the latter contained a ground squirrel (*Spermophilus tereticaudus*). Several were seen in the Santa Clara Valley, Utah, about the middle of May.

In the Panamint Mountains, California, Dr. Merriam observed it in Emigrant Cañon about the middle of April, and Mr. Bailey and the writer saw one soaring over the summit of Telescope Peak on June 23 and later in the day the former observer killed one near the 'charcoal kilns.' Its stomach contained one pocket gopher (*Thomomys*), two large lizards (*Cnemidophorus tigris* and *Sauromalus ater*), five grasshoppers, and one sand cricket (*Stenopalmatus*). In the northern part of the same mountains Mr. Nelson noted a few, and also in the White and Inyo mountains from the upper limit of the pines down to the valleys. In the Argus Range individuals were seen at Shepherd Cañon and Maturango Spring; and near the road to Lookout Mountain an adult was seen on June 25, beating back and forth over the rocky hillside, evidently hunting for the large lizards known as 'chuck-wallas' (*Sauromalus ater*), which were common in the locality.

It was observed in the Coso Mountains, and in Owens Valley it was found at a number of places, both in winter and summer. It was seen at Old Fort Tejon, Walker Pass, Walker Basin, South Fork of Kern River, and in the High Sierra at Sequoia National Park, Horse Corral, Cottonwood, and Whitney meadows, and Round Valley.

In the San Joaquin Valley it was observed at Bakersfield and Visalia. Mr. Bailey saw it at Monterey, and Mr. Stephens at Reche Cañon near San Bernardino. Mr. Nelson saw it everywhere about the Tehachapi and Temploa mountains and found it common all along the coast from San Simeon to Santa Paula in November and December.

Buteo lineatus elegans. Red-bellied Hawk.

This species was observed mainly in the San Joaquin Valley, where one was seen near an irrigating ditch at Bakersfield, July 18, evidently watching for frogs. At Visalia a fine adult was seen among the oaks, July 22, and at the same place on September 17 and 18 the species was not uncommon. Mr. Nelson reported it as abundant among the oaks on Kings River at the base of the foothills in August, and saw it near the Mission of Santa Ynez and in Gaviota Pass, in November.

Buteo swainsoni. Swainson's Hawk.

Swainson's hawk is apparently a rare species in the region traversed by the expedition. Mr. Nelson saw a number on the western foothills of the Sierra Nevada, and Dr. Merriam shot an adult male on Kern River near Kernville, June 23. Its stomach contained one grasshopper. Several were seen catching grasshoppers in the Cañada de las Uvas, California, June 28–29. At Walker Basin, California, Mr. Bailey and the writer saw a number, and on July 15 the latter observer killed an adult female whose stomach contained about fifty grasshoppers. In Walker Basin a species of grasshopper, which Prof. C. V. Riley kindly identified for the writer as *Camnula pellucida*, was very abundant. In many places a large part of the vegetation ordinarily available as food for these insects was dried up and had lost much of its original nutritive properties, so they had to seek elsewhere for subsistence. This they found in the form of fresh horse droppings which were strewn along the roads and in the corrals. Wherever this substance occurred vast numbers of grasshoppers congregated in a struggling mass, each individual striving to reach the interior of the throng so as to partake of the food. Not only the hawks, but most other birds in the valley, including ducks, ravens, woodpeckers, and sparrows, fed almost exclusively on the grasshoppers.

Archibuteo ferrugineus. Ferruginous Rough-leg.

Very few squirrel hawks were seen by the expedition. Mr. Nelson secured a specimen at Pahrump ranch, and saw others in Vegas and Pahrump valleys and Vegas Wash, March 3–16. A few were seen at Ash Meadows, Nevada, about the same time, but none were secured. Dr. Merriam saw a pair circling over the summit of the highest peak of Mount Magruder, Nevada, June 8, and several times afterward saw them hunting in company in the nut pine groves of the same mountains.

Aquila chrysaëtos. Golden Eagle.

The golden eagle was observed sparingly in a number of widely separated localities by different members of the expedition. One was seen at Ash Meadows, Nevada, March 18, circling over a shallow pond in which a large number of ducks were feeding. Mr. Nelson saw several

in Vegas Valley and about the Charleston Mountains, Nevada, March 3-16, and Dr. Merriam saw three among the tree yuccas on the east side of Pahrump Valley, April 29, and one on the Charleston Mountains the following day. One was seen in the Juniper Mountains May 19, and another at Oasis Valley the 1st of June. In California Dr. Merriam observed a pair in Owens Valley, June 10-19, and he and Mr. Palmer saw one near Alamo ranch, in the Sierra Liebre, June 30. According to the Indians, this eagle breeds rarely in the higher portions of the Grapevine, Panamint, Inyo, and White mountains.

In the main Sierra Nevada one was seen on the east slope of Walker Pass, July 2; a pair on the South Fork of the Kern River, July 3-11; one near Little Cottonwood Creek, August 23; a number in Whitney Meadows; and several at and above timber line near Mineral King, September 8-11. At the latter place they probably fed on woodchucks (*Arctomys*) and grouse (*Dendragapus*).

Haliæetus leucocephalus. Bald Eagle.

Two adult bald eagles were seen sitting on a dead mesquite at Ash Meadows, Nevada, about the middle of March. They were the only ones noted during the season.

Falco mexicanus. Prairie Falcon.

Prairie falcons were seen in a number of localities throughout the desert regions as well as among the mountain ranges of southern California and Nevada. In Death Valley, between Bennett Wells and Furnace Creek, one was seen January 22, and at the latter place one was shot from its perch on a haystack where it sat watching a flock of Gambel's quail, January 27, and another was seen in summer on June 20. One was secured at Resting Springs in the Amargosa Desert, February 12, and another at Ash Meadows, Nevada, March 16. At the latter place, where ducks were abundant, this falcon was seen on several occasions to chase single birds, which escaped by dropping in the water among the tules. Mr. Nelson saw a number in Pahrump and Vegas valleys, Nevada, and at the Bend of the Colorado, and one was seen on a cliff in Vegas Wash eating a duck. In the Panamint Mountains one was shot from the top of a cut bank at the mouth of Johnson Cañon, March 26; others were seen in Emigrant Cañon, April 14-15, and in the higher mountains near Telescope Peak, April 17-19. Mr. Nelson found it sparingly about the bases of both the Panamint and Grapevine ranges, where old nests were found on the cliffs. In Nevada Dr. Merriam saw it on Mount Magruder, June 8; in Pahranagat Valley, May 22-26 (breeding in both the Pahranagat and Hyko mountains), and in the Virgin Valley near Bunkerville, May 8. In the Lower Santa Clara Valley, Utah, he saw a pair several times about the cliffs a short distance from the village of St. George, May 11-15.

In Panamint Valley it was seen at Hot Springs April 20, and in the lower end of the valley, January 12. A female was seen in the Coso

Mountains chasing doves, May 19. In Owens Valley the species was seen at a number of localities, and undoubtedly breeds in both the Inyo range and the Sierra Nevada. On the eastern slope of Walker Pass a pair of these falcons were seen flying along the hillsides where quail were abundant.

In the High Sierra a specimen was shot at Big Cottonwood Meadows, August 26; one was seen at Whitney Meadows in the same month, and another at the summit of the pass at the head of Kings River. Mr. Palmer noted the species at Old Fort Tejon, June 28; Mr. Nelson saw it occasionally in the San Joaquin Valley, October 5–27; and saw several along the route from San Simeon to Santa Maria in November, and a few at Cañada de las Uvas and up to the summit of the Temploa Mountains.

Record of specimens collected of Falco mexicanus.

Collector's No.	Sex.	Locality.	Date.	Collector.	Remarks.
83	♂	Panamint Valley, Calif	Jan. 12, 1891	E. W. Nelson	
	♂	Death Valley, Calif	Jan. 27, 1891	A. K. Fisher	Furnace Creek.
110	♀	Resting Springs, Calif	Feb. 12, 1891	....do	
131	♀	Ash Meadows, Calif	Mar. 16, 1891	....do	
141	♂	Panamint Mountains, Calif	Mar. 25, 1891	....do	Johnson Cañon.

Falco peregrinus anatum. Duck Hawk.

The only true duck hawk seen by the expedition was observed by Mr. Nelson near the coast west of San Luis Obispo, in November.

Falco columbarius. Pigeon Hawk.

The only records of the pigeon hawk made by the expedition are the following, all in California: Two seen by Mr. Stephens at Little Owens Lake early in May; the remains of one found by the writer near the reservoir at Furnace Creek, Death Valley, June 21; a few seen on the coast by Mr. Nelson between San Simeon and Carpenteria in November, and one in the Ojai Valley, Ventura County, in December.

Falco sparverius deserticolus. Desert Sparrow Hawk.

The sparrow hawk was common in but few places and was nowhere numerous as a summer resident. In Nevada it was not observed except at Ash Meadows, and in Pahrump and Vegas valleys, where it was found in March.

In California one was seen in Cajon Pass in the San Bernardino Mountains, January 1, and another, March 30. In Death Valley it was seen at Mesquite Well, January 21, Bennett Wells at the same date, and again about the middle of April; a pair among the cottonwoods at Furnace Creek, March 22, and one in Mesquite Valley, April 12.

In the Panamint Mountains, Dr. Merriam saw one in Emigrant Cañon, April 14, another on the north side of Telescope Peak, April 17–19, and Mr. Nelson found it rare in this range as well as in the Grapevine range in May. He found a pair nesting at the summit of the divide at the head of Cottonwood Creek in the former range, and a few in the Inyo

Mountains from the upper edge of the piñon belt up to the summit. In the latter range a pair occupied a cavity in a dead *Pinus flexilis* on the divide east of Lone Pine. Dr. Merriam saw a male on the summit of the White Mountains between Deep Spring Valley and Owens Valley, June 9, and Mr. Nelson saw the species in the same mountains and on the plateau at head of Owens Valley the following month.

In the Argus range, above Maturango Spring, a male was seen with a snake in its talons, which was carried to a height of several hundred yards and dropped, for what reason was not evident.

In Owens Valley the sparrow hawk was common at Lone Pine in December, 1890, and was found sparingly in the summer from Little Owens Lake to the head of the valley in the White Mountains. It was seen along the South Fork of Kern River, July 3-10; at Kernville, July 11-12, and was common in Walker Basin, where it was feeding on grasshoppers, July 13-16.

Mr. Palmer found it common on Peru Creek and in Castac Cañon, near Newhall, June 30, and in San Francisquito Pass, July 1. In the High Sierra it was seen at Menache Meadows, May 24-26; was common at Big Cottonwood Meadows during the summer; common at Whitney Meadows from below timberline to some distance above it during the last of August; at Round Valley, 12 miles south of Mount Whitney August 28; at Soda Springs or Kern River Lakes, early in September; and along the Kaweah River in August. Mr. Bailey found it common at Monterey, September 28 to October 9, and Mr. Stephens at Reche Cañon, September 22-24.

Mr. Nelson found it common in the San Joaquin Valley October 5-27 and abundant along the route from San Simeon to Carpenteria and Santa Paula in November and December.

It was common near San Luis Obispo, where one was seen with a small snake in its talons. It was sitting on a fence post eating the snake, and when startled flew off, carrying the reptile.

Record of specimens collected of Falco sparverius deserticolus.

Collector's No.	Sex.	Locality.	Date.	Collector.	Remarks.
33	♂	Sierra Nevada, Calif.	Aug. 12, 1891	B. H. Dutcher	Big Cottonwood Meadows.
428	♂	......do............	Aug. 28, 1891	A. K. Fisher	Round Valley.

Pandion haliaëtus carolinensis. Osprey.

The fish hawk was observed by Dr. Merriam in two localities, Death Valley, California, and Pahranagat Valley, Nevada. In the former place a single individual was seen at Furnace Creek just before dark on April 10. In Pahranagat Valley he saw several at the lake May 24, and in the evening of the same day shot one by mistake for an owl, as it hovered over the camp fire after dark.

At Furnace Creek a specimen was nailed upon the side of the house at the ranch, where it was killed a year or so before our arrival.

Strix pratincola. Barn Owl.

The only barn owl found east of the Sierra Nevada was a dead one seen by Mr. Stephens at Alvord, the last of June. Dr. Merriam and Mr. Palmer found the species abundant at Old Fort Tejon the latter part of June, where a family of young, in one of the large oaks near camp, proved a great nuisance on account of the hissing and shrieking which was kept up all night. The old birds were seen flying in and out among the large oaks on several occasions, as if in pursuit of bats. It is altogether likely that they were thus occupied, as the remains of this mammal have been found repeatedly among their stomach contents, both in Europe and this country. A pouched gopher and a chipmunk, left on the table, disappeared one night, probably through the agency of these birds.

On the South Fork of the Kern River Mr. Bailey secured two specimens July 4, and the species was common at Bakersfield and Visalia, in the San Joaquin Valley, in the latter part of July. Dr. Merriam found it common in the old mission of San Luis Rey, in San Diego County, and Mr. Stephens saw one in Reche Cañon, near San Bernardino. Mr. Nelson found it very common about San Emigdio, Morro Bay, and San Luis Obispo in October and November.

Record of specimens collected of Strix pratincola.

Collector's No.	Sex.	Locality.	Date.	Collector.	Remarks.
	♂	Kern River, Calif	July 4, 1891	V. Bailey	South Fork.
	♂	......do......	......do......	......do......	Do.
402	♀	Visalia, Calif	July 23, 1891	A. K. Fisher	

Asio wilsonianus. Long-eared Owl.

The long-eared owl was seen at a few places only. Mr. Nelson found a flock of eight living in a willow patch at Pahrump ranch, Nevada, February 12-28. All were flushed in an area less than 50 yards in diameter, and each bird had evidently occupied the same place for a considerable time, as the little groups of several dozen pellets plainly showed. Mr. Bailey secured a specimen at Bakersfield, in the San Joaquin Valley, July 18, and another near timber line north of Mineral King in the Sierra Nevada, September 9.

Asio accipitrinus. Short-eared Owl.

Several short-eared owls were seen at Ash Meadows, Nevada, during the early part of March, and Mr. Stephens shot a specimen in Temecula Cañon, San Diego County, California, January 30.

Syrnium occidentale. Spotted Owl.

This species was not met with by any member of our expedition, though the type came from Old Fort Tejon, California, where it was obtained March 6, 1858, by John Xantus.

Syrnium occidentale   Specimens taken in southern Calif.
                        (Auk, XIII p. 265)

Megascops flammeolus.

A specimen of this owl was captured in the San Bernardino Mtts. at an elevation of 5000 ft. May 26 1893 E.D. Palmer (Auk XI Jan., 1894 p. 78).

Mr. Brewster who examined the San Luis Obispo specimen considers it <u>saturatus</u>

Megascops asio bendirei. California Screech Owl.

No screech owls were seen or heard east of the Sierra Nevada in California. On the ridge above Walker Basin one was flushed from among the oaks July 14, but was not secured. At Bakersfield, in the San Joaquin Valley, the species was common and was heard at short intervals from dark to daylight, and Mr. Bailey secured a specimen about midnight of July 19, as it sat in the moonlight on a low limb over his bed. At Visalia, in the same valley, it was heard commonly among the big oaks July 22-24, and again September 17 and 18.

Mr. Nelson heard screech owls in different parts of the San Joaquin Valley in October, and along the route from San Simeon to Carpenteria and Santa Paula in November and December.

Record of specimens collected of Megascops asio bendirei.

Collector's No.	Sex.	Locality.	Date.	Collector.	Remarks.
399	♂	Bakersfield, Calif	July 20, 1891	A. K. Fisher	
463	♀	Visalia, Calif	July 24, 1891	do	

Bubo virginianus subarcticus. Western Horned Owl.

Great horned owls were often heard and occasionally seen at different localities in California and Nevada—in the latter State at Ash Meadows and in the Grapevine and Charleston mountains.

In California, in the Panamint Mountains, it was heard almost nightly in Johnson and Surprise cañons during the first half of April, and by Dr. Merriam in Emigrant Cañon about the same time. In the Argus Range at Shepherd Cañon an individual on several occasions was seen to fly from a certain ledge, where it probably had young; and at Maturango Spring one was flushed from among some boulders on May 7. It was heard all along the South Fork of the Kern River, July 3-11, and at Walker Basin, where two started from a rocky ledge among the hills, and one secured, July 14. Its stomach contained the remains of a wood rat (*Neotoma*) and a scorpion. In the San Joaquin Valley the species was heard at Bakersfield and Visalia in the latter part of July, and in the High Sierra at Sequoia National Park, Horse Corral and Whitney meadows, Soda Springs, and along the Kaweah River, in August and September.

Mr. Bailey heard it at Monterey, September 28 to October 9, and Mr. Stephens at Reche Cañon, September 22-24. Mr. Nelson heard great horned owls in the Tehachapi and Temploa mountains, in the San Joaquin Valley, and secured a specimen near San Luis Obispo.

Record of specimens obtained of Bubo virginianus subarcticus.

Collector's No.	Sex.	Locality.	Date.	Collector.	Remarks.
	im.	Soda Springs, Kern River, Calif.	Aug. 13, 1891	V. Bailey	Fragments.
	♀	San Luis Obispo, Calif	Nov. 29, 1891	E. W. Nelson	

Speotyto cunicularia hypogæa. Burrowing Owl.

The burrowing owl was not met with in any great numbers east of the Sierra Nevada in California or in Nevada. In the latter State several were seen in Ash Meadows, and one was caught at the mouth of the hole of a kangaroo rat (*Dipodomys deserti*) in Oasis Valley in March. In California several were seen about badger holes at Daggett, on the Mohave Desert, January 8–10; a few at Granite Wells January 15 and April 5, and a pair at Lone Willow Spring April 25. Mr. Bailey saw a pair at Bennett Wells, in Death Valley, June 21. A pair was seen in Coso Valley, below Maturango Spring, May 11. In Owens Valley one was seen at Lone Pine June 11; a pair with young at Alvord June 26–29; one at Morans July 4–7, and a few at the head of the valley, near the White Mountains, in July. Mr. Stephens saw it at various places in Salt Wells Valley, where it probably was breeding, May 1–5, and Mr. Bailey and the writer found it common at Indian Wells, in the same valley, July 1. A pair was seen on the eastern slope of Walker Pass July 1, where one was caught in a trap the following morning. A number of times burrowing owls were caught in steel traps set at the holes of badgers, foxes, spermophiles, and kangaroo rats.

Dr. Merriam and Mr. Palmer saw several pairs with full-grown young in the upper part of the Cañada de las Uvas and near Gorman Station, at the west end of Antelope Valley, during the latter part of June and the first week of July. They were living in the burrows of Beechey's spermophile and were catching grasshoppers in the daytime. They saw the species also at Caliente June 24, and in Tehachapi Valley June 25. At Bakersfield, in the San Joaquin Valley, and on the dry plains between Bakersfield and Visalia it was abundant, and as many as a dozen or fifteen were often in sight at once, perched on the mounds in front of the burrows, or on the tops of the telegraph poles.

Mr. Nelson found it generally distributed in the lowlands bordering the coast, between San Simeon and Carpenteria.

Record of specimens collected of Speotyto cunicularia hypogæa.

Collectors' No.	Sex.	Locality.	Date.	Collector.	Remarks.
48	♀	Daggett, Calif	Jan. 10, 1891	A. K. Fisher	Mohave Desert.
49	♂	do	do	do	Do.
7	♀	do	Feb. 7, 1891	F. Stephens	Do.
62	♂	Granite Wells, Calif	Jan. 15, 1891	A. K. Fisher	Do.
103	♀	Mojave, Calif	Sept. 9, 1891	F. Stephens	35 miles northeast.
120	♂	Owens Valley, Calif	June 20, 1891	do	
	♀ im	Walker Pass, Calif	July 2, 1891	V. Bailey	
31	♂	Oasis Valley, Nev	Mar. 15, 1891	F. Stephens	

Geococcyx californianus. Road-runner.

The road-runner or chaparral cock is tolerably common in many of the desert and foothill regions visited by members of the expedition, but on account of its more or less retiring habits comparatively few were seen, though their tracks were common. In Nevada it was very common among the sand dunes and mesquite patches at Ash Meadows, as well as in Vegas Valley and at the Bend of the Colorado, in March, and Mr. Stephens heard it in Oasis Valley.

In California the species is resident in Death Valley, as its numerous tracks seen around the mesquite and other thick growths at Furnace Creek during January and in June conclusively demonstrate.

At Resting Springs in the Amargosa Desert, where it was tolerably common, Mr. Bailey caught one in a steel trap, February 12, and Mr. Nelson found indications of its presence in Mesquite and Saline valleys. In Owens Valley it was very common, judging from the tracks; Mr. Nelson found it common and secured a specimen at Lone Pine in December, 1890; and Dr. Merriam saw one three miles south of that town, June 18, and others at the lower end of the valley on the following day. He saw one in Walker Pass June 22, and Mr. Bailey secured a specimen in the same place July 3. Several were seen along the South Fork of Kern River and at Kernville, June 22-23 and July 3-10, and near Alamo ranch in the Sierra Liebre, June 30. Dr. Merriam saw two near the north end of Cajon Pass in the San Bernardino Mountains, March 29, and found it common in the southern part of San Diego county in Escondido and San Marcos valleys, where it was breeding in patches of branching cactus.

In the Cañada de las Uvas, Mr. Palmer saw one near Castac Lake July 9, and shot one the following day at Old Fort Tejon. In the San Joaquin Valley tracks were seen frequently in the river bottoms and along the borders of thickets near Bakersfield in July, and Mr. Nelson found it common about the foothills at the south and west sides of the valley, October 5-27. The same observer found it along the coast from Morro to Carpenteria in November, and Mr. Bailey at Monterey, September 28 to October 9.

Record of specimens collected of Geococcyx californianus.

Collector's No.	Sex.	Locality.	Date.	Collector.	Remarks.
	♀	Resting Springs, Calif.	Feb. 12, 1891	V. Bailey	
	♂	Walker Pass, Calif.	July 3, 1891	....do	

Coccyzus americanus occidentalis. California Cuckoo.

At Furnace Creek ranch in Death Valley, a cuckoo was seen among the willows at the edge of the reservoir about sunrise on June 20, and later in the day Mr. Bailey succeeded in securing it (an adult female). In the San Joaquin Valley the species was common at Bakersfield July 17-20, and was heard several times at Visalia among the live oaks July 22-25. In Owens Valley, Mr. Stephens saw one August 11, two miles west of Bishop. No others were recorded.

Ceryle alcyon. Belted Kingfisher.

A kingfisher was seen at San Bernardino, Calif., December 29, 1890. The species was not again met with until the party reached Ash Meadows, Nevada, where a few were seen along the streams during the early part of March. One was seen by Mr. Burnett at Furnace Creek, Death Valley, flying about the reservoir, April 15. Dr. Merriam saw one at Hot Springs, Panamint Valley, April 20, and another in Vegas Wash, Nevada, near the Colorado, May 2.

At Lone Pine, in Owens Valley, it was not uncommon along the river, and Mr. Stephens noted it at Alvord, in the same valley, the last of June. In the Sierra Nevada it was not uncommon at Soda Springs or Kern River lakes, the first of September, and was noted at Three Rivers, in the western foothills, about the middle of the month. Mr. Nelson observed it at the head of the Merced and San Joaquin rivers, and later saw a few individuals along the Kern River, in San Joaquin Valley, in October, and along the streams flowing into the sea between San Simeon, Carpenteria, and Santa Paula, in November and December. Mr. Bailey found it common at Monterey September 28 to October 9.

Dryobates villosus hyloscopus. Cabanis's Woodpecker.

Cabanis's woodpecker was found nowhere common in California, and was not observed at all in Nevada. One was seen above Johnson Cañon in the Panamint Mountains, April 18; Dr. Merriam observed several on the north side of Telescope Peak in the same range, April 17–19, and Mr. Nelson found the species very rare in the northern part of the Panamint and Grapevine Mountains during May and the first part of June. In the Coso Mountains it was seen on several occasions during the last half of May; in the upper part of the Inyo Range a few were seen the last of June; and others on the summit of the White Mountains June 9.

In the Sierra Nevada a few were seen on the east slope, at the head of Owens River, in July; several at Bishop Creek August 4–11; and the species was rather common at Menache Meadows May 24-26. Several were seen on the western slope of Walker Pass July 2; a number along the valley of Kern River July 3–10; and they were not uncommon in Walker Basin, from the bottom of the valley to summit of the ridge, July 13–16. Several were seen in the Sequoia National Park during the first week in August; a few at Horse Corral Meadows August 9–13; one was observed in Kings River Cañon August 15; the species was common at Big Cottonwood Meadows through the summer, at Whitney Meadows September 1, and several were noted from timber line down to below Mineral King September 10–13.

In the Cañada de las Uvas Mr. Palmer saw one or two back of Old Fort Tejon July 6, and a number near the summit of Frazier Mountain July 9.

At Monterey Mr. Bailey found a race of the hairy woodpecker, probably the present subspecies, common from September 28 to October 9; and Mr. Nelson found it sparingly at Mount Piños in October, and in the mountains between San Simeon and Carpenteria November 4 to December 18.

Record of specimens collected of Dryobates villosus hyloscopus.

Collector's No.	Sex.	Locality.	Date.	Collector.	Remarks.
365	♂ ad.	White Mountains, Calif	June 9, 1891	V. Bailey	
375	♀ im.	Walker Pass, Calif	July 2, 1891	A. K. Fisher	
143	♂ im.	Kern River, Calif	July 5, 1891	....do	South Fork.
30	♀ im.	Sierra Nevada, Calif	July 27, 1891	F. Stephens	
31	♂ im.	......do	Aug. 11, 1891	B. H. Dutcher	Big Cottonwood Meadows.
	im.	......do	....do	......do	Do.

Dryobates pubescens gairdnerii. Gairdner's Woodpecker.

Dr. Merriam shot a specimen of this species on the north side of Tehachapi Pass, California, a few miles below the summit, June 25. Mr. Nelson found it rare in the piñon belt of the Panamint and Grapevine mountains May 4 to June 15, and reported a few seen near San Luis Obispo the last of October. These are the only records we have for the species.

Dryobates scalaris bairdi. Baird's Woodpecker.

The known range of this woodpecker was extended considerably by the observations of the expedition. In the Mohave Desert it was not uncommon among the giant yuccas at Hesperia, east of Cajon Pass, where a pair was secured January 4 and 5. Dr. Merriam saw one at the Upper Cottonwood Springs at the east base of the Charleston Mountains, Nevada, April 30, one in Vegas Wash May 2, another near the mouth of the Santa Clara, Utah, May 14, and shot an adult male and saw others in the cottonwoods where Beaverdam Creek joins the Virgin in northwestern Arizona, May 9.

In 1889 Mr. Bailey found it common in the timber along the Santa Clara in January, among the yuccas at Dolan and Mud springs in Detrital Valley, Arizona, in February, and in the river bottom at Fort Mohave in March.

Record of specimens collected of Dryobates scalaris bairdi.

Collector's No.	Sex.	Locality.	Date.	Collector.	Remarks.
31	♂	Beaverdam, Ariz	May 9, 1891	C. Hart Merriam	
41	♂	Hesperia, Calif	Jan. 4, 1891	A. K. Fisher	
	♀	......do	Jan. 5, 1891	....do	

Dryobates nuttallii. Nuttall's Woodpecker.

This species was first observed in Cajon Pass in the San Bernardino Mountains, Calif., where a fine adult male was secured January 2. Mr. Palmer saw several at Old Fort Tejon, July 1, and Dr. Merriam secured a specimen between Walker Basin and Caliente, June 24. In the Sierra Nevada several were seen on the western slope of Walker Pass, July 2—13; it was not uncommon along the valley of Kern River

July 3–13; was common at Walker Basin, July 13–16; and at Three Rivers it was not uncommon, and was found along the East Fork of the Kaweah River as high as the lower edge of the conifers. It was seen on several occasions at Bakersfield, in the San Joaquin Valley, July 17–20; and Mr. Nelson saw several around San Emigdio, and a few along the coast from San Simeon to Carpenteria in November and December, 1891.

Record of specimens collected of Dryobates nuttallii.

Collector's No.	Sex.	Locality.	Date.	Collector.	Remarks.
20	♂	Cajon Pass, Calif.	Jan. 2, 1891	A. K. Fisher	
366	♂ im	Walker Pass, Calif.	July 2, 1891	....do	

Xenopicus albolarvatus. White-headed Woodpecker.

The white-headed woodpecker was rather common in the higher parts of the Sierra Nevada, in California. Mr. Nelson noted a few at the head of Owens River, and found it common on the divide between the Merced and San Joaquin rivers, on the western slope. In the Sequoia National Park it was common, going in pairs and frequenting the more open pine woods. Several were seen at Horse Corral Meadows, August 9–13, and in Kings River Cañon, August 15.

It was seen also at Big Cottonwood Meadows, August 26; at Whitney Meadows the last of August; at Soda Springs or Kern River Lakes, September 3; and along the East Fork of the Kaweah River, from the lower edge of the pines to and above Mineral King, the last of July and September 13–14. Mr. Palmer saw one in Tejon Pass, July 12, and Mr. Nelson observed several near the summit of Mount Piños, in October.

Record of specimens collected of Xenopicus albolarvatus.

Collector's No.	Sex.	Locality.	Date.	Collector.	Remarks.
	♀	Sierra Nevada, Calif.	July 30, 1891	V. Bailey	East Fork of Kaweah River.
408	♂	....do	Aug. 6, 1891	A. K. Fisher	Sequoia National Park.

Sphyrapicus varius nuchalis. Red-naped Sapsucker.

The single record of this woodpecker is a male, killed by Mr. Nelson among the piñons on the west slope of the mountains northwest of Charleston Peak, Nevada, February 12, 1891.

Sphyrapicus ruber. Red-breasted Sapsucker.

The red-breasted woodpecker was not met with east of the Sierra Nevada. Mr. Palmer secured a specimen at Halsted Meadows, in the Sequoia National Park, where it was not uncommon, August 3. It was common at Horse Corral Meadows, around the edges of clearings and in the willow clumps, August 9–13; was seen at Soda Springs or Kern

River Lakes by Mr. Bailey and the writer in August and September; and on the Kaweah River, below the pines, September 12. Mr. Nelson noted it at the head of Owens River and on the western slope, where it was rather more common. He also saw a few at Mount Piños about the middle of October, and Mr. Palmer say a few in Tejon Pass, July 12.

Record of specimens collected of Sphyrapicus ruber.

Collector's No.	Sex.	Locality.	Date.	Collector.	Remarks.
140	♂	Sierra Nevada, Calif	July 24, 1891	F. Stephens	Horse Corral Meadows.
412	♂ ad.	....do	Aug. 12, 1891	A. K. Fisher	Do.
413	♂ im.	....do	....do	....do	Do.
	♂ im.	....do	....do	V. Bailey	Kern River Lakes.

Sphyrapicus thyroideus. Williamson's Sapsucker.

Williamson's woodpecker is not uncommon in a number of places in the Sierra Nevada, in California. Mr. Nelson saw one at the head of Owens River, and a few on the western slope opposite that place. Several were seen at Horse Corral Meadows, August 11–13; at Whitney Meadows about September 1; and the species was common at Big Cottonwood Meadows, August 25–27, where Mr. Dutcher killed several earlier in the season. It was noted at Soda Springs or Kern River Lakes, early in September; at Mineral King, the last of July and the second week in September, and was seen once on Mount Piños about the middle of October.

Record of specimens collected of Sphyrapicus thyroideus.

Collector's No.	Sex.	Locality.	Date.	Collector.	Remarks.
410	♂	Sierra Nevada, Calif	Aug. 11, 1891	A. K. Fisher	Horse Corral Meadows.
	im.	....do	Aug. 2, 1891	V. Bailey	Mineral King.
27	♂ im.	....do	Aug. 4, 1891	B. H. Dutcher	Big Cottonwood Meadows.
28	♂ im.	....do	....do	....do	Do.
29	im.	....do	....do	....do	Do.
423	♂	....do	Aug. 26, 1891	A. K. Fisher	Do.
156	♂ im.	....do	Aug. 24, 1891	F. Stephens	Olancha Peak.

Ceophlœus pileatus. Pileated Woodpecker.

This handsome woodpecker was not observed except in the Sierra Nevada, in California, where Mr. Nelson found it common at an altitude of about 1980 meters (6,500 feet) in the Mariposa grove of big trees near Wawona and along the Merced River. The writer heard it a number of times in the Sequoia National Park early in August, and Mr. Palmer saw a pair in Kings River Cañon, August 14.

Melanerpes formicivorus bairdi. California Woodpecker.

The California woodpecker was not seen east of the western slope of the Sierra Nevada. Dr. Merriam found it in Walker Basin June 24; in

Tehachapi Pass, June 25; and in the Cañada de las Uvas, where it was breeding abundantly, June 28-29. At Three Rivers, in the foot hills, the species was common July 25-30, and September 14-17, at which time it was feeding on acorns.

In Walker Basin the writer saw several families along a fence row where they were feeding on grasshoppers, July 13-16, and on the 14th the species was common among the pines on the ridge above the valley.

All along the road between Tulare and Visalia in the San Joaquin Valley, this woodpecker was common among the oaks, July 22-24. As many as ten individuals were seen in one tree.

Mr. Nelson found it common and generally distributed among the oaks in the San Joaquin Valley, and along the route from San Simeon to Santa Paula, during the last three months of the year.

Record of specimens collected of Melanerpes formicivorus bairdi.

Collector's No.	Sex.	Locality.	Date.	Collector.	Remarks.
389	♂	Walker Basin, Calif	June 14, 1891	A. K. Fisher	
401	♂	Visalia, Calif	July 23, 1891	do	

Melanerpes torquatus. Lewis's Woodpecker.

This woodpecker was quite common in Walker Basin, where it was seen June 24 and July 13-16. The birds were stationed along the fence rows and on trees, from which they made frequent excursions to the ground to capture grasshoppers. The stomachs of a number examined contained nothing but the remains of this insect.

It was seen by Dr. Merriam and Mr. Palmer near Old Fort Tejon, in the Cañada de las Uvas, the latter part of June. Mr. Nelson saw one on the plateau at the head of Owens Valley in July and on the east slope of the Sierra at the head of Owens River in the latter part of July. At Three Rivers, in the western foothills, it was common among the oaks September 12-17.

Record of specimens collected of Melanerpes torquatus.

Collector's No.	Sex.	Locality.	Date.	Collector.	Remarks.
388	im	Walker Basin, California	July 13, 1891	A. K. Fisher	
	im	......do......	....do......	V. Bailey	
	♂ im	......do......	....do......	....do......	
	♀ ad	......do......	....do......	....do......	

Melanerpes uropygialis. Gila Woodpecker.

A specimen of this woodpecker was taken by Mr. Bailey near Fort Mohave, Ariz., in March, 1889.

Colaptes cafer. Red-shafted Flicker.

The red-shafted flicker was seen in many places, though it was comparatively rare over the greater part of the country traversed.

In Nevada, Mr. Nelson saw this woodpecker in Pahrump and Vegas valleys during the latter part of February and first of March. Mr. Stephens observed it in the Grapevine Mountains March 20-26 and found it common at the Queen mine July 11-16. Dr. Merriam saw two in the nut pine zone on Mount Magruder June 6, and the writer shot an individual, the only one seen, at Ash Meadows, March 2. At Pahrump ranch, Mr. Nelson saw where one had drilled four holes through the boards in the gable end of a building used as a granary, and each time a piece of tin had been placed over the hole. When he was there, the bird had just completed a fifth hole, close to the others.

In California, it was common just outside of the town of San Bernardino the last of December, 1890, and was observed in Cajon Pass January 1-2. At Hesperia, in the Mohave Desert, a number were seen among the tree yuccas January 3-4.

Mr. Nelson found the species in the Inyo Mountains the latter part of June, and stated that it occurred wherever there was moisture enough to support a growth of the higher pines in the mountains or of cottonwoods in the valleys. He also found it common from the head of Owens Valley up to timber line in the White Mountains in July. Dr. Merriam saw a red-shafted flicker at Furnace Creek, in Death Valley, April 10, among the willows and mesquite; one at Hot Springs, Panamint Valley, about April 20, and another in the Panamint Mountains a few days earlier. In the Argus Range, the writer saw one at Maturango Spring May 14, several in the Coso Mountains during the latter part of the same month, and a number in the higher portions of the Panamint Mountains the last week in June. In Owens Valley, it was seen by Mr. Nelson at Lone Pine, in December, 1890, and by Mr. Stephens at Independence Creek, Bishop Creek, and Benton during the summer.

This woodpecker was not uncommon in Walker Pass, along the valley of the Kern River, at Kernville, and in Walker Basin during the first half of July. On the High Sierra it was seen in the Sequoia National Park the first week in August; at Horse Corral Meadows August 9-13; in Kings River Cañon August 13-16; at Menache Meadows May 24-26; at Big Cottonwood Meadows June 15 to September; at Whitney Meadows the last of August; Soda Springs or Kern River Lakes, August and first part of September; and at Mineral King and down the west slope to Three Rivers in the foothills during the first two weeks in September.

Dr. Merriam saw it in the Cañada de las Uvas June 28-29, and the writer observed it at Bakersfield July 17-20. Mr. Bailey recorded the species from Monterey September 20 to October 9, and Mr. Nelson reported it common in the Tejon Mountains, in the San Joaquin Valley, at San Luis Obispo, and along the route between San Simeon and Carpenteria during the fall and early winter.

Phalænoptilus nuttalli. Poor-will.

The poor-will was common in a number of localities visited by the expedition. In Death Valley a specimen was obtained at Bennett Wells January 28, another at Saratoga Springs February 4; and the species was seen and heard by Dr. Merriam at Furnace Creek April 10, and in Mesquite Valley April 13. One was seen in the Funeral Mountains March 21. At Ash Meadows, Nevada, one or two were seen and others heard during the first part of March. In Nevada Dr. Merriam found it common on Mount Magruder June 4-9, where he saw and heard one or more every evening and obtained a specimen. On Gold Mountain he heard it at the deserted mining camp June 3, in Pahranagat Valley May 22-26, at Sheep Spring in the Juniper Mountains, May 18, and at Vegas ranch May 1. In Utah he heard it along Shoal Creek, near the Escalante Desert, May 17.

Mr. Nelson found the species in the Panamint and Grapevine mountains, where it was a rare breeder in the sage-brush belt. He saw and heard a few from the bottom of Saline Valley up to the piñons in the Inyo Mountains, found it as high as 2,650 meters (8,700 feet) in the White Mountains, and also on the plateau at the head of Owens Valley. In Owens Valley a specimen was taken at the mouth of the cañon at Lone Pine, June 12; Mr. Stephens saw two at Olancha May 16-23, and others at Independence Creek June 18-23, and at the Queen mill and mine, Nevada, July 11-16. The same observer saw one at Borax Flat, near the southern end of the Argus Range, the last of April. Mr. F. W. Koch collected two fresh eggs May 6 above Maturango Spring, where it was common. At Coso it was heard or seen every evening during the latter half of May. It was common at Hot Springs in Panamint Valley, April 10-25; and at Wild Rose Spring, in the Panamint Mountains, June 25.

Record of specimens collected of Phalænoptilus nuttalli.

Collector's No.	Sex.	Locality.	Date.	Collector.	Remarks.
	♀	Death Valley, Calif	Jan. 28, 1891	E. W. Nelson	Bennett Wells.
	♂	...do...	Feb. 14, 1891	...do...	Saratoga Springs.
246	♂	Coso Mountains, Calif	May 22, 1891	A. K. Fisher	
337	♀	Owens Valley, Calif	June 12, 1891	...do...	Lone Pine.
41	♂	Grapevine Mountains, Calif	Apr. 1, 1891	F. Stephens	Grapevine Spring.
	♀	Mount Magruder, Nev	June 4, 1891	C. Hart Merriam	

Phalænoptilus nuttalli californicus. California Poor-will.

This race of the poor-will was common in Kern Valley, where Mr. Bailey secured a specimen July 8. One was seen on the road from Kaweah to the Sequoia National Park July 31. It would await until the horse nearly stepped on it, then fly ahead some distance and alight on the road again, which manœuver it repeated several times. Mr. Bailey saw a poor-will at Trout Meadows in the High Sierra, which probably belonged to this race. Dr. Merriam shot one at Twin Oaks, at the foot of the Granite range, in San Diego County, July 10, where several were observed to alight in the same place every evening in a dusty road under the spreading branches of a live-oak tree.

Record of specimens collected of Phalænoptilus nuttalli californicus.

Collector's No.	Sex.	Locality.	Date.	Collector.	Remarks.
	♂	Kern River, Calif. Twin Oaks, San Diego County, Calif.	July 8, 1891 July 10, 1891	V. Bailey C. Hart Merriam	South Fork.

Chordeiles virginianus henryi. Western Nighthawk.

It is a source of great regret that specimens of nighthawks were not secured at the various places where they were found by the members of the expedition. This neglect makes it impossible to properly separate the range of the present from that of the following species in the region under consideration.

The only specimen of the western nighthawk secured was one collected by the writer in Death Valley, at Furnace Creek, June 19. At this place the nighthawks began to fly just after sunset and were very common over the alfalfa fields at the ranch. Nighthawks supposed to belong to this species were seen in Pahranagat Valley, Nevada, May 22-26, on Mount Magruder, Nevada, June 4-8, and in the High Sierra, at Trout, Whitney, and Big Cottonwood meadows, during the summer and autumn.

Chordeiles texensis. Texas Nighthawk.

Fortunately, a larger number of specimens of this night-hawk was taken than of the preceding species, though not enough to enable the satisfactory mapping of its distribution in California and Nevada.

The Texas nighthawk was a very common breeder in most parts of Owens Valley, where it occurred as far north at least as Bishop. Around Owens Lake and Lone Pine large numbers were observed every night, and at the former place many were seen skimming close to the water in pursuit of a small fly (*Ephydra hians*), which was swarming on and near the shore.

The species was not uncommon along the South Fork of the Kern River, where Mr. Bailey secured a specimen July 8, and at Bakersfield, in the San Joaquin Valley, where several were seen and one secured about the middle of the month.

Dr. Merriam saw it during the breeding season in Oasis Valley and Ash Meadows, Nev., and at other points in the Amargosa Desert, and also in the Mohave Desert, in California. He saw one at Saratoga Springs at the south end of Death Valley, April 26, and two at Resting Springs in the Amargosa Desert, April 27. He found it common at the mouth of Beaverdam Creek, Arizona, May 9, and secured two fresh eggs at St. George, in the Lower Santa Clara Valley, Utah, May 13. Another was shot in the Virgin Valley, near the eastern boundary of Nevada, May 8. Nighthawks which probably belonged to this species were seen in Pahrump and Vegas valleys, Nevada, and Saline Valley, California. This nighthawk had the habit of alighting on the dusty roads, just at dusk, where it sat motionless for a time, though in a few instances it was observed to make a series of hopping flights, alighting at short intervals for a moment only.

Record of specimens collected of Chordeiles texensis.

Collector's No.	Sex.	Locality.	Date.	Collector.	Remarks.
125	♂	Beaverdam Creek, Ariz.	May 10, 1891	V. Bailey	
319	♀	Owens Valley, Calif.	June 29, 1891	P. Stephens	Bishop.
327	♂	......do......	June 8, 1891	A. K. Fisher	Lone Pine.
335	♀	......do......	June 10, 1891	....do....	Do.
336	♀	......do......	June 12, 1891	....do....	Do.
	♂	......do......	...do...	....do....	Do.
285	♀	......do......	June 13, 1891	C. Hart Merriam	Do.
69	♀	......do......	June 2, 1891	A. K. Fisher	Keeler.
	♂	......do......	May 31, 1891	F. Stephens	Ash Creek.
398	♀	Kern River, Calif.	July 8, 1891	V. Bailey	South Fork.
		Bakersfield, Calif.	July 19, 1891	A. K. Fisher	

Cypseloides niger. Black Swift.

The black swift was first observed at Owens Lake near Keeler, Calif., where a number were seen flying back and forth over the salt meadows on May 31. On June 2, twenty or more were seen feeding over the same meadow and five specimens were collected. From the condition of the ovaries of the female secured, it was evident that the eggs had been laid. When the flock left the marsh, it rose high in the air and went in the direction of the cliffs in the Inyo Mountains, near Cerro Gordo, where a colony evidently was breeding. Near the upper end of the lake, and about 6 miles north of Keeler, several were seen on June 4 and again on June 15. At Lone Pine, five passed over camp early on the morning of June 7, and a number were seen at the mouth of the cañon above the town June 12. Dr. Merriam saw a number and secured one at the north end of Owens Lake, June 12, and saw half a dozen at Olancha, at the south end of the lake, June 20. Mr. Stephens saw a dozen or more at the latter place May 23 and secured two June 4. On the former date they were flying high out of range, in company with white-throated swifts and white-bellied swallows. The same observer saw this species at Independence Creek, June 20, and at Bishop Creek, August 6.

On the South Fork of Kern River three swifts were seen which undoubtedly belonged to this species, and on several occasions black swifts were seen in Kings River Cañon, August 13–16.

Record of specimens collected of Cypseloides niger.

Collector's No.	Sex.	Locality.	Date.	Collector.	Remarks.
279	♂	Keeler, Inyo County, Calif.	June 2, 1891	A. K. Fisher	
280	♂	......do......	...do...	....do....	
281	♀	......do......	...do...	....do....	
282	♀	......do......	...do...	....do....	
	♂	......do......	...do...	T. S. Palmer	
	♂	Owens Lake, Calif.	June 12, 1891	C. Hart Merriam	
73	♀	......do......	June 4, 1891	F. Stephens	Olancha.
74	♂	......do......	...do...	....do....	Do.

Chætura vauxii. Vaux's Swift.

Vaux's swift was seen a few times only in the valleys on each side of the Sierra Nevada. Mr. Stephens saw it nearly every day and secured a specimen at Olancha, near the south end of Owens Lake, where it was migrating, May 16–23.

Mr. Belding saw large flocks in the Yosemite Valley. The writer saw a few at Three Rivers, in the western foothills of the Sierra, September 13–14, and at Visalia on September 18.

Aëronautes melanoleucus. White-throated Swift.

White-throated swifts were common at a number of places in the desert valleys and ranges during the spring and summer. In Johnson Cañon, in the Panamint Mountains, Calif., Mr. Palmer saw one March 26, and Mr. Nelson secured one near the same place, April 12. The latter observer found the species to be a common summer resident in portions of the Panamint and Grapevine mountains visited. The last of May he saw them going in and out of crevices in the steep walls above Willow Creek, and in June found them frequenting the cliffs in Cottonwood Cañon, 750 meters (2,500 feet) above Salt Wells, and observed them about the cliffs in Boundary Cañon in the Grapevine Range. They were frequently seen in the morning and evening hunting over Saline Valley. In the Panimint Mountains north of Telescope Peak, Mr. Bailey and the writer saw several hundred of these swifts flying back and forth over a hillside, and a few above the summit of the peak, June 23. The males uttered at short intervals a series of notes which, when a number joined in the performance, produced a not unpleasant impression. In Death Valley Dr. Merriam saw a flock at Mesquite Wells, April 8; Mr. Burnett saw individuals flying over the reservoir at Furnace Creek, April 15; and the writer killed a number of specimens at the latter place, June 20. In the Argus Range swifts were seen in Shepherd Cañon the last of April, and along the divide above Maturango Spring during the first half of May.

In Nevada Dr. Merriam saw several at Pahroc Spring, May 22; at Ash Meadows, May 30; and in Oasis Valley and the upper part of Amargosa Desert, June 1, when they were observed in aërial coition. In Utah Dr. Merriam saw several small flocks in the Lower Santa Clara Valley, May 11–15. Mr. Nelson found it breeding in the Inyo Mountains, Calif., June 24–July 4, and sparingly in the White Mountains in July. White-throated swifts were common in many places in Owens Valley, especially about the meadows at Owens Lake and at the mouth of the cañons. Along the South Fork of the Kern River they were tolerably common the first week in July, and a few were seen flying over the Sequoia National Park the first week in August. Mr. Nelson found them at the head of Owens River; also along all the streams visited on the western slope of the Sierra, and in the Yosemite Valley up to timber line. They bred everywhere in crevices in the cañon walls. He saw several flocks in the Ojai Valley in December.

Record of specimens collected of Aëronautes melanoleucus.

Collector's No.	Sex	Locality	Date	Collector	Remarks
43	♀	Panamint Mountains, Calif	Apr. 11, 1891	E. W. Nelson	
	♀	Death Valley, Calif	Apr. 9, 1891	F. Stephens	Furnace Creek.
345	♀	......do......	June 20, 1891	A. K. Fisher	Do.
346	♀	......do......	...do...	...do...	Do.
347	♀	......do......	...do...	...do...	Do.
	♂	Keeler, Calif	June 2, 1891	T. S. Palmer	
95	♂	Owens Lake, Calif	June 12, 1891	F. Stephens	Olancha.

Trochilus alexandri. Black-chinned Hummingbird.

The black-chinned hummingbird is common in Owens Valley, California, where it was found at the following localities: At Lone Pine a number of specimens were secured in June; At Olancha Mr. Stephens found it common, May 16–23; at Ash Creek, May 30–June 3; a few at Independence Creek, June 18–23; Alvord, June 26–28; and young of the year were common at Fish Slough, July 2–3. At Olancha he secured a very interesting specimen which in its specific characters was intermediate between this species and Costa's hummer, and was probably a hybrid. He found a nest containing three eggs in an orchard at the same place, May 16. Mr. Nelson found it common on both slopes of the Inyo Mountains from the valleys up to the piñons, wherever there was water enough to produce a growth of willows and other deciduous trees. In Walker Basin, where it was not common, Mr. Bailey secured a specimen, July 14, and another was taken at Bakersfield in the San Joaquin Valley, July 19. At Old Fort Tejon Mr. Palmer secured an immature bird in July, which he referred to this species.

Dr. Merriam saw several and secured two at the mouth of Beaverdam Creek, Arizona, May 9, and found the species common in the Lower Santa Clara Valley, Utah, where four nests containing fresh eggs were found, May 11–14. All the nests (one of which contained three eggs) were placed on low branches of cottonwoods, generally within easy reach from the ground.

Record of specimens collected of Trochilus alexandri.

Collector's No.	Sex	Locality	Date	Collector	Remarks
	♀	Santa Clara, Utah	May 11, 1891	C. Hart Merriam	
58	♂	Beaverdam Creek, Ariz	May 9, 1891	V. Bailey	
65	♀	Owens Valley, Calif	May 16, 1891	F. Stephens	Olancha, set 3 eggs.
	♂	......do......	May 20, 1891	...do...	Ash Creek.
80	♂	......do......	June 10, 1891	...do...	Olancha.
	♂	Walker Basin, Calif	July 14, 1891	V. Bailey	
400	♂	Bakersfield, Calif	July 19, 1891	A. K. Fisher	
311	♂	Owens Valley, Calif	June 7, 1891	...do...	Lone Pine.
312	♂	......do......	...do...	...do...	Do.
314	♂	......do......	June 8, 1891	...do...	Do.

Calypte costæ. Costa's Hummingbird.

Costa's hummingbird is the common species of the desert valleys and mountains of southern California and Nevada. One was seen at

Resting Springs in the Amargosa Desert, California, February 13; a number were seen in the Funeral Mountains March 22; at Furnace Creek, Death Valley, April 12; and in Emigrant Cañon, in the Panamint Mountains, April 14. It was common in Johnson and Surprise cañons, where it was seen near all the springs and streams during April, and in the latter cañon a half-completed nest was found April 19. Several were seen at Hot Springs in Panamint Valley, April 19–25, and at Leach Point Spring April 25. Costa's hummingbird was the only species met with by Mr. Nelson in the Panamint and Grapevine Mountains, where he found it a common breeder, during May and June.

In Nevada, Dr. Merriam found it tolerably common on Mount Magruder June 4–8; in Pahranagat Valley May 22–25; at Mountain Spring, Charleston Mountains, and at Upper Cottonwood Springs at the eastern base of these mountains, April 30. In Vegas Wash he found a nest containing two full-fledged young May 3; at the Bend of the Colorado one containing two fresh eggs May 4; and at Bitter Spring in the Muddy Mountains, another containing two fresh eggs, May 5. Mr. Nelson saw one in Vegas Wash, Nevada, March 10; and Mr. Stephens reported it from the Grapevine Mountains and Oasis Valley from the middle to the latter part of the month. Dr. Merriam found it common among the junipers on the eastern side of the Beaverdam Mountains, Utah, May 11.

In the Argus Range, California, the species was very common at Maturango Spring, and in Shepherd Cañon, where several nests were found in the low bushes along the edges of the cañon. Those containing two fresh eggs each were taken April 27, April 28, and May 7, and one containing full-fledged young, April 27. At Coso the species was very abundant and several of its nests were found. Various kinds of plants were used as nesting sites, though the branching cactus (*Opuntia echinocarpa*) was most commonly chosen. Usually the structure was placed on the top of a lower branch, a foot or so from the ground, and under an overhanging mass of thick spiny branches, which formed a protection for the parent bird from the sun and weather, as well as its enemies. At Coso one of these hummers was seen on a bright moonlight evening hovering about a bunch of flowers, and was heard again later in the same night. During our last trip to Death Valley Mr. Bailey saw one at Furnace Creek June 19, and the species was abundant all through the Panamint Mountains. Just at daylight on the morning of June 25, before the shadow had risen out of Wild Rose Cañon, a Costa's hummingbird came and hovered within a foot of our camp fire, probably mistaking it from the distance for a bunch of bright flowers. It was observed on several occasions that any bright-colored object placed in a conspicuous position attracted this bird. In Owens Valley this hummingbird was more or less common, especially along the eastern slope of the Sierra Nevada, where it was associated with the black-chinned hummer. Several were seen on the eastern slope of Walker Pass July 1, and in Reche Cañon September 22–24.

The male Costa's hummingbird has a peculiar habit, probably closely associated with the season of courtship, of flying up in the air to a considerable height and then swooping down with great velocity until near the ground, when it rises to its former position, to repeat the manœuver fifteen or twenty times before settling on some perch to rest. The course taken by the bird forms a parabolic curve, and when on the descent a booming, rushing noise is made, which can be heard at a considerable distance.

Record of specimens collected of Calypte costæ.

Collector's No.	Sex.	Locality.	Date.	Collector.	Remarks.
59	♂	Owens Valley, Calif..........	May 20, 1891	F. Stephens.....	Olancha. Hybrid between *T. costæ* and *T. alexandri*.
63	♀	......do....................	May 31, 1891	....do..........	Ash Creek. Parent of nest and eggs.
139	♂	Panamint Mountains, Calif...	Mar. 26, 1891	A. K. Fisher....	Johnson Cañon.
155	♂	......do....................	Apr. 14, 1891	....do..........	Surprise Cañon.
163	♂	......do....................	Apr. 16, 1891	....do..........	Do.
166	♂	......do....................	Apr. 20, 1891	....do..........	Do.
167	♂	......do....................	...do......	....do..........	Do.
	♂	......do....................	Mar. 27, 1891	E. W. Nelson....	Johnson Cañon.
	♂	......do....................	Mar. 28, 1891	....do..........	Do.
	♂	......do....................	April 4, 1891	....do..........	Do.
	♂	......do....................	Apr. 11, 1891	....do..........	Do.
	♂	......do....................	Apr. 14, 1891	....do..........	Surprise Cañon.
	♀	......do....................	May 12, 1891	....do..........	
	♀	......do....................	May 23, 1891	....do..........	Willow Creek. Parent of nest and eggs.
192	♀	Argus Range, Calif..........	Apr. 29, 1891	A. K. Fisher....	Shepherd Cañon. Parent of No. 191.
191	♂ juv.	......do....................	...do......	....do..........	Shepherd Cañon.
204	♀	......do....................	May 7, 1891	....do..........	Shepherd Cañon. Nest and eggs.
268	♀	Coso Mountains, Calif.......	May 28, 1891	....do..........	Nest and eggs.
	♂	Ash Meadows, Nev..........	May 30, 1891	V. Bailey.......	
	♂	Charleston Mountains, Nev...	Apr. 30, 1891	....do..........	
	♂	Panaca, Nev................	May 19, 1891	....do..........	

Calypte anna. Anna's Hummingbird.

A large hummer was seen in the Cajon Pass in the San Bernardino Mountains on January 2, which was probably this species. Mr. Stephens saw a number, mostly immature males, on the side of Reche Cañon, September 22–24; Mr. Bailey found the species common at Monterey, where he secured specimens October 3 and 6, and Mr. Nelson found it common at Morro Bay, and saw a few south of that place in November.

Record of specimens collected of Calypte anna.

Collector's No.	Sex.	Locality.	Date.	Collector.	Remarks.
	♂	Monterey, Calif..............	Oct. 3, 1891	V. Bailey........	
	♂	......do.....................	Oct. 6; 1891	....do..........	

Selasphorus platycercus. Broad-tailed Hummingbird.

The broad-tailed hummer was found by Dr. Merriam at Sheep Spring in the Juniper Mountains, Nevada, where an adult male was secured and many others seen May 19. Mr. Nelson reported it as common on the western slope of the Sierra Nevada, California, opposite the head of Owens River, and Mr. Palmer secured a specimen in the Sequoia National Park August 4.

Selasphorus rufus. Rufous Hummingbird.

The Rufous hummingbird was seen only in the Sierra Nevada, in California. Mr. Nelson found it common at the head of Owens River, and on the western slope from timber line down into the Yosemite Valley. While crossing the divide between the heads of the San Joaquin and Merced rivers he saw a number of these birds crossing from the latter to the former river. The species was common in the Sequoia National Park, where a specimen was taken August 4; and at Horse Corral Meadows August 9–13; one was seen in Kings River Cañon August 15, and one at Kearsarge Pass August 18.

At Mineral King it was common from above timber-line down to the lower part of the pines early in August and again in September. It was unusually common on the south side of Farewell Gap, on September 8, where large numbers were observed flying about in the attempt to dry and warm themselves, after a cold rain and hail storm.

Stellula calliope. Calliope Hummingbird.

None of our party obtained this hummingbird. Mr. Belding observed it at Crocker's, near the Yosemite Valley, in May 1891, and Dr. W. J. Hoffman reported it from Owens Valley, where it was found breeding in July. "One nest with eggs was found perched over and within a short distance of a noisy mountain stream, where it was no doubt frequently subjected to the dashing spray" (Bull. U. S. Geol. and Geog. Sur., Hayden, VI, 1881, 237).

Mr. Henshaw saw a single individual in the Tejon Mountains, August 17, 1875.

Tyrannus tyrannus. Kingbird.

At Olancha, near the southern end of Owens Lake, Mr. Bailey and the writer saw a common kingbird, June 29. It was so near that identification was positive. The Arkansas flycatchers seemed to be ill disposed towards the stranger and were chasing and diving at it whenever it took wing.

Tyrannus verticalis. Arkansas Kingbird.

The Arkansas flycatcher was common in most of the valleys traversed by the expedition. In California one was seen at Raymond Well, in Salt Wells Valley, and another in the Coso Valley, May 1, in which latter place it became common a few days later. Mr. Nelson saw a few in Panamint, Saline, and Mesquite Valleys, in May and June; near the valleys on both slopes of the Inyo Mountains, the last of June; and at the head of Owens Valley, near the White Mountains, in July. In Owens Valley, it was common at Lone Pine, where many young were seen June 4–15; at Olancha, June 29; at Big Pine, June 26–28; and more or less common at various other places in the valley throughout the summer. Dr. Merriam found it breeding commonly in the tree yuccas in Antelope Valley at the west end of the Mohave Desert, June 26–27, and saw one at Resting Springs in the Amargosa Desert, April 27. At Walker Pass a pair was seen on the east slope July 1, and the species was common on the west slope the following day. It was common also along the valley of Kern River July 3–13; at Walker Basin, July 13–16; at Bakersfield, in the San Joaquin Valley, July 17–20, and at Three Rivers and along the lower part of the Kaweah River, the last of July. Mr. Palmer found it abundant at Old Fort Tejon in July, and Mr. Nelson saw several near Nordhoff the last of December.

In Nevada, Dr. Merriam saw it on Gold Mountain, June 3; found it tolerably common in Pahranagat Valley May 22–26; in Meadow Creek Valley, May 19; in the Valley of the Virgin near Bunkerville, May 8; at the Bend of the Colorado, May 4; at Vegas Ranch, May 1; and at Yount's ranch in Pahrump Valley, April 29. In the Lower Santa Clara Valley, Utah, he found it breeding and tolerably common, May 11–15.

Record of specimens collected of Tyrannus verticalis.

Collector's No.	Sex.	Locality.	Date.	Collector.	Remarks.
205	♂	Vegas Valley, Nev	May 1, 1891	C. Hart Merriam	
225	♀	Argus Range, Calif	May 7, 1891	A. K. Fisher	Maturango Spring.
	♂	...do	May 11, 1891	...do	Do.
304	♂	Owens Valley, Calif	June 6, 1891	...do	Lone Pine.
91	♂	...do	June 12, 1891	F. Stephens	Olancha.
92	♀	...do	...do	...do	Do.

Tyrannus vociferans. Cassin's Kingbird.

Dr. Merriam found this flycatcher breeding commonly among the live oaks at Twin Oaks, in western San Diego County, in the early part of July and secured a specimen July 10. One was seen at San Bernardino January 1.

Myiarchus cinerascens. Ash-throated Flycatcher.

The ash-throated flycatcher is a common resident of the desert regions of southern California, Nevada, Utah, and northern Arizona, and is common also west of the Sierra Nevada. In California it was first seen in Panamint Valley, at Hot Springs, where it arrived April 22 and became common almost immediately. In the Argus Range it was common in Shepherd Cañon and at Maturango Spring, where it was seen along the hillsides, hovering over the flowers in search of small moths and other insects, during the first half of May. At Coso several pairs were seen, and an individual was observed to devote considerable time to examining the open end of a 2-inch water pipe, which protruded from the side of an old building, evidently with an idea of using it for a nesting site. Mr. Nelson found it a widely distributed species, breeding from the bottom of Mesquite, Panamint, and Saline valleys, up to at least 2,130 meters (7,000 feet) in the Panamint and Grapevine mountains, where it appeared to be equally at home on the open slopes of the valleys, among the mesquite and larrea bushes, or in the mountains, in the midst of a tolerably abundant growth of piñons. He found it breeding as high as the upper border of the piñons in the Inyo Mountains the last of June.

In Nevada Dr. Merriam saw it in the tree yuccas on the east side of Pahrump Valley, April 29; at the Bend of the Colorado, May 4; near Bunkerville, in the Valley of the Virgin, May 8; on the west slope of the Juniper Mountains, May 19; in Pahranagat Valley, May 23; on the Timpahute Mountains, May 26; found it common among the yuccas in Indian Spring Valley, May 28; on the south side of Gold Mountain, June 3; and tolerably common and evidently breeding among the nut pines on Mount Magruder, June 4-8. In Utah he found it breeding commonly in the Santa Clara Valley, May 11-15, and among the tree yuccas on the west side of the Beaverdam Mountains, May 10. In northwestern Arizona he saw several at the mouth of Beaverdam Creek the same day. On the summit connecting the White and Inyo mountains, in California, several were seen on June 9.

At Furnace Creek, Death Valley, a pair of these birds was seen just above the ranch at the mouth of the cañon, June 21, and the species was not uncommon in the Panamint Mountains up to an altitude of more than 2,450 meters (8,000 feet). In Owens Valley it was not uncommon at Lone Pine, June 4-15; at Olancha, May 16-23; at Ash Creek, May 30-June 3; and at Benton, July 9-10.

It was seen among the tree yuccas in Walker Pass, June 22 and July 2-3; was common in the valley of the Kern, July 3-13; abundant in Walker Basin, June 24 and July 13-16; in Tehachapi Pass, June 25; and in the Cañada de las Uvas, June 28. A few were seen among the live oaks in the Granite Range in the western part of San Diego County, July 1-10. It was common at Bakersfield, July 17-20, and at Three Rivers, July 25-30.

Record of specimens collected of Myiarchus cinerascens.

Collector's No.	Sex.	Locality.	Date.	Collector.	Remarks.
	♂	Panamint Valley, Calif.	Apr. 22, 1891	C. Hart Merriam	Hot Springs.
181	♂	do	Apr. 23, 1891	A. K. Fisher	Do.
305	♂	Owens Valley, Calif.	June 6, 1891	do	Lone Pine.
101	♀	do	June 13, 1891	F. Stephens	Olancha.

Sayornis saya. Say's Phœbe.

Say's phœbe is a common species throughout the desert regions, and was also found west of the Sierra Nevada. It was common in the vicinity of Owens Lake in December, 1890; was seen near Daggett, in the Mohave Desert, January 10, 1891, and at Lone Willow Spring, January 15. In Death Valley, it was observed at Bennett Wells and Furnace Creek the latter part of January; again, April 9-12 and June 19-22.

In Nevada it was observed at Ash Meadows in March, sparingly in Pahrump and Vegas valleys, and thence down to the Bend of the Colorado, and was rather common and mating in Oasis Valley in the same month. Dr. Merriam found it in Fish Lake Valley, June 8; on the north slope of Gold Mountain, June 3; at the east end of Grapevine Cañon, June 2, where a nest was observed in an old well at an abandoned mining shaft known as Thorp's mill; in Ash Meadows, where a nest was found in an old adobe, May 30; in Pahranagat Valley, May 22-26; at Pahroc Spring, May 22; at the Bend of the Colorado, May 4; and in the Virgin Valley near Bunkerville, May 8. He saw two at the mouth of Beaverdam Creek, Arizona, May 9-10, and in Utah found it common in the lower Santa Clara Valley, breeding along the cliffs near St. George, May 10-11, and among the junipers on the eastern slope of the Beaverdam Mountains, May 10-11.

In the Panamint Mountains the species was not seen in Johnson Cañon, but was common in Surprise Cañon, where a nest and eggs was found April 19, and also at Hot Springs, in Panamint Valley, April 20-25. Mr. Nelson found it commonly distributed in the bottoms of Saline, Panamint, and Mesquite valleys, ranging up in the Panamint and Grapevine mountains. He found the species breeding in various sheltered places, such as holes in clay banks, niches in rocky ledges, sides of old walls, and in crevices in deserted mining shafts. In the Argus Range it was common in Shepherd Cañon and at Maturango Spring, and at Coso a nest containing three nearly grown young was found in one of the deserted buildings the last of May. The species was found in the Inyo Range up to and among the piñons, and was a rather common breeding species in Owens Valley.

Several were seen in Walker Pass, July 1-3. Say's phœbe was common through Kern River Valley, July 3-13, and occurred in Walker Basin in about equal numbers with the black phœbe, July 13-16. One was seen at timber line near Mineral King, September 10, and the species was observed along the route to Three Rivers, September 12-16. Mr. Bailey found it common at Monterey, September 28 to October 9, and Mr. Stephens at Reche Cañon, near San Bernardino, September 22-24.

Mr. Nelson found it common and generally distributed along the coast from San Simeon to Carpenteria and Santa Paula, in November and December, and sparingly in the San Joaquin Valley, October 5-27.

Record of specimens collected of Sayornis saya.

Collector's No.	Sex.	Locality.	Date.	Collector.	Remarks.
71	♂	Death Valley, Calif	Jan. 24, 1891	A. K. Fisher	Furnace Creek.
76	♂	......do........	Jan. 25, 1891	...do......	Do.
	♀ im.	......do........	June 19, 1892	V. Bailey	Do.
12	♀	Daggett, Calif.	Feb. 8, 1891	F. Stephens	
257	♂ juv.	Coso Mountains, Calif.	May 26, 1891	A. K. Fisher	
102	♂ im.	Owens Valley, Calif.	June 15, 1891	F. Stephens	Olancha.

Sayornis nigricans. Black Phœbe.

The black phœbe was rare in the desert regions east of the Sierra Nevada, though more or less common west of this range. At San Bernardino one was seen among some willows, associated with other birds, December 28, 1890. It was seen in Cajon Pass, March 30; at Furnace Creek, Death Valley, April 12; at Hot Springs, in the Panamint Valley, April 22; and in the Argus Range, at Shepherd Cañon, April 27. Mr. Stephens found a pair apparently breeding at Little Owens Lake the first week in May, and an immature individual at Bishop Creek, August 4-10. On the western slope, it was common along the valley of Kern River, near the water, July 3-13; common and in about equal numbers with Say's phœbe, at Walker Basin, July 13-16; common in the Cañada de las Uvas, June 28-29; and in the Sierra Liebre, June 30. It was common at Bakersfield, in the San Joaquin Valley, in July; at Three Rivers, in the foothills, July 25-30 and September 13-16; and in Kings River Cañon, August 13-16. Mr. Bailey saw one at timber line near Mineral King, August 4, and found it common at Monterey, September 18 to October 9. Mr. Nelson observed it commonly about San Emigdio, sparingly along the southern and western sides of the San Joaquin Valley, commonly and in about equal numbers with Say's phœbe along the coast from San Simeon to Carpenteria, and not numerous between Carpenteria and Santa Paula, in November and December.

Contopus borealis. Olive-sided Flycatcher.

The olive-sided flycatcher was found nowhere common. Mr. Nelson observed it migrating in considerable numbers at the head of Willow Creek in the Panamint Range, during the third week in May. The same observer found it on the east side of the Sierra Nevada, at the head of Owens River, from an altitude of 2,500 to 2,900 meters (8,200 to 9,500 feet), and on the west slope up to 3,050 meters (10,000 feet).

In the Sierra Nevada Mr. Stephens found it at Menache Meadows, May 24-26; Mr. Dutcher secured two specimens and reported it as more or less common at Big Cottonwood Meadows; and Mr. Bailey saw several at an altitude of about 2,650 meters (8,700 feet) near Mineral King, and secured a brood of young just able to fly, August 4.

The writer secured a specimen in the Coso Mountains, California, May 23; Dr. Merriam observed one on the south side of Gold Mountain, Nevada, June 3; and Mr. Palmer saw one near the summit of Frazier Mountain, California, July 9.

Record of specimens collected of Contopus borealis.

Collector's No.	Sex.	Locality.	Date.	Collector.	Remarks.
248	♂	Panamint Mountains, Calif.	May 21, 1891	E. W. Nelson	
	♂	Coso Mountains, Calif.	May 23, 1891	A. K. Fisher	
8	♀	Sierra Nevada, Calif.	June 23, 1891	B. H. Dutcher	Big Cottonwood Meadows.
26	♂	do	Aug. 4, 1891	do	Do.
	♂	do	do	V. Bailey	Mineral King.
	im	do	do	do	Do.

Contopus richardsonii. Western Wood Pewee.

The western wood pewee was a common species in many of the localities visited. Mr. Nelson found it a rather common breeding bird in Cottonwood, Willow Creek, and Mill Creek cañons in the Panamint Mountains, Calif., and saw it also in the Grapevine Mountains, Nevada.

In Coso Valley, California, it first appeared May 16, and by May 25 was common in the Coso Mountains. It was common all through Owens Valley, and on the White Mountains. At Keeler, on the east side of Owens Lake, it was not uncommon the 1st of June. One day when the wind was very high, a number were seen sitting on the bare alkaline flats near the lake, where they were picking up from the ground the flies which swarmed there, as grain-eating birds do seeds. On the summit of the divide in the White Mountains, between Deep Spring Valley and Owens Valley, Dr. Merriam killed two June 9. At Old Fort Tejon it was common about the 1st of July.

It was common in Walker Pass, where a nest was observed, July 2; at Kernville, July 11; Walker Basin, July 13–16; and at Bakersfield, in the San Joaquin Valley, July 17–20. In the High Sierra it was not uncommon in the Sequoia National Park, the first week in August; at Horse Corral Meadows, August 9–13; Kings River Cañon, August 13–16; Big Cottonwood Meadows, during the summer; at Menache Meadows, May 24–26; and was common along the Kaweah River from Mineral King down to Three Rivers, in September.

In Nevada, Dr. Merriam saw it among the cottonwoods at Vegas ranch, May 1; at Pahranagat Valley, May 23 (common); at Oasis Valley, June 1; and on Mount Magruder, June 8. He also saw the species at the mouth of Beaverdam Creek, Arizona, May 10.

Record of specimens collected of Contopus richardsonii.

Collector's No.	Sex.	Locality.	Date.	Collector.	Remarks.
251	♀	Coso Mountains, Calif	May 24, 1891	A. K. Fisher	
6	♂	Sierra Nevada, Calif	June 19, 1891	B. H. Dutcher	Big Cottonwood Meadows.
89	♀	Owens Lake, Calif	June 12, 1891	F. Stephens	
	♀	White Mountains, Calif	June 9, 1891	V. Bailey	
	♂	....do........	do.	....do....	
	♂	Mount Magruder, Nev	June 4, 1891	....do....	

Empidonax difficilis. Western Flycatcher.

The western flycatcher was seen in a few localities only. Dr. Merriam secured an adult male at Ash Meadows, Nevada, May 30, and a female at Mount Magruder in the same State, June 5. Mr. Palmer reported the species as common and secured one at Old Fort Tejon, July 6. Mr. Nelson saw it along the San Joaquin River in August, but does not state how common it was.

Record of specimens collected of Empidonax difficilis.

Collector's No.	Sex.	Locality.	Date.	Collector.	Remarks.
	♂ ad.	Ash Meadows, Nev	May 30, 1891	V. Bailey	
	♀	Mount Magruder, Nev	June 5, 1891	C. Hart Merriam	

Empidonax pusillus. Little Flycatcher.

In a few localities the little flycatcher was not rare. Dr. Merriam found it tolerably common where Beaverdam Creek joins the Virgin River in northwestern Arizona, May 9, and in Pahranagat Valley, Nevada, May 22–26.

In Owens Valley, California, Mr. Stephens found it a rather common migrant at Olancha, May 16–23, and the writer secured two specimens in a willow thicket along Owens River, at Lone Pine, June 11. Mr. Palmer shot one near Old Fort Tejon July 3, and Mr. Nelson saw a few among the willows along streams from 2,940 to 2,900 meters (9,000 to 9,500 feet) altitude, in the White Mountains, in the same month.

Record of specimens collected of Empidonax pusillus.

Collector's No.	Sex.	Locality.	Date.	Collector.	Remarks.
77	♂	Pahranagat Valley, Nev	May 23, 1891	C. Hart Merriam	
	♂	Owens Valley, Calif	June 9, 1891	F. Stephens	Olancha.
99	♀	do	June 12, 1891	do	Do.
333	♂	do	June 11, 1891	A. K. Fisher	Lone Pine.
334	♂	do	do	do	Do.

Empidonax hammondi. Hammond's Flycatcher.

Hammond's flycatcher was seen in two localities only. In the Argus Range several were seen and two secured among the piñons above Maturango Spring on May 8. Dr. Merriam secured a specimen in Pahranagat Valley, Nevada, May 23.

Record of specimens collected of Empidonax hammondi.

Collector's No.	Sex.	Locality.	Date.	Collector.	Remarks.
208	♀	Argus Range, Calif	May 8, 1891	A. K. Fisher	Maturango Spring.
209	♂	do	do	do	Do.
	♀	Pahranagat Valley, Nev	May 23, 1891	C. Hart Merriam	

Empidonax wrightii. Wright's Flycatcher.

Wright's flycatcher was the only one of the small flycatchers found in winter in any of the region traversed. Mr. Nelson secured a specimen at Hot Springs in Panamint Valley, January 3, and the writer obtained one in the same place April 22. A specimen was secured among the willows at the edge of the reservoir at Furnace Creek, Death Valley, February 1, and two small flycatchers, probably this species, were seen there about the middle of April.

A specimen was secured in the Argus Range, at Maturango Spring, May 5, and another was seen in Shepherd Cañon a few days before. In Owens Valley Mr. Stephens found the species at Olancha about the middle of May, and at Bishop Creek August 4–10. In the High Sierra it was seen at Big Cottonwood Meadows, August 29; at Whitney Meadows, August 20; and at Kern River Lakes or Soda Springs, September 5. Dr. Merriam secured a specimen in the Virgin Valley in eastern Nevada, May 6.

Record of specimens collected of Empidonax wrightii.

Collector's No.	Sex.	Locality.	Date.	Collector.	Remarks.
95	♂	Panamint Valley, Calif	Jan. 3, 1891	E. W. Nelson	
	♀	Death Valley, Calif	Feb. 1, 1891	A. K. Fisher	Furnace Creek.
180	♂	Panamint Valley, Calif	Apr. 23, 1891	do	Hot Spring.
50	♀	do	Apr. 26, 1891	F. Stephens	
108	♂	Argus Range, Calif	May 5, 1891	A. K. Fisher	Maturango Spring.
	♀	do	May 12, 1891	T. S. Palmer	Do.
		St. Thomas, Nev	May 6, 1891	V. Bailey	
	im.	Sierra Nevada, Calif	Aug. 20, 1891	do	Whitney Meadows.

Pyrocephalus rubineus mexicanus. Vermilion Flycatcher.

Dr. Merriam shot an adult female of this species at St. George, in the Lower Santa Clara Valley, Utah, May 13. She was killed in an orchard at Dodge Spring, about a mile from the settlement, and contained large ova nearly ready for the shell. This record extends the known range of the species very materially, since it had not previously been recorded north of Fort Mohave, Arizona.

Otocoris alpestris arenicola. Desert Horned Lark.

So far as specimens go, this race of the horned lark was the only one found breeding east of the Sierra Nevada in the region traversed by the expedition. A flock of twenty or more was seen at Hesperia, in the Mohave Desert, January 4, and the subspecies also was seen in the same desert at Daggett January 8–10, and Granite Wells January 13–15. Dozens were seen by Dr. Merriam, who traveled over the same ground during the latter part of March and first week in April. In January Mr. Nelson saw about one hundred at the southern end of Panamint Valley. Horned larks were not seen at any time in Death Valley.

In Nevada they were common at Ash Meadows, in the plowed fields and sand plains, and about the middle of March had mated and were preparing to nest. In Pahrump and Vegas valleys Mr. Nelson found small parties in February and March. Dr. Merriam found it common in Meadow Creek Valley May 19; in Desert and Pahroc valleys May 20–22; in the valley between Gold Mountain and Mount Magruder June 4, where it was common and two nearly full grown young were shot; on Mount Magruder, June 4–8, where it was common on the sage plain on top of the mountain. In Utah, it was not seen in

Pyrocephalus in Los Angeles Co. in Winter
Auk XIII July 1896 p. 258

the Santa Clara Valley, but several were observed in Mountain Meadows May 17.

In the north end of Panamint Valley, Mr. Nelson saw several the last of May, and others on the high tableland between Saline and Panamint valleys, in May and June. Dr. Merriam found it common in the sage brush north of Telescope Peak, April 15. Horned larks were found during the breeding season in the sage plains on the Inyo and White mountains, and in Saline and Deep Spring valleys. Below Maturango Spring, in Coso Valley, it was quite common May 11, and others were seen along the valley as far north as Darwin. In Owens Valley, the subspecies was found as a summer resident from the lower to the upper end. Mr. Palmer found it very abundant in Antelope Valley, and a few near Gorman Station the last of June.

Record of specimens collected of Otocoris alpestris arenicola.

Collector's No.	Sex.	Locality.	Date.	Collector.	Remarks.
227	♂	Coso Valley, Calif.	May 11, 1891	A. K. Fisher	
228	♂	do	do	do	
229	♀	do	do	do	
8	♂	Mohave Desert, Calif.	Feb. 7, 1891	F. Stephens	Daggett.
52	♂	do	Jan. 13, 1891	A. K. Fisher	Granite Wells.
53	♂	do	do	do	Do
54	♀	do	do	do	Do
55	♂	do	do	do	Do
56	♂	do	do	do	Do
57	♂	do	do	do	Do
	♂	do	Apr. 25, 1891	V. Bailey	Leach Point Valley.
	♂	do	June 27, 1891	T. S. Palmer	25 miles southwest of Mojave.
51	♂	Salt Wells Valley, Calif.	Apr. 29, 1891	F. Stephens	Borax Flat.
125	♂	Ash Meadows, Nev.	Mar. 14, 1891	A. K. Fisher	
136	♂	do	Mar. 19, 1891	do	
	♀	do	do	E. W. Nelson	
	♂	Pahrump Valley, Nev.	Feb. 17, 1891	do	
	♂	do	do	do	
	♂	Indian Spring Valley, Nev.	May 28, 1891	V. Bailey	
	♂	Pauaca, Nev.	May 19, 1891	do	
	♂ im.	Gold Mountain Valley, Nev.	June 4, 1891	C. Hart Merriam	Valley between Gold Mountain and Mount Magruder.
	♂ im.	do	do	do	San Rafael Mountains.
	♀	Mount Piños, Calif.	Oct. 16, 1891	E. W. Nelson	
70	♀	Owens Valley, Calif.	June 1, 1891	F. Stephens	Ash Creek.
83	♀	do	June 10, 1891	do	Olancha.
270	♂	do	May 31, 1891	A. K. Fisher	Keeler.
271	♂	do	June 1, 1891	do	Do.
288	♂	do	June 2, 1891	do	Do.
289	♀	do	do	do	Do.
290	♀	do	June 3, 1891	do	Do.
153	♀	do	Aug. 16, 1891	F. Stephens	Do.
154	♀ juv.	do	do	do	
135	im.	do	July 20, 1891	do	Casa Diablo Spring.
136	♀	do	July 21, 1891	do	Do.
	♂	White Mountains, Calif.	July 12, 1891	E. W. Nelson	
197	♂	Darwin, Calif.	May 5, 1891	A. K. Fisher	
	♂	Coso Valley, Calif.	May 11, 1891	T. S. Palmer	Maturango Spring.
	♂	do	do	do	Do.

Otocoris alpestris chrysolæma. Mexican Horned Lark.

Mr. Nelson obtained a number of specimens of this race at Keeler, on the shore of Owens Lake, December 28, 1890, though specimens taken at the same place during the breeding season are referable to *arenicola*. Mr. Stephens took one in the Panamint Mountains in April, and Mr. Bailey secured a specimen at Kernville, where the subspecies was common, July 13. The birds seen by Mr. Nelson in the San Joaquin Valley and in the vicinity of the Cañada de las Uvas probably should be referred to this race. He found it excessively abundant on the San Joaquin Plain, where it is locally known as the 'wheat bird' in the grain districts, owing to its habit of following the farmer and eating the newly-sown wheat at seeding time.

Record of specimens collected of Otocoris alpestris chrysolæma.

Collector's No.	Sex.	Locality.	Date.	Collector.	Remarks.
44	♂	Panamint Mountains, Calif	Apr. 15, 1891	F. Stephens	5,200 feet altitude.
	♂	Kernville, Calif	July 13, 1891	V. Bailey	
	♂	Owens Valley, Calif	Dec. 28, 1890	E. W. Nelson	Keeler.
	♂	......do......	......do......	......do......	Do.
	♂	......do......	......do......	......do......	Do.
	♂	......do......	......do......	......do......	Do.
	♂	......do......	......do......	......do......	Do.
	♀	......do......	......do......	......do......	Do.
	♀	......do......	......do......	......do......	Do.
	♀	......do......	......do......	......do......	Do.

Pica pica hudsonica. Black-billed Magpie.

Mr. Bailey saw three individuals of this species 10 miles east of Toquerville, Utah, December, 31, 1888. The black-billed magpie was not seen by the expedition, but is known to be a common resident in the neighborhood of Carson, in western Nevada.

Pica nuttalli. Yellow-billed Magpie.

The Yellow-billed magpie is common in a number of places west of the Sierra Nevada, in California. At Visalia, several were seen among the oaks, July 23, as well as along the route from that place to Three Rivers, July 25. Near Cottage post-office, in Tulare County, about half-way between these two places, the species was common September 17.

Mr. Nelson found it common in the foothills of the Sierra Nevada, in August; and also among the oaks from La Panza to San Luis Obispo, October 28 and November 3; and from the latter place to the Santa Ynez River, beyond which places it was not noted.

Cyanocitta stelleri. Steller's Jay.

Steller's jay was met with along the coast of California, in two localities only. Mr. Bailey found it common in the thick woods in the vicinity of Monterey, where he secured a pair, October 1; and Mr. Nelson observed a few in the mountains near San Simeon in November.

Record of specimens collected of Cyanocitta stelleri.

Collector's No.	Sex.	Locality.	Date.	Collector.	Remarks.
	♂	Monterey, Calif	Oct. 1, 1891	V. Bailey	
	♀	......do......	......do......	......do......	

Pica nuttalli. Jamesburg: "Very common, Nests now in oaks here (?) the head of Carmel valley" (McLellan Field Notes, Dec. 16-20, 1894).

Cyanocitta stelleri frontalis. Blue-fronted Jay.

The blue-fronted jay was not found in the desert ranges, although it was common in many places along the east slope of the Sierra Nevada, in California. Mr. Nelson found it common at the head of Owens River at an altitude of from 2,500 to 2,900 meters (8,200 to 9,500 feet), and Mr. Stephens found it at Bishop Creek, August 4-10, and at Menache Meadows, May 24-26. The writer secured one among the pines above Walker Basin, July 14; found it common in Sequoia National Park the first week in August; at Horse Corral Meadows, August 9-13; in Kings River Cañon, August 13-16; and Big Cottonwood Meadows, Round Valley, and Whitney Meadows, the last of the month. It was very common among the sugar and yellow pines at Soda Springs or Kern River Lakes, the first week in September. Mr. Dutcher found it common during the breeding season at Big Cottonwood Meadows, and Mr. Bailey and the writer found it common at Mineral King and down along the Kaweah River to the lower limit of the pines, in September. Mr. Palmer reported it common on Frazier Mountain, near Old Fort Tejon, July 6.

Record of specimens collected of Cyanocitta stelleri frontalis.

Collector's No.	Sex.	Locality.	Date.	Collector.	Remarks.
75	♂	Owens Lake, Calif	June 7, 1891	F. Stephens	Altitude, 4,000 feet.
141	♂	Sierra Nevada, Calif	July 25, 1891	do	
17	im.	....do....	July 12, 1891	B. H. Dutcher	Big Cottonwood Meadows.
	♂ im.	....do....	Aug. 3, 1891	E. W. Nelson	South Fork Merced River.
390	♀	Walker Basin, Calif	July 14, 1891	A. K. Fisher	
409	♂ im.	Sierra Nevada, Calif	Aug. 7, 1891	do	Sequoia National Park.
434	♀	....do....	Sept. 3, 1891	do	Soda Springs.

Aphelocoma woodhousei. Woodhouse's Jay.

Woodhouse's jay was found on all the desert ranges which furnish a growth of piñon or junipers. In California it was observed in the White Mountains, Inyo, Argus, Coso, and Panamint ranges; in Nevada, in the Charleston, Grapevine, Juniper, and Pahroc mountains, and in Utah, in the Beaverdam Mountains. In the latter part of June, young which were able to fly were found among the willows along the streams in the Panamint Mountains, north of Telescope Peak.

Record of specimens collected of Aphelocoma woodhousei.

Collector's No.	Sex.	Locality.	Date.	Collector.	Remarks.
39	♂	Grapevine Mountains, Nev.	Mar. 24, 1891	F. Stephens	
147	♀	Panamint Mountains, Calif.	Mar. 29, 1891	A. K. Fisher	Johnson Cañon.
172	♂	....do....	Apr. 20, 1891	...do...	Surprise Cañon.
173	♀	....do....	....do....	...do...	Do.
355	♀ im.	....do....	June 23, 1891	...do...	Wild Rose Cañon.
356	♀ im.	....do....	....do....	...do...	
		Inyo Mountains, Calif	June 27, 1891	E. W. Nelson	
	im.	White Mountains, Calif	July 8, 1891	...do...	

Aphelocoma californica. California Jay.

The California jay was not found east of the Sierra Nevada, it being replaced in the desert ranges by Woodhouse's jay. Although abundant on the west slope of the main Sierra, it was common in few places on the east side. Mr. Stephens found it rather common on the latter slope at Independence Creek, June 18–23; at Menache Meadows, May 24–26; and Mr. Nelson, at the head of Owens River, in the latter part of July.

The species was common in Cajon Pass in the San Bernardino Mountains, January 2–3, where it was seen and heard among the chaparral at all times of the day. Dr. Merriam found it common in the Sierra Liebre, San Bernardino, Tejon, and Tehachapi ranges, as well as in the southern Sierra from Walker Pass southward. It was tolerably common on the west slope of Walker Pass, June 21 and July 2–3; in the valley of Kern River, June 21–22 and July 3–13; thence southward to Havilah and Caliente, June 23–24; and was abundant and noisy at Old Fort Tejon late in June and early in July.

Dr. Merriam found it common in the coast ranges south of the San Bernardino plain, and in large numbers in the Granite Range between Twin Oaks and Escondido, Calif., early in July.

In the San Joaquin Valley it was common at Visalia and up along Kaweah River to the lower edge of the pines, in August and September, and a few were seen in the Sequoia National Park during the first week of August. Mr. Bailey found it common in the brush and open woods at Monterey, Calif., September 28 to October 9.

Mr. Nelson reported this jay as abundant in the Tejon and Temploa mountains and around San Luis Obispo in October, and along the route from San Simeon to Carpenteria and Santa Paula, in November and December.

Record of specimens collected of Aphelocoma californica.

Collector's No.	Sex.	Locality.	Date.	Collector.	Remarks.
62	♀	Owens Valley, Calif.	May 23, 1891	F. Stephens	Olancha.
	♂	Walker Pass, Calif.	July 3, 1891	V. Bailey	
363	♀ im.	...do...	July 2, 1891	A. K. Fisher	
383	♀	Kern River, Calif.	July 9, 1891	...do...	South Fork.

Corvus corax sinuatus. Raven.

Ravens were seen in more or less abundance in most, if not all, of the localities visited by members of the expedition, from above timber line on the High Sierra to the bottom of Death Valley and the other desert valleys, and undoubtedly breed in all the desert ranges of southern California and Nevada. Ravens were seen in Cajon Pass in the San Bernardino Mountains, and on the Mohave Desert during the first week in January. At Daggett fifty or more remained about the

Corvus americanus

"For several days in succession it was noticed that the crows would gather together in the grounds of the Hotel Del Norte (Crescent City) in the afternoon about four o'clock in straggling flocks for some hours down the coast" (McLellan, Field Notes Feb 27, 1864, 1894).

"At a sharp bend among upper one of the tributaries of the Big Sur opposite Potts in the redwoods in which the cold, chilly north wind from the Ocean Shore not extreme is a large crow roost" (McLellan, Field Notes, Mch 6-12, 1894).

Jamesburgh. They gather in flocks of several hundreds and feed on the wheat in the grain fields" (McLellan, Field Notes, Mch 16-23, 1894).

slaughter house feeding on the refuse. In Death Valley they were observed by every party that visited the place from the first week in January to the last in June. In the Coso Mountains, two adults with their five young were seen flying high in the air May 25, the old birds being readily distinguished by their worn primaries.

In Nevada they were common at Ash Meadows and Pahrump Valley, and at the latter place a pair was secured the last of February. Dr. Merriam observed one, together with a large nest, on the shelf of a high cliff in Vegas Wash, May 3. He found ravens tolerably common about the Bend of the Colorado, May 4, and saw several in the Valley of the Virgin, near Bunkerville, May 8; others in the Juniper Mountains, May 19; in Desert Valley, May 20, and in Pahranagat Valley, May 22-26. In Utah he found several pairs in the Lower Santa Clara Valley, May 11-15, and thence northward to Mountain Meadows, where several were seen May 17.

Ravens were common all through Owens Valley. At Walker Basin flocks of several hundred were observed every day flying about the fields and roads, feeding on the grasshoppers which occurred in vast numbers there. All the specimens shot had nothing in their stomachs except the remains of these insects. Dr. Merriam and Mr. Palmer observed large numbers catching grasshoppers in the western part of the Mohave Desert, known as Antelope Valley, June 27-28, and near Gorman Station no less than forty-four were seen catching grasshoppers on the grassy hillsides at one time.

In the High Sierra ravens were seen at Menache, Whitney, and Big Cottonwood meadows, and at the head of Owens River. Mr. Nelson saw a few about Mount Piños and at Buena Vista Lake in October, and found them sparingly along the route from San Simeon to Carpenteria and Santa Paula, in November and December.

Record of specimens collected of Corvus corax sinuatus.

Collector's No.	Sex.	Locality.	Date.	Collector.	Remarks.
113	♀	Lone Willow Spring, Calif	Jan. 14, 1891	E. W. Nelson	
	♀	Pahrump Valley, Calif	Feb. 24, 1891	A. K. Fisher	
114	♂	do	do	do	

Corvus americanus. Crow.

At one place only was the common crow seen by any member of the expedition east of the Sierra Nevada. In Pahrump Valley, Nevada, a flock of crows kept around the ranch during February and March.

At Bakersfield, in the San Joaquin Valley, crows were common along the river bottoms, in flocks of from five to fifty, July 17-20. Crows were observed among the oaks at Visalia, July 23, and a flock of about one hundred was seen and a specimen secured near Three Rivers, the latter part of the same month. Dr. Merriam saw a flock of half a dozen in Tehachapi Valley, California, June 25, and Mr. Palmer found them common at Tejon ranch, where they were feeding on figs, early in July. At Monterey, Mr. Bailey heard them cawing in the grounds of the Hotel Del Monte, September 28 to October 9. Mr. Nelson found crows common in the San Joaquin Valley in October, along the route from San Simeon to Carpenteria, and in the Ojai Valley in November and December.

Picicorvus columbianus. Clarke's Nutcracker.

Clarke's crow was common in the High Sierra in California, as well as in a few of the higher desert ranges to the eastward. It was numerous about the camp in the Charleston Mountains, Nevada, in February. In the Panamint Mountains, California, a solitary individual was seen near the top of the ridge south of Telescope Peak, April 2, and on the north slope of the same peak several were heard, June 23. A pair was seen later in the same day which, from their actions, appeared to be parent and young. Mr. Nelson found it rather common among the *Pinus flexilis* on the Inyo Mountains, and in the same belt of the White Mountains as well as on the plateau at the head of Owens Valley; and Mr. Stephens reported it common at Queen mine, in the White Mountains, Nevada, July 11–16. Along the eastern slope of the Sierra, it was abundant at Monache Meadows, May 24–26; at Kearsarge Pass, June 18–23; at Bishop Creek, August 4–10; and from 2,450 meters (8,000 feet) altitude to timber line at the head of Owens River the latter part of July; at Big Meadows and Horse Corral Meadows it was seen August 8–13; in Big Cottonwood Meadows it was very common all summer; at Round Valley, 12 miles south of Mount Whitney, August 28; and along the route from Soda Springs or Kern River Lakes to Mineral King, early in September. Mr. Nelson found it numerous among piñons on Mount Piños the later part of October.

Record of specimens collected of Picicorvus columbianus.

Collector's No.	Sex.	Locality.	Date.	Collector.	Remarks.
63	♂	Sierra Nevada, Calif.	May 27, 1891	F. Stephens	Summit Meadows, near Olancha Peak.
421	♂	......do......	Aug. 28, 1891	A. K. Fisher	Big Cottonwood Meadows.
430	♀	......do......	Aug. 28, 1891	......do......	Round Valley.
		......do......	Sept. 4, 1891	......do......	Soda Springs, Kern River.

Cyanocephalus cyanocephalus. Piñon Jay.

The piñon jay is more or less common on all the desert ranges of southern California and Nevada which are high enough to support a growth of piñons (*Pinus monophylla*), and was found in a few places on the Sierra Nevada, though in limited numbers. Mr. Nelson found it breeding in the piñon belt in the Panamint, Inyo, White, and Grapevine mountains, and Mr. Stephens saw a flock of a hundred or more in the latter range toward the end of March.

Nut pine or piñon (Pinus monophylla)
Twelve or 15 miles west of Bishop Creek village, Calif.
August 1891

The writer found it common in the Argus Range above Maturango Spring. The stomach and gullet of one shot at this place about the middle of May contained the kernels of the pine nut, which it evidently had picked up from the ground, as some of them had already sprouted. The species was common on the Coso Mountains the last half of May. Dr. Merriam saw it on Mount Magruder and Gold Mountain, Nevada, early in June; in the Juniper Mountains, near the boundary between Nevada and Utah, May 18-19, and in the juniper belt on the east slope of the Beaverdam Mountains, in Utah, May 11.

Mr. Palmer saw a single bird in the Charleston Mountains among the tree yuccas, February 14.

In the Sierra Nevada Mr. Nelson saw it at the head of Owens River, though it was not numerous, and Mr. Stephens observed it at Bishop Creek, August 4-10, and noted one individual at Benton, July 9-10.

Record of specimens collected of Cyanocephalus cyanocephalus.

Collector's No.	Sex.	Locality.	Date.	Collector.	Remarks.
201	♂	Argus Range, Calif.	May 6, 1891	A. K. Fisher.	Maturango Spring.
206	♂	do	May 8, 1891	do	Do.
207	♂	do	do	do	Do.
233	♀	do	May 12, 1891	do	Do.
249	♂	Coso Mountains, Calif.	May 23, 1891	do	

Molothrus ater. Cowbird.

Dr. Merriam saw several cowbirds in the Lower Santa Clara Valley, Utah, May 11-15, and a few in Pahranagat Valley, Nevada, May 22-26. The writer shot an adult male at Furnace Creek, Death Valley, June 20, which was the only one seen there.

Xanthocephalus xanthocephalus. Yellow-headed Blackbird.

Yellow-headed blackbirds were seen sparingly at a number of localities. Mr. Bailey secured a specimen at Bennett Wells in Death Valley, April 1, and an individual came and alighted on the wagon while the party was at Darwin, in the Coso Valley, May 5. Dr. Merriam saw a few about the spring at Yount's ranch in Pahrump Valley, Nevada, April 29, and a number in the valley of the lower Muddy, May 6. Others were seen by him in Meadow Creek Valley, Nevada, near Panaca, May 19, and the species was said to breed in Pahranagat Valley, though he did not see it there, May 22-26. In the Lower Santa Clara Valley, Utah, it was tolerably common about the junction of the Santa Clara with the Virgin, May 11-15. In Salt Wells Valley, Mr. Stephens saw a small flock at Raymond Well, and at Borax Flat the last of April and first of May. At Lone Pine, in Owens Valley, one was seen among a flock of redwings in December, 1890. A number were observed in June, and several small flocks among the tules and along the fence rows, August 22. The species was seen sparingly at Bakersfield, in the San Joaquin Valley, July 17-20.

Record of specimens collected of Xanthocephalus xanthocephalus.

Collector's No.	Sex.	Locality.	Date.	Collector.	Remarks.
325	♂ ad.	Death Valley, Calif.	Apr. 1, 1891	V. Bailey	Bennett Wells.
	♂ ad.	Lone Pine, Calif.	June 9, 1891	A. K. Fisher	

Agelaius phœniceus. Red-winged Blackbird.

The red-winged blackbird is probably resident in most if not all of the tule marshes in southern California and Nevada. A small flock of eight or ten individuals was seen at Furnace Creek, Death Valley, during the latter part of January; a single specimen was secured at Resting Springs, California, in February. In Nevada a large flock was found during March around the corral of Mr. George Watkins, at Ash Meadows, where the birds fed upon grain left by the stock. Mr. Nelson stated that several hundred of these birds came to roost each night in the tules growing near the main spring at Pahrump Ranch, February 12-28. Mr. Stephens found it common in Oasis Valley, March 15-19, and at Grapevine Spring, California, the first week in April. Dr. Merriam saw it at Yount's ranch, in Pahrump Valley, April 29, and at the Bend of the Colorado, May 4. He found it breeding abundantly in the valley of the Muddy, in eastern Nevada, May 6; in Meadow Creek Valley, near Panaca, May 19; in Pahranagat Valley, May 23 and 24; in Oasis Valley, June 1; along the Santa Clara and Virgin, near St. George, Utah, May 14, and saw a few at the west end of Antelope Valley, near Gorman Station, California, June 28.

At Hot Springs, in Panamint Valley, Calif., several were seen April 20-24. In Owens Valley, Mr. Stephens found the species not common at Little Owens Lake, May 6-11; at Olancha May 16-23; abundant at Alvord, June 26-28; common at Bishop, June 30; at Fish Slough, July 2-3; at Moraus, July 4-7; at Benton, July 9-10, and a few at Haway Meadows, May 12-14; and on the meadow at Bishop Creek, August 4-10. Mr. Nelson observed it at the head of Owens River up to an altitude of 2,130 meters (7,000 feet) during the latter part of July, and found it abundant about the farms at Lone Pine, in Owens Valley, December, 1890, where the writer saw numbers which were breeding in the tule marshes, the following June. The same observer also found it common along the South Fork of the Kern River, California, July 3-11; and Bakersfield, in the San Joaquin Valley, July 17-20.

Mr. Bailey saw flocks of redwings at Monterey, September 28 to October 9. Mr. Nelson found this species common and associated with *A. gubernator* about Buena Vista Lake in the San Joaquin Valley; in the wet places near San Emigdio, and along the coast between San Simeon and Carpenteria.

Record of specimens collected of *Agelaius phœniceus*.

Collector's No.	Sex.	Locality.	Date.	Collector.	Remarks.
138	♂ ad.	Ash Meadows, Nev	Mar. 18, 1891	A. K. Fisher	
	♂ ad.	......do......	...do......	E. W. Nelson	
111	♂ ad.	Resting Springs, Calif	Feb. 14, 1891	A. K. Fisher	
503	♂	Owens Valley, Calif	June 6, 1891	...do......	Lone Pine.
317	♂	......do......	June 8, 1891	...do......	Do.
118	♂	......do......	June 26, 1891	F. Stephens	Alvord.
124	♀	......do......	June 28, 1891	...do......	Do.
	♀	Fresno, Calif	Sept. 25, 1891	V. Bailey	

Agelaius gubernator. Bicolored Blackbird.

Although this species was common, if not abundant, in some localities west of the Sierra Nevada, one specimen only was collected during the season, and this was shot by Mr. Stephens at Olancha, at the southern end of Owens Lake, California, June 11.

Mr. Nelson found a few in the Ojai Valley in December; found it common and associated with the common redwing on the border of Buena Vista Lake in the San Joaquin Valley, near San Luis Obispo, and along the route from San Simeon to Carpenteria, in November and December.

Mr. Belding recorded it from the Yosemite Valley.

Sturnella magna neglecta. Western Meadowlark.

The meadowlark is a more or less common resident in most of the valleys in the desert region, as well as in those west of the Sierra Nevada. It was common and singing at San Bernardino, December 28-29, 1890, and was seen in Cajon Pass, January 1. In Death Valley it was not uncommon at Bennett Wells, near the old Eagle borax works, at Saratoga Springs, and at Furnace Creek, where it was common in the alfalfa fields the last of January. On the last trip to the valley Mr. Bailey and the writer found it not uncommon at Furnace Creek, June 19-21. The meadowlark was not uncommon at Resting Springs in the Amargosa Desert, the first half of February and April 27, and was common about the ranches at Ash Meadows and in Pahrump and Vegas valleys, Nevada, in March. In the same State Dr. Merriam found it common in the sage-covered plateau of Mount Magruder, June 5-8; and in Oasis Valley, where it was abundant and singing in great numbers in the early evening, June 1. He also found it abundant and musical in Pahranagat Valley, May 22-26; along the valleys of the Virgin and lower Muddy May 6-8, and at Ash Meadows, May 30. In Utah it was common in alfalfa fields along the Lower Santa Clara, near its junction with the Virgin, May 11-15; thence northerly to Mountain Meadows and the Escalante Desert, May 17; and one was seen on the western side of the Beaverdam Mountains, May 10.

In California Mr. Nelson observed a few pairs breeding on the tableland between Saline and Panamint valleys, at the base and among the piñons of the Inyo Mountains, and on the plateau at the head of Owens Valley, at the base of the White Mountains. In the Coso Valley and

Mountains it was rare, only a few individuals being seen in May. It was common all through Owens Valley and on the lower part of the eastern slope of the Sierra Nevada. It was common all along Kern River Valley, July 3–13; at Walker Basin, July 13–16; in Tehachapi Valley, June 25; at Old Fort Tejon the last of June; and at Bakersfield, in the San Joaquin Valley, July 17–20. Mr. Bailey found it in flocks consisting of several hundred individuals at Monterey, September 28 to October 9, and Mr. Nelson reported it as common in the San Joaquin Valley, October 5–27, and along the route from San Simeon to Carpenteria and Santa Paula in November and December.

Record of specimens collected of Sturnella magna neglecta.

Collector's No.	Sex.	Locality.	Date.	Collector.	Remarks.
28	♂	Resting Springs, Calif	Feb. 6, 1891	A. K. Fisher	
69	♀	Death Valley, Calif	Jan. 23, 1891	....do	Furnace Creek.
84	♂	....do	Jan. 28, 1891	....do	Do.
	♂	....do	June 19, 1891	V. Bailey	Do.
79	♂	Owens Lake, Calif	June 9, 1891	F. Stephens	

Icterus parisorum. Scott's Oriole.

Scott's oriole is one of a number of birds whose known range has been greatly extended by the observations of the different members of the expedition. It was first observed at the summit of Shepherd Cañon in the Argus Range, Calif., May 1. All along the western slope of this range and in Coso Valley it was common, and males were in full song. On May 5 a female was secured, which contained an egg in the oviduct, and on May 7 a nest containing two eggs was found. It was placed on the lower side of a branch of a tree yucca about 8 feet from the ground, and was firmly attached to the bayonet-shaped leaves of the tree by threads of plant fiber and tough grasses. A number of old nests were seen in many places through the valley. In the Coso Mountains it was also common up to the summit among the yuccas, junipers, and piñons, where, on May 27, a nest containing an egg and three young was found in a yucca in Mill Cañon.

Mr. Nelson found it breeding in the Inyo, Panamint, and Grapevine mountains in the piñon belt. On the eastern slope of the Inyo Mountains, near Cerro Gordo, one was noted on June 15. On both slopes of the Panamint Mountains, near Cottonwood Cañon, he found it ranging from the yucca belt up to the summit of the divide, and in the Grapevine Mountains found it among the piñons. Everywhere he found it in pairs, the males singing from the tops of piñons. Above the 'charcoal kilns' in Wild Rose Cañon in the Panamint Mountains, Mr. Bailey and the writer saw the species and heard the males singing, June 24–25. Mr. Stephens heard it near the Queen mine in the White Mountains, Nevada, July 11–16. In the same State Dr. Merriam secured specimens in the Charleston Mountains April 30, and in the Juniper

Salpinctes guadalupensis in western San Diego County, Calif. A.W. Anthony
Auk., XI, Oct 1894, pp. 327-328.

A male was shot in Reche Cañon April 1, 1895 (Auk XIII July 1896

Mountains, east of Panaca, May 19, when several pairs were seen mating. On Mount Magruder, Nevada, he found it tolerably common among the nut pines, where the birds seemed to be hunting for nesting sites, and were very difficult to approach. Several fine specimens were taken there June 4-11. The same observer found the species in the juniper belt of the Beaverdam Mountains, in Utah, May 10-11. In Walker Pass, on the east slope of the Sierra Nevada, several were seen and one shot among the yuccas June 21, and another on the western slope of the same pass in a *Pinus sabiniana* July 2.

Record of specimens collected of Icterus parisorum.

Collector's No.	Sex.	Locality.	Date.	Collector.	Remarks.
195	♀	Argus Range, Calif	May 5, 1891	A. K. Fisher	Maturango Spring.
	♂	....do....	May 9, 1891	T. S. Palmer	Do.
	♂	....do....	May 11, 1891	....do....	Do.
243	♀	Coso Mountains, Calif	May 21, 1891	A. K. Fisher	
261	♂	....do....	May 27, 1891	....do....	
	♂	Panamint Mountains, Calif	May 8, 1891	E. W. Nelson	
	♂	....do....	May 12, 1891	....do....	
	im	Walker Pass, Calif	June 21, 1891	C. Hart Merriam	
	♀	Charleston Mountains, Nev	Apr. 30, 1891	....do....	
	♀	Mount Magruder, Nev	June 4, 1891	....do....	
	♀	....do....	....do....	....do....	
	♂	....do....	June 8, 1891	....do....	

Icterus bullocki. Bullock's Oriole.

Bullock's oriole was tolerably common in several localities, where streams large enough to nourish a more or less extensive growth of trees were found. In Owens Valley it was common at Lone Pine, where a number of nests were observed in the willows, and several specimens secured, June 4-15. In the same valley, Mr. Stephens saw a solitary male at Little Owens Lake the first week in May; at Haway Meadows May 12-14; found the species rather common at Olancha May 16-23; common and a nest containing young at the mouth of the cañon at Independence Creek June 19; not common at Bishop, Fish Slough, and Morans July 1-7; and Benton July 9-10. Dr. Merriam saw one among the cottonwoods at Furnace Creek in Death Valley about the middle of April; in the Amargosa Cañon, and at Resting Springs, April 27. In Nevada, he saw it at Vegas Ranch, May 1; in the Valley of the Virgin and lower Muddy, May 6-8, and in Meadow Creek Valley, near Panaca, May 19. He found it tolerably common also in the Lower Santa Clara Valley, Utah, where it was breeding, May 11-15. On the western slope of the Sierra Nevada it was seen in Walker Pass, July 2; was common along the valley of the Kern June 22-23 and July 3-10; at Walker Basin July 13-16; and at Bakersfield July 17-20. It was common at Old Fort Tejon, and was seen in other parts of the Cañada de las Uvas in June and July. Mr. Nelson saw it in the Yosemite Valley, and Mr. Bailey, along the Kaweah River, in August.

Record of specimens collected of Icterus bullocki.

Collector's No.	Sex.	Locality.	Date.	Collector.	Remarks.
297	♂	Death Valley, Calif.	April 7, 1891	V. Bailey	
298	♂	Owens Valley, Calif.	June 5, 1891	A. K. Fisher	Lone Pine.
309	♂	......do......	..do..	......do......	Do.
322	♂ ad	......do......	June 7, 1891	......do......	Do.
323	♂ ''	......do......	June 9, 1891	......do......	Do.
324	♀ ''	......do......	..do..	......do......	Do.
87	♀	......do......	June 12, 1891	F. Stephens	Owens Lake.
		Walker Pass, Calif.	July 3, 1891	V. Bailey	

Scolecophagus cyanocephalus. Brewer's Blackbird.

Brewer's blackbird was not a common species in many localities visited by the expedition, either in the desert region or among the mountains. At San Bernardino a number of flocks were seen, together with redwings, December 29, 1890. A few individuals were found about the ranch at Furnace Creek, in Death Valley, in the latter part of January, and at Resting Springs, in the Amargosa Desert, early in February.

In Nevada a few were seen at Ash Meadows and in Pahrump and Vegas valleys, where they kept about inclosures and out-houses, in March. Dr. Merriam found it in the same valleys April 29-30; at the Bend of the Colorado May 4; at Bunkerville in the Virgin Valley, May 8; in Meadow Creek Valley near Panaca, May 19; and in Pahranagat Valley May 22. A few were seen at Hot Springs, in Panamint Valley, April 20-25; in Saline Valley the latter part of June, and on the plateau at the foot of the White Mountains in July. In Owens Valley it was common at Olancha June 29; at Alvord June 26-28; at Morans July 4-7; at Benton July 9-10; rather common at Bishop Creek August 4-10; and a few were seen at Little Owens Lake May 6-11; at Haway Meadows May 12-14; and at Ash Creek May 30 to June 3.

In the High Sierra it was common at Menache Meadows May 24-26; at the head of Owens River the latter part of July; at Whitney Meadows, where Mr. Nelson saw a flock of twenty or more sitting on the backs of sheep, August 30. A dozen or fifteen were seen at Trout Meadows September 7, and it was found breeding at Big Cottonwood Meadows during the summer. It was common in Walker Pass July 2; along the valley of the Kern July 3-13; at Walker Basin, where it was feeding on grasshoppers, July 13-16; and at Bakersfield, in the San Joaquin Valley, July 17-20. Dr. Merriam saw many catching grasshoppers in Antelope Valley, at the west end of the Mohave Desert, June 27; found the species common in the Cañada de las Uvas June 27-28; and saw a few in the San Marcos Valley, San Diego County, July 1-10.

Mr. Bailey found it common at Monterey September 28 to October 9; and Mr. Nelson saw flocks in San Joaquin Valley, and found it generally distributed along the route from San Simeon to Carpenteria, in November and December.

Record of specimens collected of Scolecophagus cyanocephalus.

Collector's No.	Sex.	Locality.	Date.	Collector.	Remarks.
77	♀	Death Valley, Calif.	Jan. 25, 1891	A. K. Fisher	Furnace Creek.
82	♀	......do............	Jan. 27, 1891	....do........	Do.

Coccothraustes vespertinus montanus. Western Evening Grosbeak.

The evening grosbeak was seen but once by the expedition. Mr. Bailey saw a small flock at Auburn, Calif., and secured two specimens October 22.

Record of specimens collected of Coccothraustes vespertinus montanus.

Collector's No.	Sex.	Locality.	Date.	Collector.	Remarks.
	♂	Auburn, Placer Co., Calif.	Oct. 22, 1891	V. Bailey	
	♀	......do............	....do........	....do........	

Pinicola enucleator. Pine Grosbeak.

Mr. Nelson saw a fine adult male pine grosbeak in brilliant plumage on the head of the San Joaquin River July 30. This individual was the only one seen during the year.

Carpodacus purpureus californicus. California Purple Finch.

Not obtained by any member of the expedition. Mr. Henshaw secured a single specimen near Mount Whitney, Calif., October 10, 1875.

Carpodacus cassini. Cassin's Purple Finch.

Cassin's purple finch was seen only in the higher parts of the White and Inyo mountains, and in the Sierra Nevada. Mr. Nelson saw two pairs in the *Pinus flexilis* belt on Waucoba Peak, in the Inyo Mountains, during the latter part of June, and secured two specimens at about 2,650 meters (8,700 feet) altitude in the White Mountains July 7. The same observer found it very abundant on the eastern slope, from 2,500 to 2,900 meters (8,200 to 9,500 feet) at the head of Owens River, and also at the head of the San Joaquin River, on the western slope.

It was also observed or secured at the following places in the High Sierra: at Horse Corral Meadows, August 11; at Cottonwood Meadows during the summer and as late as September 1; at Round Valley, which is 12 miles south of Mount Whitney, August 26–28; at Menache Meadows May 24–26; at Whitney Meadows the latter part of August, and near Mineral King during the latter part of August and early September.

Record of specimens collected of Carpodacus cassini.

Collector's No.	Sex.	Locality.	Date.	Collector.	Remarks.
137	♂ im.	White Mountains, Calif	July 7, 1891	E. W. Nelson	
	♂	do	do	do	
	♂	Sierra Nevada, Calif	July 22, 1891	F. Stephens	
	♂ im.	do	Aug. 11, 1891	T. S. Palmer	Horse Corral Meadows.
1	♂	do	June 19, 1891	B. H. Dutcher	Big Cottonwood Meadows.
7	♂	do	June 23, 1891	do	Do.
420	♀ im.	do	Aug. 24, 1891	A. K. Fisher	Do.
432	♂ im.	do	Aug. 30, 1891	do	Whitney Meadows.
	♂ im.	do	Aug. 1, 1891	V. Bailey	East Fork of Kaweah River, Calif.

Carpodacus mexicanus frontalis. House Finch.

The house finch was found wherever water was present in all localities visited by the expedition, except in the higher mountains among the pines, and undoubtedly bred wherever found. There was no other species of bird, with the possible exception of the dove, whose presence was so indicative of the nearness of water as the one under consideration. The writer never saw it more than a few hundred yards from water, except when flying high overhead.

After leaving Daggett on the Mohave Desert, Calif., house finches were seen at all the springs or water holes on the road to Death Valley. At Granite Wells flocks were found about the water at all times of day. In Death Valley a few were seen at Bennett Wells and between that place and Furnace Creek during the latter part of January. Dr. Merriam saw it at the latter place about the middle of April, and Mr. Bailey and the writer found it at both places on their last trip to the valley, June 19-22.

In the Panamint Mountains it was abundant in Johnson, Surprise, and Emigrant cañons, in April; at Willow Creek and Cottonwood Creek, in May; and in Wild Rose and Death Valley cañons, in June. In the Argus Range, the species was very abundant in Shepherd Cañon and at Maturango Spring, where it bred commonly, as it did in the Panamint Mountains.

As many as a dozen nests were found from April 25 to May 1, in various situations. A few were placed in crevices in the rocky sides of the cañon, while the majority were in bushes on the sloping hillsides, from one to several feet above the ground. The nests among the rocks were more compact, as they contained a larger amount of lining than those in the bushes, which in many cases were very loosely put together. The full complement of eggs in the different nests was four, five, and six. The species was common in the Coso, Inyo, and White mountains. It was everywhere common in Owens Valley from the lower to the upper part. In this valley, both at Independence and Lone Pine, the species was found to be very destructive to the ripened peaches during the middle of August. Flocks of birds occurred in the orchards, and in some places hardly an example of the ripe fruit could be found which was not more or less mutilated. A number of birds shot in the peach orchards at Lone Pine had little except the pulp of this fruit in their gullets or stomachs. It was known as the 'peach bird.'

It was common all along the route from Walker Pass, through the valley of Kern River, Walker Basin and Bakersfield to Visalia, June 21–23, and July 1 to 3, and at Old Fort Tejon late in June and early in July. It was seen at Ash Meadows and Pahrump Valley, Nevada, in March. In the same State, Dr. Merriam noted it among the cottonwoods at Yount's ranch in Pahrump Valley, April 29; at Mountain Spring, in the Charleston Mountains, and at Upper Cottonwood Springs near the east base of these mountains, April 30; near the summit of the Timpahute Mountains in tree yuccas, May 26; at Quartz Spring, on the west side of the Desert Mountains, May 27; at the Bend of the Colorado, May 4, and on Gold Mountain where a young one just able to fly was caught June 3, at an altitude of about 1,980 meters (6,500 feet). It was common in Tule Cañon June 4, and thence up to the plateau on top of Mount Magruder. In Arizona, he found it common at the mouth of Beaverdam Creek, May 9–10; in Utah, in the juniper belt of the Beaverdam Mountains, May 10–11, and at St. George, in the Lower Santa Clara Valley, May 11–15, where it was called 'peach bird' by the Mormons. Two nests were found at St. George, one in a cottonwood and the other in an arborescent cactus.

Mr. Nelson found the species in small numbers in the Cañada de las Uvas, at San Emigdio Creek, and in the Temploa Mountains, and rather common about the ranches in the San Joaquin Valley in October. It was common along the route from San Simeon to Carpenteria, among the farms along the coast, and not uncommon between the latter place and Santa Paula in November and December.

Record of specimens collected of Carpodacus mexicanus frontalis.

Collector's No.	Sex	Locality	Date	Collector	Remarks
45	♂	Daggett, Calif	Jan. 9, 1891	A. K. Fisher	
13	♂	do	Feb. 8, 1891	F. Stephens	
	♂	Panamint Mountains, Calif	Mch. 28, 1891	E. W. Nelson	Johnson Cañon.
158	♂	do	Apr. 19, 1891	A. K. Fisher	Surprise Cañon.
159	♀	do	do	do	Do.
187	♀	Argus Range, Calif	Apr. 27, 1891	do	Nest and eggs.
231	♂	do	May 12, 1891	do	Maturango Spring.
232	♂	do	do	do	Do.
	♂	do	do	T. S. Palmer	Do.
	♂	do	do	do	Do.
348	♀	Death Valley, Calif	June 21, 1891	A. K. Fisher	Furnace Creek.

Loxia curvirostra stricklandi. Mexican Crossbill.

Crossbills were uncommon and seen only in the Sierra Nevada. At Big Cottonwood Meadows Dr. Merriam saw them just below timber line June 18, and towards the end of the season Mr. Dutcher saw a few and shot a pair. Mr. Nelson saw some on the west slope opposite the head of Owens River in August. At Horse Corral Meadows a noisy flock passed our camp August 12. Mr. Bailey saw the species at Whitney Meadows, and it was heard at Soda Springs or Kern River Lakes, September 5.

Record of specimens collected of Loxia curvirostra stricklandi.

Collector's No.	Sex.	Locality.	Date.	Collector.	Remarks.
	♀	Sierra Nevada, Calif	Aug. 20, 1891	V. Bailey	Whitney Meadows.
	♂	do	Aug. 28, 1891	do	Do.
34		do	Aug. 22, 1891	B. H. Dutcher	Big Cottonwood Meadows.

Leucosticte tephrocotis. Gray-crowned Leucosticte.

A very interesting discovery made by the expedition was that the gray-crowned finch is a common summer resident in the higher portions of the White Mountains and the Sierra Nevada in eastern and southern California. The knowledge that this bird breeds as stated, makes its distribution in relation to the other species of the genus a little more clear.

In the Rocky Mountain region *Leucosticte atrata* is the northern and *L. australis* the southern representative, just as *Leucosticte t. littoralis* is the northern race of *L. tephrocotis* of the more western range.

Mr. Nelson found the gray crowned finch breeding abundantly on the White Mountains, the only range except the Sierra Nevada on which the species was seen. It was found above timber line about the bases of the main peaks at an elevation from 3,350 to 3,650 meters (11,000 to 12,000 feet). He found the birds easy of approach as they were feeding on seeds and insects about the border of the melting snowdrifts.

The warm west wind coming from over Owens Valley brought many insects which became benumbed by the cold and fell on the snowdrifts. These the birds devoured eagerly, and Mr. Nelson saw them pursue and tear to pieces several grasshoppers on the surface of the snow. The condition of the skin on the abdomen showed that they were incubating and that both sexes shared in this labor. He noticed when skinning the birds that they had a double craw. One located in the usual place and the other in the form of a double gular sac divided by a median constriction. The latter when full hangs down like a lobe of bare skin outside of the feathers.

In the Sierra Nevada the same observer saw the species about timber line at the head of Owens River on the eastern slope, and at the same altitude on Kern, Kings, and Kaweah rivers on the western slope. Mr. Stephens found it abundant about the lakes at the head of Independence Creek, where it was breeding June 18–23, and also saw three above timber line at Menache Meadows, May 24–26. Mr. Dutcher saw several flocks and secured a few specimens at and above timber line at

Big Cottonwood Meadows, during the summer. *Mr. Bailey found it common all along timber line and down among the *Pinus balfouriana* at Whitney Meadows. The writer did not see the species until August 18, when a flock of forty or more was seen on the west side of the Kearsarge Pass. Later in the day, during a snow storm, a flock was seen just below timber line on the east side of the Pass, and five specimens secured. The bad weather seemed to make them restless and hard to approach. At Round Valley, 12 miles south of Mount Whitney, the species was again seen just above timber line, August 28, and on the ridge north of Mineral King large flocks were seen September 8–11.

Record of specimens collected of Leucosticte tephrocotis.

Collector's No.	Sex.	Locality.	Date.	Collector.	Remarks.
	♂	White Mountains, Calif.	July 15, 1891	E. W. Nelson	
	♂	....do....	....do....	....do....	
	♂	....do....	....do....	....do....	
	♂	....do....	....do....	....do....	
	♂	....do....	....do....	....do....	
	♂	....do....	....do....	....do....	
	♂	....do....	....do....	....do....	
	♂	....do....	....do....	....do....	
	♂	....do....	....do....	....do....	
	♂	....do....	....do....	....do....	
	♂	....do....	....do....	....do....	
	♂	....do....	....do....	....do....	
	♂	....do....	....do....	....do....	
	♀	....do....	....do....	....do....	
	♀	....do....	....do....	....do....	
	♀	....do....	....do....	....do....	
	♀	....do....	....do....	....do....	
	♀	....do....	....do....	....do....	
	♀	Sierra Nevada, Calif.	July 25, 1891	E. W. Nelson	Summit of Mammoth Pass, Cal.
417	♂	....do....	Aug. 16, 1891	A. K. Fisher	Kearsarge Pass, 11,000 feet altitude.
418	♀ im	....do....	....do....	....do....	Do.
419	♀ im	....do....	....do....	....do....	Do.
112	♂	....do....	June 22, 1891	F. Stephens	Independence Creek, 10,000 feet.
113	♀	....do....	....do....	....do....	Do.
114	♀	....do....	....do....	....do....	Do.
115	♂	....do....	....do....	....do....	Do.
19	im	....do....	July 30, 1891	B. H. Dutcher	Big Cottonwood Meadows.
25	♂	....do....	Aug. 2, 1891	....do....	Do.
	♀ im	....do....	Aug. 20, 1891	V. Bailey	Do.
429	♂ im	....do....	Aug. 28, 1891	A. K. Fisher	Round Valley, above timber line.
161	♀ im	....do....	Aug. 23, 1891	F. Stephens	Olancha Peak, 12,000 feet altitude.
	♂	....do....	Aug. 7, 1891	V. Bailey	Mineral King, 9,700 feet altitude.

Leucosticte atrata. Black Leucosticte.

Mr. Bailey secured one specimen of this species at St. George, Utah, January 21, 1889. It was feeding alone on a rocky hill, among low brush.

Spinus tristis. Goldfinch.

A common species throughout southern California, though not recorded by any member of the expedition.

Spinus psaltria. Arkansas Goldfinch.

The Arkansas goldfinch was observed in a number of localities throughout the mountain and desert regions visited. At San Bernardino a flock of eight or ten was seen feeding on the seeds of a wild sunflower, December 28, 1890. Small flocks were seen in Cajon Pass, January 2, again March 29-30, and in the cottonwoods bordering the Mohave River near Victor, March 30.

In Nevada, it was not uncommon at Ash Meadows in March; at Queen station and mill in the White Mountains, July 11-16. Dr. Merriam found it at Upper Cottonwood Springs at the east base of the Charleston Mountains, April 30; at the Bend of the Colorado River, May 4; and in Pahranagat Valley, where it was breeding commonly, May 23. At the mouth of Beaverdam Creek, Arizona, and on the west side of the Beaverdam Mountains, Utah, he saw several May 9-10. As no specimens were taken for identification, the Arizona and Utah records may apply to *Spinus psaltria arizonæ*.

In the Panimint Mountains it was common in Johnson and Surprise cañons, and in the latter place Mr. Albert Koebele found a nest, just completed, April 23. In the same mountains Mr. Nelson found it a common breeding species in Cottonwood, Mill Creek, and Willow Creek cañons. In the Argus Range it was common in Shepherd Cañon, where a nest and four eggs were taken April 27, and at Maturango Spring the first half of May. At Coso Mountains a few were seen along the streams in the cañons, the last of May.

Mr. Nelson found it common in the Grapevine Mountains, and rather common in the Inyo Mountains, in willow patches along the streams up to the piñons, the latter part of June. Goldfinches were common at the head of Owens River, abundant in the Yosemite, and from the base up to the nut-pines in the White Mountains. The were more or less common in Owens Valley from the lower end, at Little Owens Lake, northward to Benton and the foot of the White Mountains. A few were seen in Walker Pass, July 2-3; the species was common along the South Fork of Kern River, July 3-10; in Walker Basin, July 13-16; and at Bakersfield, in the San Joaquin Valley, July 17-20. In the High Sierra Dr. Merriam saw the species near Big Cottonwood Meadows, June 18, and the writer observed a flock near the abandoned sawmill in Sequoia National Park, August 1.

Mr. Palmer reported it common at Old Fort Tejon during the first half of July; Mr. Stephens found it rather common at Reche Cañon September 22-24, and Mr. Bailey saw it in flocks at Monterey September 28 to October 9.

It was common at Three Rivers July 25-30, and along the route from Mineral King to that place September 12-15.

Mr. Nelson found it common and generally distributed between San Simeon and Carpenteria and Santa Paula, in November and December.

Record of specimens collected of Spinus psaltria.

Collector's No.	Sex.	Locality.	Date.	Collector.	Remarks.
7	♂	San Bernardino, Calif	Dec. 28, 1890	A. K. Fisher	
188	♀	Argus Range, Calif	April 27, 1891	....do	Shepherd Cañon, nest and 4 eggs.
193	♂	....do	April 29, 1891	....do	Shepherd Cañon.
247	♂	....do	May 13, 1891	....do	Maturango Spring.
368	♂	Walker Pass, Calif	July 3, 1891	....do	
371	♂	Kern River, Calif	July 4, 1891	....do	South Fork.
	♂	Pahranagat Valley, Nevada	May 23, 1891	C. Hart Merriam	
	♂	Santa Clara, Utah	May 11, 1891	V. Bailey	

Spinus psaltria arizonæ. Arizona Goldfinch.

This subspecies was found breeding in great abundance in the Lower Santa Clara Valley, Utah, by Dr. Merriam. Five nests with fresh eggs were found, and one with eggs nearly ready to hatch, May 11-15. In California Mr. Bailey secured a specimen from a flock at Three Rivers, in the western foothills of the Sierra Nevada, September 15.

Spinus lawrencei. Lawrence's Goldfinch.

Dr. Merriam reported Lawrence's goldfinch as common in the Cañada de las Uvas, June 28-29, and in the Granite Range in western San Diego County, July 1-10. Mr. Palmer saw a male near Old Fort Tejon, June 30, and shot one in the cañon July 6. A specimen was secured in Walker Basin July 16, and an individual was seen among the oaks above it, July 14. These are all the records we have for the species.

Spinus pinus. Pine Siskin.

At two places only was this species seen by members of the expedition, both in the High Sierra in California. Mr. Nelson saw it at the head of the San Joaquin River, in August, and the writer observed a flock of a dozen or fifteen near timber line above Mineral King, September 10. The birds were feeding upon seeds on or near the ground, and when flushed alighted on a pine branch within a few feet of the observer.

Poocætes gramineus confinis. Western Vesper Sparrow.

The vesper sparrow was seen in comparatively few places on either side of the Sierra Nevada. At Ash Meadows, Nevada, it was not uncommon in migration March 10, and a few were seen by Mr. Bailey at Vegas Ranch, March 10-13.

Mr. Nelson found a few among the sage brush above the piñons in the Inyo Mountains, in June; not uncommon on the White Mountains, and on the plateau at the head of Owens Valley, in July; and common at the head of Owens River, in the same month. Dr. Merriam found the species at Mountain Meadows, Utah, May 17. A single specimen was seen near Visalia, Calif., September 17, a few near the lower end of the Cañada de las Uvas and San Emigdio Cañon, and on the Carrizo Plain, in San Joaquin Valley, in October.

Ammodramus sandwichensis alaudinus. Western Savanna Sparrow.

This little sparrow was found nowhere common, though it breeds sparingly in various localities throughout the desert regions. The writer found it not uncommon in the alfalfa fields at Furnace Creek, Death Valley, in the latter part of January, and Dr. Merriam found a few at the same place April 9-12, but Mr. Bailey and the former observer did not detect it on their last trip to the valley, June 19-22. Mr. Nelson found a few at Saratoga Springs, in the lower end of the valley, late in January. A few were seen at Resting Spring, California early in February; a number of specimens were secured in the wet meadows at Ash Meadows, Nevada, during the first three weeks of March; and Mr. Nelson found it not uncommon about wet ground in Pahrump and Vegas valleys and in Vegas Wash March 3-16. Dr. Merriam shot one at the Great Bend of the Colorado May 4; one in Meadow Creek Valley, Nevada, May 19, and a number in Pahranagat Valley, Nevada, May 22-26.

In Owens Valley the writer found it not uncommon and breeding among the salt grass at Owens Lake May 30 to June 4, and at Lone Pine June 4-15; and Mr. Stephens found it not uncommon at Olancha, May 16-23; Alvord, June 26-28; and Morans, July 4-7.

A pair was seen by Mr. Nelson at the head of Owens Valley near the White Mountains about the middle of July, and by the writer at Three Rivers, in the western foothills, September 16. It was common along the coast from San Simeon to Santa Barbara, and a few were seen near Carpenteria in December.

Record of specimens collected of Ammodramus sandwichensis alaudinus.

Collector's No.	Sex.	Locality.	Date.	Collector.	Remarks.
	♀	Great Bend of Colorado River, Nev	May 4, 1891	C. Hart Merriam	
	♂	Pahrump Valley, Nev	Feb. 17, 1891	E. W. Nelson	
	♂	Ash Meadows, Nev	Mar. 4, 1891	....do	
	♀	....do	....do	....do	
118		....do	Mar. 8, 1891	A. K. Fisher	
120	♀	....do	Mar. 9, 1891	....do	
129	♀	....do	Mar. 15, 1891	....do	
	♂	....do	Mar. 19, 1891	E. W. Nelson	
106	♂	Resting Springs, Calif	Feb. 11, 1891	A. K. Fisher	
	♂	Death Valley, Calif	Jan. 31, 1891	E. W. Nelson	Saratoga Spring.
79	♀	....do	Jan. 26, 1891	A. K. Fisher	Furnace Creek.
91	♀	....do	Jan. 31, 1891	....do	Do.
92	♂	....do	....do	....do	Do.
170	♀	Panamint Valley, Calif	Apr. 23, 1891	....do	Hot Springs.
283	♀	Owens Valley, Calif	June 2, 1891	....do	Keeler.
291	♂	....do	June 3, 1891	....do	Do.
61	♂	....do	May 22, 1891	F. Stephens	Olancha.
88	♂	....do	June 12, 1891	....do	Do.
103	♀	....do	June 15, 1891	....do	Do.
292	♂	....do	June 5, 1891	A. K. Fisher	Lone Pine.
	♀	Fresno, Calif	Sept. 25, 1891	E. W. Nelson	

Ammodramus sandwichensis bryanti. Bryant's Marsh Sparrow.

Mr. Nelson found Bryant's sparrow common along the coast from Santa Barbara to Carpenteria during the first half of December.

Record of specimen collected of *Ammodramus sandwichensis bryanti*.

Collectors No.	Sex.	Locality.	Date.	Collector.	Remarks.
	♂	Carpenteria, Calif	Dec. 18, 1891	E. W. Nelson	
	♂	....do..............	....do.......	....do........	
	♀	....do..............	....do.......	....do........	

Chondestes grammacus strigatus. Western Lark Sparrow.

The western lark sparrow is a characteristic inhabitant of the Upper Sonoran and Transition Zones and was not found in the Lower Sonoran Zone, except west of the Sierra Nevada, and during migration. It was a common species in Owen's Valley from the lower end northward, and was breeding wherever found. The writer found it abundant along the South Fork of Kern River, at Kernville, and in Walker Basin during the first half of July. In the San Joaquin Valley it was abundant at Bakersfield, and all along the route to Visalia, July 17–23, and at Three Rivers, July 25–30 and September 14–17.

Dr. Merriam furnished the following notes on the species: "In Nevada it was common throughout the sage brush on the rolling plateau that forms the northward continuation of the Juniper Mountains, May 18, and in Desert and Pahranagat valleys, May 20–26. In Pahranagat Valley it was particularly abundant, breeding and in full song. It was common in the north part of Oasis Valley, June 1, but was not observed at the southern end of this valley. On Mount Magruder a few were seen in the sage brush June 5. Others were found at Mountain Spring in the Charleston Mountains and at Upper Cottonwood Springs at the east base of these mountains, April 30; and in the Valley of the Muddy, May 6. Several were seen in the lower edge of the junipers on both sides of the Beaverdam Mountains in southwestern Utah, May 10 and 11. It was found also in the Santa Clara Valley, Utah, May 11–15, and was common in Mountain Meadows, Utah, May 17. In Owens Valley, California, it was common in the sage brush of the Upper Sonoran Zone, June 10–19, and in Antelope Valley at the west end of the Mohave Desert, June 27–28. On the west slope of the Sierra Nevada it was abundant in the valley of Kern River, where full-grown young were conspicuous, June 22–23. It was seen in the Tehachapi Valley, June 25, and in the Cañada de las Uvas, June 28–29, where full-grown young were common."

Mr. Nelson found it rather common in the Cañada de las Uvas and San Emigdio Cañon, at various places in San Joaquin Valley and about the borders of the foothills, in October, and in the more open country along the route from San Simeon to Carpenteria, in November and part of December.

Record of specimens collected of Chondestes grammacus strigatus.

Collector's No.	Sex.	Locality.	Date.	Collector.	Remarks.
307	♀	Owens Valley, Calif.	June 6, 1891	A. K. Fisher	Lone Pine.
308	♂	......do......	...do...	...do...	Do.
320	♀	......do......	June 9, 1891	...do...	Do.

Zonotrichia leucophrys. White-crowned Sparrow.

The white-crowned sparrow was a common summer resident in the Sierra Nevada and White Mountains, but was not found in any other locality, even as a migrant—at least specimens were not taken elsewhere. There is uncertainty as to the race which breeds among the piñons in the Inyo Mountains, as no specimens were collected there. Mr. Nelson found the white-crowned sparrow on the plateau at the head of Owens Valley, and thence up to near timber line in the White Mountains, and Mr. Stephens saw it at the Queen mill and mine, Nevada, in the same range, July 11–16. Along the eastern slope of the Sierra it was common at the head of Owens River, the last of July; rather common at Menache Meadows, May 24–26; Onion Lake on Independence Creek, June 18–23; and at Bishop Creek, August 4–10. Mr. Dutcher found it very common among the willows at Big Cottonwood Meadows, where nests were taken. Mr. Palmer saw a nest containing three eggs near Mount Silliman, August 7, and Mr. Belding found the species in the Yosemite. White-crowned sparrows were common in flocks at Whitney Meadows, September 1, Farewell Gap, September 8, and from timber line above Mineral King down along the Kaweah River to below the pines, September 10–12.

Record of specimens collected of Zonotrichia leucophrys.

Collector's No.	Sex.	Locality.	Date.	Collector.	Remarks.
148	im	Sierra Nevada, California	Aug. 8, 1891	F. Stephens	Bishop Creek.
116	♂	......do......	June 22, 1891	...do...	Independence Creek.
	♀	......do......	July 31, 1891	V. Bailey	Mineral King.
	♂	White Mountains	July 10, 1891	E. W. Nelson	
162	♂	Sierra Nevada	Aug. 26, 1891	F. Stephens	Mulkey Meadows.
	♀	......do......	July 7, 1891	B. H. Dutcher	Big Cottonwood Meadows.
	♀	......do......	July 13, 1891	...do...	Do.
	♂	......do......	July 19, 1891	...do...	Do.
422	♂ im	......do......	Aug. 25, 1891	A. K. Fisher	Do.

Zonotrichia leucophrys intermedia. Intermediate Sparrow.

The intermediate sparrow was found as a migrant or winter resident only, through the desert regions, where it was often abundant among the mesquite or other thickets. In Cajon Pass it was very common January 1–2, and again March 30. In the Mohave Desert it was common at Hesperia January 4, and about Stoddard Wells January 6. In Death Valley it was common about Furnace Creek ranch the last of

January and April 9-12, and at Resting Springs the first half of February and April 27. At the latter place the flocks became very tame and came into camp to pick up the crumbs.

It was common about the ranch and among the mesquite at Ash Meadows, Nev., during the greater part of March, and Mr. Nelson found it abundant at Pahrump and Vegas ranches and among the junipers in the Charleston Mountains during the same month. Dr. Merriam found it common at Leach Point Spring, Calif., April 25; at Mountain Spring in the Charleston Mountains, Nev., April 30; in the Valley of the Virgin near Bunkerville, May 8, and a few tardy migrants in Pahranagat Valley May 22-26. In the Santa Clara Valley, Utah, the subspecies was still tolerably common May 11-15. In the Panamint Mountains it was common in Johnson, Surprise, and Emigrant cañons in April, and Mr. Nelson found a few late migrants on Willow Creek the last of May. The sparrow was abundant among the mesquite at Hot Springs, Panamint Valley, April 20-25; a few were seen at Searl's garden, near the south end of the Argus Range, about the same time, and a few in Shepherd Cañon as late as May 1. In the latter place Mr. Nelson reported it very common in January. Mr. Stephens found it rather common in the lower end of Oasis Valley, Nev., March 15-19, and at Grapevine Spring, Calif., April 1-4.

A few were observed by Mr. Nelson about the Cañada de las Uvas and San Emigdio Cañon in October, and along the coast from San Simeon to Carpenteria in November and December.

Record of specimens collected of Zonotrichia leucophrys intermedia.

Collector's No.	Sex.	Locality.	Date.	Collector.	Remarks.
26	♀ im.	Cajon Pass, Calif	Jan. 2, 1891	A. K. Fisher	
27	♀	......do	......do	......do	
38	♂	Hesperia, Calif	Jan. 4, 1891	......do	
6	♂	Daggett, Calif	Feb. 7, 1891	F. Stephens	
68	♀	Death Valley, Calif	Jan. 23, 1891	A. K. Fisher	Furnace Creek.
67	♂	......do	......do	......do	Do.
81	♂ im.	......do	Jan. 27, 1891	......do	Do.
105	♀	Resting Springs, Calif	Feb. 10, 1891	......do	
123	♂	Ash Meadows, Calif	Mar. 11, 1891	......do	
137	♀	......do	Mar. 19, 1891	......do	
	♀	Panamint Mountains, Calif	Mar. 29, 1891	E. W. Nelson	Johnson Cañon.
	♂	......do	......do	......do	Do.
	♂	......do	......do	......do	Do.
	♂	Panamint Valley, Calif	Apr. 22, 1891	......do	Hot Spring.
	♀	......do	Apr. 23, 1891	......do	Do.
	♀	......do	......do	......do	Do.
	♂	......do	Apr. 14, 1891	V. Bailey	Emigrant Spring.
48	♀	Argus Range, Calif	Apr. 22, 1891	F. Stephens	Borax Flat.
	♀	Carpenteria, Calif	Dec. 18, 1891	E. W. Nelson	

Zonotrichia leucophrys gambeli. Gambel's Sparrow.

Gambel's sparrow was not met with east of the Sierra Nevada, and on the western side as a migrant only. Mr. Bailey found it abundant at Monterey the first week in October, and Mr. Nelson reported it common in the San Joaquin Valley wherever a vigorous growth of bushes or weeds afforded attractive shelter. Along the route from

San Simeon to Carpenteria and Santa Paula it was abundant during November and December.

Zonotrichia coronata. Golden-crowned Sparrow.

The golden-crowned sparrow was found by Mr. Nelson to be abundant and generally distributed along the coast from San Simeon to Carpenteria and Santa Paula during November and December. This is the only region where the species was noted.

Zonotrichia albicollis. White-throated Sparrow.

Mr. Nelson secured a male specimen of the white-throated sparrow at the mission of Santa Ynez, December 6, 1891, which makes the fourth record for California.

Spizella monticola ochracea. Western Tree Sparrow.

The only place where the tree sparrow was seen was Pahrump ranch, Nevada, where Mr. Nelson found quite a number in the willow thickets, the latter part of February. They appeared quite suddenly one morning before a storm, which filled the valley with rain and covered the mountains with snow.

Spizella socialis arizonæ. Western Chipping Sparrow.

The chipping sparrow was not found to be a common migrant in the valleys, though it was more or less common as a summer resident in the mountains, from the piñons and junipers up to and among the other conifers. A number were seen in the cultivated fields about San Bernardino, December 28-29, 1890. Mr. Nelson saw a few on the Panamint Mountains the latter part of May and found the species breeding on the Grapevine Mountains, June 10-11. A few were seen about Maturango Spring, where the males were in full song, May 13-14. The species was found up to timber line in the White Mountains, and was common at the head of Owens River, in the Sierra Nevada. Dr. Merriam found it on the north slope of Telescope Peak in the Panamint Mountains, April 17-19; among the junipers in the Juniper Mountains, Nevada, May 18; and among the piñons on Mount Magruder, Nevada, June 5. In Walker Basin it was common among the pines above the valley, July 14, and Mr. Palmer found it quite common at Old Fort Tejon about the same time. In the High Sierra it was common in the Sequoia National Park the first week in August; at Horse Corral Meadows, August 9-13; in Big Cottonwood Meadows during the summer and fall; at Whitney Meadows, the first week in September; at Mineral King, near timber line, September 9-11; and along the Kaweah River, from Mineral King to the valley, September 11-13.

Record of specimens collected of Spizella socialis arizonæ.

Collector's No.	Sex.	Locality.	Date.	Collector.	Remarks.
1	♂	San Bernardino, Calif	Dec. 28, 1890	A. K. Fisher	
158	♀	Sierra Nevada, Calif	Aug. 22, 1891	F. Stephens	Olancha Peak.
	♂ im.	do	Aug. 29, 1891	V. Bailey	Whitney Meadows.

Zonotrichia coronata
Large numbers were found feeding among the refuse of a slaughter house" [at Monterey] (McLellan Field Notes Feb. 27 - Mch 1 1894).

Zonotrichia albicollis George F. Breninger secured a specimen (male) at Santa Cruz Jan 1 1895 — (Letter Jan 26 1895)
A specimen was secured Nov. 21, 1894 at Pasadena Calif. by Horace A. Gaylord (Auk, July, 1896 p. 260).

Spizella breweri. Brewer's Sparrow.

Brewer's sparrow was a common species throughout the desert regions during migration, and bred in most of the mountain ranges among the sagebrush. A number were seen in Vegas Wash, March 10-13, and the species arrived at Ash Meadows, Nevada, March 17. Mr. Nelson reported it as a common breeding species among the sage, both in the Panamint and Grapevine mountains, during the latter part of May and first of June. Many of its nests were found, usually containing four eggs, and built in a sage bush a couple of feet from the ground. On the north side of Telescope Peak Dr. Merriam found it common among the sage, April 17-19, and Mr. Bailey and the writer observed it near the same place, June 22-25. It was not uncommon at Hot Springs, in Panamint Valley, April 20-23; several were seen at Leach Point Spring, April 25; and one was shot in the northwest arm of Death Valley, April 13.

In Nevada Dr. Merriam found it tolerably common in parts of Pahrump Valley, April 29, and at Mountain Spring, in the Charleston Mountains, April 30. He reported it as common in the sage brush on the plateau of the Juniper Mountains; in Pahranagat Valley, May 22-26; on Gold Mountain, June 3; in Tule Cañon, June 4; and thence up to the summit of Mount Magruder, where it was the commonest bird on the sage plateau, June 4-11, breeding abundantly, and extending thence northerly into Fish Lake Valley.

In Utah Dr. Merriam did not see it in the low St. George Valley, but found it common in the upper part of the Santa Clara Valley, May 16, beginning with the sagebrush about 8 miles north of St. George and continuing northward to Mountain Meadows and the Escalante Desert, where several nests were found, May 17. In the Beaverdam Mountains it was tolerably common throughout the sage and junipers, May 10.

Returning to California, in the Argus Range, the species was common in Shepherd Cañon, and was breeding commonly at Maturango Spring, from the summit of the range to the bottom of Coso Valley, early in May. In the Coso Mountains it was common, and a number of nests containing eggs were found during the latter part of May. Mr. Nelson found the species rather common in the Inyo Mountains, from the sage up to the summit in the White Mountains, and at the head of Owens River in the Sierra Nevada. In Owens Valley it was common throughout the summer, especially along the eastern slope of the Sierra Nevada, where Mr. Stephens noted it in a number of places, even as high as Monache Meadows. It was common on the western slope of Walker Pass, June 21 and July 2-3, and in Kern River Valley, June 22-23 and July 11-13. Mr. Palmer reported it as tolerably common in the sagebrush among the piñons at Old Fort Tejon, July 9.

Record of specimens collected of Spizella breweri.

Collector's No.	Sex.	Locality.	Date.	Collector.	Remarks.
130	♂	Ash Meadows, Nev	Mar. 17, 1891	A. K. Fisher	
	♂	......do	Mar. 18, 1891	E. W. Nelson	
	♀	Panamint Valley, Calif.	Apr. 22, 1891	....do	Hot Springs.
46	♂	Panamint Mts., Calif.	Apr. 16, 1891	F. Stephens	
203	♂	Argus Range, Calif.	May 6, 1891	A. K. Fisher	Maturango Springs.
213	♂	......do	May 8, 1891	....do	Do.
81	♀	Owens Lake, Calif.	June 10, 1891	F. Stephens	
105	♂ im	......do	June 15, 1891	....do	

Spizella atrigularis. Black-chinned Sparrow.

The black-chinned sparrow is one of a number of species whose known range was much extended by the observations of the expedition. It was first observed in Johnson Cañon in the Panamint Range, where an adult male was seen among the junipers, April 6. In Surprise Cañon, of the same range, the species was first seen April 15, when two specimens were secured, and subsequently it became common.

The song, which was frequently heard, resembles closely that of the Eastern field sparrow (*Spizella pusilla*). At Maturango Spring, in the Argus Range, a male was seen among the sage (*Artemisia tridentata*) on May 12, and a female was secured among the willows near the spring, which had an egg in the oviduct, almost ready for expulsion, May 15. In the Coso Mountains the species was not uncommon, and on May 27 a female with her nest and three eggs was secured. The nest was situated in a small bush about two feet from the ground, on a gradually sloping hillside bearing a scattered growth of piñon.

On the west side of Owens Valley Mr. Stephens heard several singing on Independence Creek, near the Rex Monte mill, and secured a specimen June 20. On the western slope of Walker Pass a specimen was secured in one of the cañons, as it was washing at a pool, July 3, and at Walker Basin an immature bird was shot on the ridge above the valley, July 14.

Record of specimen collected of Spizella atrigularis.

Collectors No.	Sex.	Locality.	Date.	Collector.	Remarks.
160	♂	Panamint Mountains, Calif.	Apr. 16, 1891	E. W. Nelson	Surprise Cañon.
161	♂	......do	Apr. 15, 1891	A. K. Fisher	Do.
	♀	......do	......do	....do	Do.
241	♀	Argus Range, Calif.	May 15, 1891	....do	Maturango Spring.
259	♀	Coso Mountains, Calif.	May 27, 1891	....do	Nest and eggs.
260	♂	......do	......do	....do	
363	♀	Walker Pass, Calif.	July 3, 1891	....do	
392	♂	Walker Basin, Calif.	July 14, 1891	....do	
109	♂	Independence Creek, Calif.	June 20, 1891	F. Stephens	Owens Valley.

Junco hyemalis. Slate-colored Junco.

A specimen of the common eastern junco was secured by the writer in Johnson Cañon in the Panamint Range, April 3, and another was seen a day or two later in the same locality. Mr. Bailey took one near Fort Mohave, Ariz., March 4, 1889.

Junco hyemalis shufeldti. Shufeldt's Junco.

A specimen collected in the Charleston Mountains and another in the Grapevine Mountains, Nevada, in March, belong to this race. Whether the species remains in these ranges to breed, or passes further east for that purpose, it is impossible to say, as no specimens were collected there later in the season.

Record of specimens collected of Junco hyemalis shufeldti.

Collectors No.	Sex.	Locality.	Date.	Collector.	Remarks.
35	♀	Charleston Mountains, Nev	Mar. 7, 1891	V. Bailey	
	♀	Grapevine Mountains, Nev	Mar. 21, 1891	F. Stephens	

Junco hyemalis thurberi. Thurber's Junco.

Thurber's junco was a common species in many places throughout the desert region of southeastern California, and bred commonly in most of the desert ranges, as well as in the Sierra Nevada. It was very common in Cajon Pass in the San Bernardino Mountains, January 2, and several were seen there March 30. Mr. Nelson found juncos common at Lone Pine, in the cañons at the foot of the Sierra Nevada, also in Surprise Cañon of the Panamint, and Shepherd Cañon of the Argus range, in December and early January. The individuals which he found in considerable numbers at Pahrump ranch, and in the Charleston Mountains, in February and March, may or may not have been wholly or in part referable to this form, as a single specimen collected in the Charleston Mountains belongs to the more eastern race, *shufeldti*. The same may be said of the few pairs of birds he found breeding near the summit of the Grapevine Mountains, in June, as no specimens were collected at that time. It was common in Johnson and Surprise cañons, in the Panamint range, during the first half of April; Dr. Merriam saw many on the north base of Telescope Peak, April 16-19, and Mr. Bailey and the writer saw it from the summit of that peak down to below the 'charcoal kilns', in Wild Rose Cañon, June 23. It was tolerably common among the piñons in the Argus range, where specimens were secured during the first half of May, and Mr. Palmer saw one in the Coso Mountains May 27, and others at Cerro Gordo, in the Inyo range, May 31. Mr. Nelson found it sparingly among the *Pinus flexilis* in the latter range the last of June, and not common in the White Mountains in July. Mr. Stephens found it not common from the Rex Monte mine to timber line in Independence Cañon, June 18-23; at Queen mine, White Mountains, Nevada, July 11-16; common at Bishop Creek, August 4-10, and Menache Meadows, May 24-26. Juncos were common on the ridge above Walker Basin, July 14, and Mr. Palmer saw three back of

Old Fort Tejon July 6, which had probably descended from the mountains where they were common among the pines July 9. Mr. Nelson reported this species as abundant at the head of Owens River, where he found a nest containing four eggs nearly ready to hatch, July 25. On the western slope it was also common. On the upper Merced he found two nests on August 3, one containing a young bird and three eggs nearly ready to hatch, and the other three fresh eggs. The first mentioned nest was nicely hidden under a projecting spruce root on the side of a small gully, and the latter was placed in a clump of aspens at the base of a small sapling, was strongly made, and was lined with the long hairs of the porcupine.

Juncos were very common in the Sequoia National Park during the first week of August. One nest with three eggs was found, and young as large as their parents were seen. They were common at Horse Corral Meadows August 9–13, Big Cottonwood Meadows and Round Valley the last of August, and at Whitney Meadows and Mineral King early in September. Mr. Dutcher found them abundant at Big Cottonwood Meadows where he discovered several nests, and Mr. Bailey observed them on the Kaweah River from the lowest conifers to above timberline. A nest with young was found among the giant redwoods July 29.

Mr. Nelson reported the species as common on high ground along the route from San Simeon to Carpenteria in November and December; it was also common on the route from La Pauza to San Luis Obispo October 28 to November 3; and a few were seen at Santa Paula the last of December.

Record of specimens collected of Junco hyemalis thurberi.

Collector's No.	Sex.	Locality.	Date.	Collector.	Remarks.
	♀	Panamint Mountains, Calif.	Mar. 28, 1891	E. W. Nelson	Johnson Cañon.
	♂	......do......	......do......	......do......	Do.
149	♂	......do......	Apr. 2, 1891	A. K. Fisher	Do.
170	♀	......do......	Apr. 19, 1891	......do......	Surprise Cañon.
	♂	......do......	......do......	E. W. Nelson	Do.
353	♂	......do......	June 23, 1891	A. K. Fisher	Coal kilns.
202	♂	Argus Range, Calif.	May 6, 1891	......do......	Matarango Spring.
	♂	......do......	May 9, 1891	T. S. Palmer	Do.
	♀	......do......	......do......	......do......	Do.
111	♀	Owens Valley, Calif.	June 21, 1891	F. Stephens	Independence Creek. Sitting.
133	♂	White Mountains, Calif.	July 13, 1891	......do......	10,000 feet altitude.
	♂	......do......	July 14, 1891	E. W. Nelson	
22	♂	Cajon Pass, Calif.	Jan. 2, 1891	A. K. Fisher	
	♀	Sierra Nevada, Calif.	Aug. 7, 1891	V. Bailey	Mineral King.
5	♂	......do......	June 19, 1891	B. H. Dutcher	Big Cottonwood Meadows.
	♀	......do......	July 7, 1891	......do......	Do.
37	♂	......do......	Sept. 14, 1891	......do......	Do.
38	?	......do......	......do......	......do......	Do.
414	♀ ad.	......do......	Aug. 12, 1891	A. K. Fisher	Horse Corral Meadows.
144	♂ im.	......do......	July 27, 1891	F. Stephens	
	♀	......do......	July 22, 1891	E. W. Nelson	
	♂	......do......	July 25, 1891	......do......	Nest and eggs.
	♂	San Emigdio Cañon, Calif.	Oct. 18, 1891	......do......	

Turdus jamaicensis (Plate) Ibis XI Oct 1869 pp. 265-266.

Junco pinosus. Point Pinos Junco.

This species has been described by Mr. Leverett M. Loomis since the return of the expedition. Juncos which were seen at Monterey by Dr. Merriam and Mr. Bailey undoubtedly belong to this species.

Amphispiza bilineata. Black-throated Sparrow.

The black-throated desert sparrow is one of the most abundant and characteristic birds of the Lower Sonoran zone, in which it breeds abundantly. The writer first observed the species in the Funeral Mountains, at the summit of Furnace Creek Cañon, on March 22, while on the return trip to Death Valley from Ash Meadows, Nevada. The four or five males which were seen evidently had just arrived, as Mr. Bailey and Mr. Nelson, who had passed over the same route a few days before, saw none. The bird was common on both slopes of the Panamint Mountains, in Johnson and Surprise cañons, during the first three weeks of April, where it was in full song most of the time. It was common in the Argus range from the valley to the summit. In Coso Valley, below Maturango Spring, Mr. Palmer and the writer found several nests. On May 12 two were discovered, one containing three young and the other four eggs, and on May 13 a nest was found just completed. In the Coso Mountains this sparrow was common, and its nest was found in various kinds of bushes, though the branching cactus (*Opuntia echinocarpa*) seemed to be the most common site. A nest containing eggs was found near the road between Darwin and Keeler as late as May 30.

When Mr. Bailey and the writer returned to Death Valley in the latter part of June, they did not find this bird in the valley proper, but found it a few hundred feet above, in Death Valley Cañon, and all through the Panamint Mountains. The same observers found it common both on the east and west slope of Walker Pass, in the Sierra Nevada, on July 1–3, and the former saw several on the South Fork of the Kern River July 3–10.

Dr. Merriam furnishes the following notes on the species as observed by him on the trip to and from St. George, Utah: "In California it was common on the Mohave Desert, between the mouth of Cajon Pass and Pilot Knob, in the early part of April; and at the west end of the desert (Antelope Valley) June 27, and was found also near Lone Willow Spring, in Windy Gap, in Death Valley, in Emigrant Cañon, and in Leach Point Valley. In Owens Valley, California, it was common in the Lower Sonoran zone where it ranges north on the east side of the valley as far as Alvord, and was found in Deep Spring Valley, Nevada (June 9). In Nevada it was common also in Pahrump Valley (the commonest sparrow April 29), in Vegas Valley, at the Great Bend of the Colorado (where a nest containing two fresh eggs was collected May 4), along the Virgin River Valley (nests containing fresh eggs found at Bunkerville early in May), in Desert Valley just east of the Pahroc Mountains (May 20), on the plain below Pahroc Spring (May 22), in Pahranagat

Valley (May 22–26), in Indian Spring Valley, where a nest containing three eggs was found in a bush of *Atriplex canescens* May 28, and at the extreme west end of this valley, where it slopes down toward the Amargosa Desert, young just able to fly were secured May 29. It was tolerably common on the Amargosa Desert, but rare in Oasis Valley (one seen June 1). On Sarcobatus Flat, at the mouth of Grapevine Cañon, a few were seen June 2, and a few were seen on both sides of Gold Mountain (where young nearly full-grown were secured June 3). It was common in Tule Cañon, at the extreme north end of the northwest arm of Death Valley, June 4, though it does not reach the sage plain of the Mount Magruder plateau. It reappears, however, a short distance below Pigeon Spring on the northwestern slope of Mount Magruder, and ranges thence across Fish Lake Valley (June 8). In southwestern Utah it was found on both slopes of the Beaverdam Mountains, ranging up into the junipers slightly above the upper limit of the lower division of the Lower Sonoran zone. In the Lower Santa Clara Valley, Utah, it is abundant, breeding in the greasewood bushes (*Atriplex*) and in the branching cactuses (*Opuntia echinocarpa*), where several nests were found containing two or three fresh eggs each (May 11–15)."

Mr. Nelson found it breeding from the middle of the sage brush belt on the slopes of the Panamint, Grapevine, Inyo, and White mountains, down into Panamint, Mesquite, Saline, and Owens valleys. Mr. Stephens found it common near the lower end of the Argus Range, at Borax Flat, April 28–30; and in Owens Valley, at Little Owens Lake, May 6–11; at Haway Meadows, May 12–14; at Olancha, May 16–23; at Morans, July 4–7, and at Benton July 9–10.

Record of specimens collected of Amphispiza bilineata.

Collectors' No.	Sex.	Locality.	Date.	Collector.	Remark.
162	♂	Panamint Mountains, Calif	Apr. 15, 1891	A. K. Fisher	Surprise Cañon.
171	♀	do	Apr. 20, 1891	do	Do.
180	♀	Argus Range, Calif	Apr. 27, 1891	do	
332	♂	Owens Valley, Calif	June 11, 1891	do	Lone Pine.
	♀	Coso Valley, Calif	May 11, 1891	T. S. Palmer	Nest and 4 eggs.
	♂ im.	Owens Valley, Calif	June 9, 1891	do	Lone Pine.
127	♀ juv.	do	July 6, 1891	F. Stephens	Morans.
	♀ juv.	Amargosa Desert, Nev	May 29, 1891	V. Bailey	
	juv.	Gold Mountain, Nev	June 3, 1891	C. Hart Merriam	
	♂ juv.	Mount Magruder, Nev	June 4, 1891	do	

Amphispiza belli. Bell's Sparrow.

Mr. Nelson found Bell's sparrow abundant in the bushes of the arid district bordering the southern and western sides of Buena Vista Lake, in San Joaquin Valley, during October.

Amphispiza belli nevadensis. Sage Sparrow.

The sage sparrow is one of the few birds characteristic of the sage plains of the Upper Sonoran and Transition zones, but does not breed in the Lower Sonoran zone, though it winters in this zone and passes through it in great numbers during migration.

In winter it was common along the entire route of the expedition. It was seen at Cajon Pass in the San Bernardino Mountains, January 2, and on the Mohave Desert, at Hesperia, in flocks of from ten to twenty, January 4-5; at Victor, Stoddard Wells, and Daggett, January 6-10; at Granite Wells, January 13-15; at Lone Willow Spring, January 15-19. It was found in Death Valley from the lower end to Furnace Creek, January 21 to February 4; at Resting Springs, February 6-17, and at Ash Meadows, Nevada, the first three weeks in March.

Mr. Stephens found it common in Oasis Valley, Nevada, March 15-19; not common at Grapevine Spring, California, April 1-4; and Mr. Nelson found it everywhere common in Pahrump Valley about the ranch, and along the route down through Vegas Valley and Wash, to the Bend of the Colorado, March 3-16. Dr. Merriam saw a few in tree yuccas on the Mohave Desert near the mouth of Cajon Pass, March 30, and a number near Daggett, April 4-6. He noted the species at Windy Gap, April 7; in Death Valley, near Bennett Wells, April 9-12; in Mesquite Valley, April 13; Emigrant Cañon, in the Panamint Mountains, April 14 and 15, and found it common in Perognathus Flat, April 15. Perognathus Flat is a high basin in the Panamint Mountains, at the lower edge of the Upper Sonoran zone, and the species may remain there to breed. At the mouth of Johnson Cañon, in the Panamint Mountains, the writer saw this species March 25, and Mr. Bailey saw one in Wild Rose Cañon, near the 'charcoal kilns,' in the same mountains, June 25. At Hot Springs, in Panamint Valley, a few were seen in *Atriplex* bushes by Dr. Merriam, April 19-24, and one was seen at Leach Point Spring, April 25. He did not find it in the Lower Santa Clara Valley near St. George, Utah, but met with it in great abundance in passing north from this valley towards the Escalante Desert. It was one of the most characteristic birds at the upper Santa Clara Crossing, Utah, May 17, thence northward through Mountain Meadows to the Escalante Desert and Shoal Creek, and westerly across the low rolling plateau of the Juniper Mountains to Meadow Creek Valley, Nevada. It was common also in Desert Valley, Nevada, and in the neighboring Pahroc Mountains, May 20-21. A few were seen in the sage plain on Mount Magruder plateau, Nevada, June 5, and in the sage brush in Owens Valley, June 10-19. In this valley Mr. Stephens found it not common at Ash Creek, May 30-June 3; at Morans, July 4-7; and common at Olancha toward the mountains and breeding; at Independence Creek, June 18-23; at Benton, July 9-10; and was seen at Bishop Creek, August 4-10. Mr. Nelson found it common at the head of Owens River the latter part of July; on both slopes of the Inyo Mountains, from the valleys up to the middle or upper part of the piñon belt, June 24-July 4; and common in the White Mountains, up to the middle of the same belt. He did not find it in the north end of the Panamint Mountains nor in Saline Valley, but noted it on the eastern slope of the Panamint Mountains, in Cottonwood Creek, and thence down to Mesquite Valley, and also in the Grapevine Mountains, May 4 to June 15. Mr. Nelson reported the sage sparrow as very common along the route from Lone Pine to Keeler, and through the Coso and Panamint valleys to Lone Willow Spring, and thence to Death Valley, during December 1890, and January 1891.

The specimens collected along the east slope of the Sierra Nevada in Owens Valley are almost intermediate, both in size and color, between *Amphispiza belli* and *Amphispiza belli nevadensis*.

Record of specimens collected of Amphispiza belli nevadensis.

Collector's No.	Sex.	Locality.	Date.	Collector.	Remarks.
25	♂	Hesperia, Calif	Jan. 4, 1891	A. K. Fisher	Mohave Desert.
36	♂	....do....	....do....	....do....	Do.
42	♀	Victor, Calif	Jan. 6, 1891	....do....	Do.
43	♀	Stoddard Wells, Calif	Jan. 7, 1891	....do....	Do.
46	♀	Daggett, Calif	Jan. 9, 1891	....do....	Do.
47		....do....	....do....	....do....	Do.
2	♂	....do....	Feb. 6, 1891	F. Stephens	Do.
3	♂	....do....	....do....	....do....	Do.
4	♂	....do....	Feb. 7, 1891	....do....	Do.
5	♂	....do....	....do....	....do....	Do.
10	♂	....do....	Feb. 8, 1891	....do....	Do.
11	♀	....do....	....do....	....do....	Do.
58	♂	Granite Wells, Calif	Jan. 13, 1891	A. K. Fisher	Do.
63	♀	Lone Willow Spring, Calif	Jan. 16, 1891	....do....	
66		Death Valley, Calif	Jan. 21, 1891	....do....	Furnace Creek.
80		....do....	Jan. 27, 1891	....do....	Do.
112	♂ ad.	Resting Springs, Calif	Feb. 17, 1891	....do....	
27	♀	12-mile Spring Calif	Feb. 21, 1891	F. Stephens	North of Resting Springs.
	♂	Mountain Meadows, Utah	May 17, 1891	V. Bailey	
331	♂ ad.	Owens Valley, Calif	June 11, 1891	A. K. Fisher	Lone Pine.
52	♂	Salt Wells Valley, Calif	May 1, 1891	F. Stephens	
84	♂	Owens Valley, Calif	June 10, 1891	....do....	Olancha.
96	♂	....do....	June 15, 1891	....do....	Do.
97	♀	....do....	....do....	....do....	Do.
98	♀	....do....	....do....	....do....	Do.
99	♀	....do....	....do....	....do....	Do.
	Im.	Sierra Nevada, Calif	Aug. 20, 1891	V. Bailey	Whitney Meadows.

Peucæa cassini. Cassin's Sparrow.

The only specimen of this species noted during the entire expedition was shot by Dr. Merriam in Timpahute Valley, Nevada, May 26. It was an old male in worn breeding plumage, and attracted his attention by flying up from the desert brush and singing in the air.

Peucæa ruficeps. Rufous-crowned Sparrow.

An immature specimen of this sparrow was secured on a rocky hillside on the South Fork of Kern River, California, July 8. Mr. Palmer saw one on the west fork of Castac Cañon June 30, and Mr. Stephens saw several migrants in Reche Cañon, near San Bernardino, Calif., September 22–24. These are all the records we have of the specis.

Melospiza fasciata fallax. Desert Song Sparrow.

The writer did not meet with this race, and quotes the following from Dr. Merriam's notes:

"The desert song sparrow was not found anywhere in California, but was common in suitable valleys in southeastern Nevada, south-western Utah, and northwestern Arizona. It was found in the valley of the Muddy near St. Joe, Nev., May 7, and was a common breeder in Pahranagat Valley, Nevada, May 23. A specimen was shot and others seen at the mouth of Beaverdam Creek, Arizona, May 9, and it was common in the Lower Santa Clara Valley near the junction of the Santa Clara and Virgin, May 11-15, where a nest was found near a marshy meadow."

Record of specimens collected of Melospiza fasciata fallax.

Collector's No.	Sex.	Locality.	Date.	Collector.	Remarks.
	♂	Pahranagat Valley, Nev.	May 23, 1891	C. Hart Merriam.	
	♂	Beaverdam, Ariz	May 9, 1891	do	

Melospiza fasciata montana. Mountain Song Sparrow.

This song sparrow was tolerably common about the ranch at Furnace Creek, and among the reeds at Saratoga Springs, in Death Valley, in January, but was not seen at the former place in June. It was quite common at Resting Springs in the Amargosa Desert, February 6-17, and at Ash Meadows, Nevada, in March. Mr. Nelson found it common along the willow-grown banks of the ditches in Pahrump and Vegas valleys, and Mr. Stephens found it rather common in the lower end of Oasis valleys, March 15-19. Mr. Bailey reported it abundant at St. George, Utah, in January, 1889.

Record of specimens collected of Melospiza fasciata montana.

Collector's No.	Sex.	Locality.	Date.	Collector.	Remarks.
78	♂	Death Valley, Calif.	Feb. 3, 1891	E. W. Nelson	Saratoga Springs.
	♂	do	Jan. 25, 1891	A. K. Fisher	Furnace Creek.
117	♂	Ash Meadows, Nev	Mar. 4, 1891	do	
118	♂	do	Mar. 9, 1891	do	
128	♀	do	Mar. 15, 1891	do	
33	♀	Oasis Valley, Nev	Mar. 16, 1891	F. Stephens	
34	♀	do	do	do	
	♂	Pahrump Valley, Nev	Mar. 4, 1891	E. W. Nelson	
	♂	do	do	do	
	♀	Vegas Valley, Nev	Mar. 12, 1891	do	

Melospiza fasciata heermanni. Heermann's Song Sparrow.

This Californian subspecies was quite common at San Bernardino, where it was singing in the brush along streams, December 28-29, 1890. It was tolerably common in suitable localities in Owens Valley, along the South Fork of Kern River, July 3-10, and was heard singing at Kernville July 11-13. At Walker Basin it was seen along the sloughs, July 13-16, and at Bakersfield it was common along the river bottom, July 17-20. Mr. Palmer found it common near Old Fort Tejon early in July; Mr. Nelson observed it commonly in the Cañada de las Uvas and in San Emigdio Cañon the last of October; and along the route from La Panza to San Luis Obispo, October 28 to November 3.

Record of specimens collected of Melospiza fasciata heermanni.

Collector's No.	Sex.	Locality.	Date.	Collector.	Remarks.
5	♂	San Bernardino, Calif	Dec. 28, 1890	A. K. Fisher	
	♀ ad	San Emigdio Cañon, Calif	Oct. 22, 1891	E. W. Nelson	
396	♀ ad	Bakersfield, Calif	July 19, 1891	A. K. Fisher	
378	♀ im	Kern River, Calif	July 5, 1891	....do	25 miles above Kernville.
	♂ im	......do	July 4, 1891	V. Bailey	Do.
119	♂	Owens Valley, Calif	July 26, 1891	F. Stephens	Alvord.
67	♂	......do	May 30, 1891	...do	Ash Creek.
205	♂	......do	June 5, 1891	A. K. Fisher	Lone Pine.
303	♂	......do	June 6, 1891	...do	Do.
321	♂	......do	June 9, 1891	...do	Do.

Melospiza fasciata guttata. Rusty Song Sparrow.

Mr. Bailey secured a specimen of this song sparrow at Santa Clara, Utah, January 13, 1889. It was undoubtedly an accidental straggler from the northwest coast.

Melospiza fasciata rufina Sooty Song Sparrow.

Mr. Bailey took a specimen of this subspecies at Boulder Creek, California, on October 13, 1891, and stated that it was common there.

Melospiza fasciata graminea. Santa Barbara Song Sparrow.

Specimens of this new race, indistinguishable from Mr. Townsend's type, were taken by Mr. Nelson at Morro and Carpenteria, Calif. He found them common near the streams and wet places along the coast, and a few as far inland as Santa Paula. Whether it is a resident or a migrant from the Santa Barbara Islands, can not be decided at present.

Record of specimens collected of Melospiza fasciata graminea.

Collector's No.	Sex.	Locality.	Date.	Collector.	Remarks.
	♂	Carpenteria, Calif	Dec. 18, 1891	E. W. Nelson	
	♀	......do	...do	...do	
	♀	Morro, Calif	Nov. 8, 1891	...do	

Melospiza lincolni. Lincoln's Sparrow.

A few Lincoln's sparrows were seen at Ash Meadows, Nevada, and Mr. Nelson found it common in wet places among bushes at Vegas ranch and in Vegas Wash in March, where Dr. Merriam again saw it May 1. It was not uncommon in Johnson and Suprise cañons in the Panamint Range, April 1–20. The species was common at Hot Springs in Panamint Valley, April 20–23, and a few were seen in Shepherd Cañon, in the Argus Range, the last of April. Mr. Stephens found it breeding, but not commonly, at Independence Creek, June 18-23, and the writer saw several in the high grass at Horse Corral Meadows, August 9-13. Mr. Belding found a pair breeding in the meadow at Crockers, near the Yosemite Valley, in May, and Mr. Bailey saw a few at Monterey, September 28 to October 9.

Record of specimens collected of Melospiza lincolni.

Collector's No.	Sex.	Locality.	Date.	Collector.	Remarks.
154	♀	Panamint Mountains, Calif.	Mar. 27, 1891	E. W. Nelson	Johnson Cañon.
	♀	do	Apr. 11, 1891	A. K. Fisher	Do.
175	♀	Panamint Valley, Calif.	Apr. 21, 1891	do	Hot Springs.
177	♂	do	Apr. 22, 1891	do	Do.
117	♀	Sierra Nevada, Calif.	June 22, 1891	F. Stephens	

Passerella iliaca unalaschcensis. Townsend's Sparrow.

Townsend's sparrow was not uncommon in Cajon Pass in the San Bernardino Mountains January 2. It was not reported again until Mr. Bailey found it common at Monterey, September 28 to October 9. Mr. Nelson found it common and generally distributed wherever thickets occurred along the coast from San Simeon to Carpenteria, November 4 to December 18.

Record of specimens collected of Passerella iliaca unalaschcensis.

Collector's No.	Sex.	Locality.	Date.	Collector.	Remarks.
21	♂	Cajon Pass, Calif.	Jan. 2, 1891	A. K. Fisher	
		Morro, Calif.	Nov. 8, 1891	E. W. Nelson	

Passerella iliaca megarhyncha. Thick-billed Sparrow.

The thick-billed sparrow was found commonly in a number of places in the High Sierra. Mr. Nelson reported it as rather common at the head of Owens River, and on the western slope, in July and August. Mr. Stephens saw it among the thickets at Menache Meadows May 24-26; found it common at Independence Creek, where young were taken June 20; and at the lake on Bishop Creek August 4-10. In the Sequoia National Park it was common, and several broods of young just able to fly were seen the first week in August. On the East Fork of the Kaweah River Mr. Bailey found it breeding from the lower edge of the conifers up to where *Pinus monticola* grows. It was seen at Horse Corral Meadows, August 9-13; at Whitney Meadows and Soda Springs or Kern River Lakes, the last of August; at Mineral King, September 8-11, and on the brushy hillsides about the Cañada de las Uvas and San Emigdio, October 14-28.

Record of specimens collected of Passerella iliaca megarhyncha.

Collector's No.	Sex.	Locality.	Date.	Collector.	Remarks.
64	♀	Sierra Nevada, Calif.	May 27, 1891	F. Stephens	Summit Meadow, near Olancha Peak.
108	♀	......do.............	June 20, 1891	......do......	Independence Creek.
	♀ Im.	......do.............	July 30, 1891	V. Bailey	East Fork of Kaweah River.
407	♂	......do.............	Aug. 6, 1891	A. K. Fisher	Sequoia National Park.
411	♂ Im.	......do.............	Aug. 11, 1891	......do......	Horse Corral Meadows.

Passerella iliaca schistacea. Slate-colored Sparrow.

The slate-colored sparrow was not uncommon, according to Mr. Nelson, about the heads of streams on the eastern slope of the White Mountains, where a specimen was taken, July 14. A few were seen in Johnson and Surprise cañons, in the Panamint Mountains, where a specimen was taken in the former cañon, March 28. This sparrow was not detected elsewhere by members of the expedition.

Record of specimens collected of Passerella iliaca schistacea.

Collector's No.	Sex.	Locality.	Date.	Collector.	Remarks.
	♀ ♂	Panamint Mountains, Calif. White Mountains, Calif.	Mar. 28, 1891 July 14, 1891	E. W. Nelson ......do......	Johnson Cañon.

Pipilo maculatus megalonyx. Spurred Towhee.

The spurred towhee is common over much of the Great Basin, and also in California west of the Sierra Nevada. Mr. Nelson reported it as common among the junipers on the Charleston Mountains in the early part of March. A pair was seen in one of the cañons in the Coso Mountains, May 23, and subsequently Mr. Palmer saw others in the brush along the streams. Mr. Nelson found a few at Lone Pine in Owens Valley, in December, 1890, and the writer saw a few in the brush along the river at the same place, June 11. Dr. Merriam found it common in the northern part of the valley on the latter date. Mr. Stephens reported it as common in the lower part of the cañon at Independence Creek, where young were seen June 18-23; as not common among the piñons at Benton, July 9-10; he also saw three at Bishop Creek, August 4-10. In the Panamint Mountains, Mr. Nelson saw it in Surprise Cañon in December, 1890, and found it sparingly in the vicinity of water, where thickets of willows and rose bushes afforded it shelter, in both this range and the Grapevine Mountains during the latter part of May and the first of June. The same observer found a few in the Inyo Mountains among the piñons at Hunter's arastra, and again in willows bordering the creek near Waucoba Peak, the latter part of June; found it rather common on the west slope of the Sierra, mainly along streams; and found a few in the upper parts of the streams in the White Mountains.

In Nevada, Dr. Merriam found it in the following localities: At Mountain Spring in the Charleston Mountains, April 30; in the Juniper Mountains May 19, where it was common throughout the scrub oak and juniper down to the very edge of Meadow Creek Valley near Panaca; at Tule Cañon and on Mount Magruder, where it was abundant and a full-fledged young was shot, June 5. In Utah, he found it common among the junipers on the Beaverdam Mountains, May 11, and saw a number between the Upper Santa Clara Crossing and Mountain Meadows, in thickets of *Amelanchier* and scrub oak, May 17.

On the western slope of Walker Pass, in California, it was common July 2 and 3; along the South Fork of the Kern, July 3-10; on the hillsides in chaparral at Walker Basin, July 13-16; and at Bakersfield in the San Joaquin Valley, July 17-20.

Mr. Bailey reported it as common below the conifers on the Kaweah River the last of July, and Dr. Merriam found it common in the Granite Range in western San Diego County, July 1-10.

Record of specimens collected of *Pipilo maculatus megalonyx*.

Collector's No.	Sex.	Locality.	Date.	Collector.	Remarks.
	♂	Mountain Meadows, Utah	May 17, 1891	C. Hart Merriam	
	♂	Charleston Mountains, Nev	Mar. 7, 1891	V. Bailey	
	im.	Mount Magruder, Nev	June 5, 1891	do	
26	♂	Grapevine Mountains, Nev	Mar. 21, 1891	F. Stephens	
329	♂ ad.	Lone Pine, Calif	June 11, 1891	A. K. Fisher	Owens Valley.
374	♂ im.	Kern River, Calif	July 5, 1891	do	South Fork.

Pipilo maculatus oregonus. Oregon Towhee.

Mr. Nelson found the Oregon towhee sparingly along the coast of California from La Panza to San Luis Obispo the last of October; between San Simeon and Carpenteria November 4 to December 18, and common between the latter place and Santa Paula December 18 to January 4.

Pipilo chlorurus. Green-tailed Towhee.

The green-tailed towhee is a common summer resident in the mountain ranges visited by of the expedition. It was first observed in Johnson Cañon on the east slope of the Panamint Mountains, April 12, but was not seen in Surprise Cañon on the west slope during the following fortnight. In May and June Mr. Nelson found it common among the sage brush on the Panamint and Grapevine mountains, where it was associated with Brewer's sparrow. It was most numerous among the rank growth of vegetation along small streams and about springs, though it was not uncommon on the high benches among the *Artemisia tridentata*. On Willow Creek, May 24, he found a nest containing four eggs which was placed in a sage bush 15 inches from the ground. It was composed externally of rather coarse plant stems, and lined with fine fibrous rootlets and horsehair. On the north slope of

Telescope Peak, it was common as high as the upper limit of the sage brush, June 22-25.

In the Argus Range, it was common in Shepherd Cañon, where numbers were migrating the last week in April, and at Maturango Spring among the willows and other vegetation at the spring the first two weeks in May. Among the Coso Mountains it was very common along the streams and on the slopes among the sage and piñons, where the males often were heard singing from their perches on the tops of some dead brush or trees, the latter part of May. Dr. Merriam saw it on the northward continuation of the Kingston Range, between the Amargosa Desert, California, and Pahrump Valley, Nevada. He found it also in the following localities in Nevada: Tolerably common in the Charleston Mountains, April 30; at the Bend of the Colorado, May 4; very abundant on Mount Magruder, where it was breeding from the upper part of Tule Cañon up to 2,600 meters (8,500 feet) or higher, and where a dozen or more were often seen at one time, singing from the tops of sage brush and nut pines, and they were heard singing several times at night; a few were seen in the Juniper Mountains, May 19; in the Beaverdam Mountains, Utah, he found them tolerably common among the junipers, May 10-11, and in the Santa Clara Valley, Utah, May 11-15.

Mr. Nelson found the species from among the piñons up to the summit in the Inyo Mountains the latter part of June, and in the White Mountains and on the plateau at the head of Owens Valley, in July. Along the eastern slope of the Sierra Nevada it was common at the head of Owens River the last of July; at Independence Creek, where a nest containing two eggs just ready to hatch was found at the Rex Monte mill, June 18-23; at Bishop Creek, August 4-10; not common at Benton, July 9-10; and at Menache Meadows where it occurred nearly to timber line, May 24-26. The species was seen at Walker Pass, July 2; at Soda Springs or Kern River Lakes, September 3; and was common in the Sequoia National Park, during the first week of August; and in the vicinity of Mineral King, the last of August and 1st of September. Mr. Dutcher saw a few at Big Cottonwood Meadows during the summer, and Mr. Palmer found it common on Frazier Mountain among the pines, July 9, and in Tejon Pass, July 12.

Record of specimens collected of Pipilo chlorurus.

Collector's No.	Sex.	Locality.	Date.	Collector.	Remarks.
186	♂	Argus Range, Calif	Apr. 27, 1891	A. K. Fisher	Shepherd Cañon.
230	♀	....do....	May 12, 1891	....do....	Maturango Spring.
258	♂	Coso Mountains, Calif	May 27, 1891	....do....	
110	♀	Owens Valley, Calif	June 20, 1891	F. Stephens	Independence Creek.
154	♂	White Mountains, Nev	July 14, 1891	....do....	Queen mine.

Pipilo fuscus mesoleucus. Cañon Towhee.

Mr. Bailey found the cañon towhee abundant among the hills at Mineral Park, in western Arizona, during the middle of February, 1889; and later in the same month saw a few near Fort Mohave.

Pipilo fuscus crissalis. California Towhee.

The California towhee was common among the chaparral in a number of localities west of the Sierra Nevada. At Cajon Pass, in the San Bernardino Mountains, it was very common from the lower part of the valley, well up on the divide among the oaks, January 2-3, and Dr. Merriam found it abundant at the same place, March 29-30. It was common on the western slope of Walker Pass, July 2-3; along the valley of the Kern River, July 3-13, and abundant in Walker Basin, July 13-16. Mr. Palmer reported it as abundant at Old Fort Tejon in July; Mr. Stephens at Reche Cañon, September 22-24, and Mr. Nelson as very abundant in the western foothills of the Sierra Nevada in August. It was common at Three Rivers, July 25-30, and September 12-15, and Mr. Bailey noted it along the East Fork of the Kaweah River nearly up to the lower edge of the pines. The same observer found it common at Monterey the first week in October; Mr. Nelson reported it as abundant among the brush along the western edge of the San Joaquin Valley in October, and along the coast from San Simeon to Carpenteria and Santa Paula in November and December.

Record of specimens collected of Pipilo fuscus crissalis.

Collector's No.	Sex.	Locality.	Date.	Collector.	Remarks.
3	♀	San Bernardino, Calif	Jan. 1, 1891	A. K. Fisher	
18	♂	do	do	do	
49	♂	Argus Range, Calif	Apr. 25, 1891	F. Stephens	Searl's Garden.
364	♀ ad.	Walker Pass, Calif	July 2, 1891	A. K. Fisher	
	Im.	do	July 3, 1891	V. Bailey	
	♀ im.	do	do	do	
372	♂ ad.	Kern River, Calif	July 4, 1891	A. K. Fisher	South Fork.
	♂	Ventura River, Calif	Dec. 20, 1891	E. W. Nelson	

Pipilo aberti. Abert's Towhee.

The westernmost locality at which Dr. Merriam and Mr. Bailey saw Abert's towhee is the Bend of the Colorado River, in Nevada, where it was common, and a full grown young was secured, May 4. Thence northward they found it common in the valleys of the Virgin and lower Muddy, May 6-8, where Beaverdam Creek joins the Virgin in northwestern Arizona, May 9-10, and in the Lower Santa Clara Valley, Utah, near St. George, May 11-15, where it was breeding commonly.

Habia melanocephala. Black-headed Grosbeak.

The black-headed grosbeak was first observed in Shepherd Cañon in the Argus Range, where a specimen was secured April 26. A week later it was common among the willow patches at Maturango Spring and among the tree yuccas at the western base of the range. In the Coso Mountains several were seen in the cañons during the latter part of May. Mr. Nelson found it a common breeding bird both in the Panamint and Grapevine mountains, and the writer saw a fine male in full song at the 'charcoal kilns' in Wild Rose Cañon, north of Telescope Peak, June 23. In Owens Valley Mr. Stephens found it rather common at Olancha, May 16-23; not common at Ash Creek, May 30 to June 3, and saw one male at Independence Creek, June 18-23. Mr. Nelson found it sparingly among the willows in the Inyo Mountains, June 24 to July 5, and along the western slope of the Sierra Nevada in August. Mr. Bailey reported this grosbeak as common among the pines along the East Fork of the Kaweah River, July 25 to August 10. It was observed on the western slope of Walker Pass, June 21; was common in Kern Valley, June 22-23 and July 3-10; on the ridge above Walker Basin, July 14; in the Sierra Liebre, June 30; and in Cañada de las Uvas, June 28-29.

In Nevada Dr. Merriam found a pair breeding in a thicket near Log Spring on Mount Magruder, June 8; saw it in Oasis Valley, June 1; in the valley of the Virgin near Bunkerville, May 8; and found it common in Pahranagat Valley, where it was singing in the tall cottonwoods, May 22-26. In Utah he found it breeding plentifully along the Lower Santa Clara River, May 11-15.

Record of specimens collected of Habia melanocephala.

Collector's No.	Sex.	Locality.	Date.	Collector.	Remarks.
184	♂	Argus Range, Calif	Apr. 26, 1891	A. K. Fisher	Shepherd Cañon.
240	♂	......do......	May 14, 1891	......do......	Maturango Spring.
	♀	......do......	May 15, 1891	T. S. Palmer	Do.

Guiraca cærulea eurhyncha. Western Blue Grosbeak.

The blue grosbeak is tolerably common in many of the valleys of California and Nevada. In Nevada, Dr. Merriam found it breeding commonly in Pahranagat Valley, May 22-26, and along the Lower Muddy and Virgin rivers, May 7 and 8. He saw several where Beaverdam Creek joins the Virgin River in northwestern Arizona, May 9-10, and found the species common in the Lower Santa Clara Valley, Utah, May 11-15. Several were seen in the Cañada de las Uvas, California, June 28-29. At Lone Pine, in Owens Valley, it was quite common among the fruit orchards and thick growth along streams, where two young just out of the nest were secured, June 14. Mr. Stephens found it more or less common in the same valley, at Olancha, May 16-23; Ash Creek, May 30 to June 3; Alvord, June 26-28; and at Morans, July 4-7. Mr. Bailey secured an adult male at Furnace Creek ranch, Death Valley, June 19, and Mr. Nelson saw the species in Saline Valley the latter part of the same month. Blue grosbeaks were very common along the South Fork of the Kern, where they frequented the oat fields and the thick vegetation in the river bottoms, July 3-10. They were also common at Kernville, July 11-13; at Walker Basin, July 13-16; and at Bakersfield in the San Joaquin Valley, July 17-20.

Record of specimens collected of Guiraca cærulea eurhyncha.

Collector's No.	Sex.	Locality.	Date.	Collector.	Remarks.
	♂	St. George, Utah	May 14, 1891	V. Bailey	
	♀	Beaverdam, Ariz	May 9, 1891	...do	
	♂	Bunkerville, Nev	May 8, 1891	C. Hart Merriam	
	♂	Death Valley, Calif	June 19, 1891	V. Bailey	Furnace Creek.
	♂	Owens Valley, Calif	June 5, 1891	T. S. Palmer	Lone Pine.
313	♂	...do	June 7, 1891	A. K. Fisher	Do.
316	♂	...do	June 8, 1891	...do	Do.
338	♀ juv	...do	June 11, 1891	...do	Do.
339	♀ juv	...do	...do	...do	Do.
66	♂	...do	May 30, 1891	F. Stephens	Ash Creek.
85	♀	...do	June 11, 1891	...do	Olancha.
93	♂	...do	June 12, 1891	...do	Do.
104	♀	...do	June 15, 1891	...do	Do.
121	♂	...do	June 27, 1891	...do	Alvord.
373	♂	Kern River, Calif	July 4, 1891	A. K. Fisher	South Fork.
379	♂ ad	...do	July 5, 1891	...do	Do.
384	♂ ad	...do	July 10, 1891	...do	Do.

Passerina amœna. Lazuli Bunting.

The lazuli bunting is a common breeder in many places in the Great Basin wherever there is sufficient water to produce a growth of willow or other thickets suitable for nesting sites.

In Nevada, Dr. Merriam found it breeding commonly on Mount Magruder, and in the thickets in Tule Cañon, June 4-8; in Pahranagat Valley, May 22-26, and saw a few in the Juniper Mountains, May 18, and in Oasis Valley, June 1. He found it common at the Bend of the Colorado, May 4, and at a few points in the valleys of the Muddy and Virgin rivers, May 7-8. In the Santa Clara Valley, Utah, it was an abundant breeder, May 11-15.

The writer first met with the species at Coso, Calif., where a male was secured May 25. At Furnace Creek, Death Valley, a female was secured in the brush near the ranch, June 19, and the species was common in Wild Rose Cañon in the Panamint Mountains, June 24 and 25. Mr. Nelson found it common in both the Panamint and Grapevine mountains, wherever willow thickets occurred. It was nesting in Mill Creek, Willow Creek, and Cottonwood cañons in the former, and in Wood Cañon in the latter range of mountains. The same observer found it from the bottom of the valley up to the piñons in the Inyo Mountains; at the head of Owens Valley, near the White Mountains, and along borders of streams from the foothills up to 2,450 meters (8,000 feet) altitude at the head of Owens River. In Owens Valley it was common about the orchards at Lone Pine in June; and Mr. Stephens saw several at

Olancha, May 16-23; found it common at Ash Creek, May 30-June 3; at Morans, July 4-7; abundant in the lower part of the cañon of Independence Creek, June 18-23; not common at Alvord, June 26-28; at Benton, July 9-10; at Queen station in the White Mountains, Nev., June 11-16; and saw a male at about 2,450 meters (8,000 feet) altitude, at Bishop Creek, August 4-10. Mr. Palmer secured a specimen at Horse Corral Meadows, August 11, and saw another in Kings River Cañon, August 15; and Mr. Bailey saw two at 2,450 meters (8,000 feet) altitude on the Kaweah River, about the same time. Mr. Palmer found it common at Old Fort Tejon, where a nest containing three fresh eggs was found in a willow tree 6 feet from the ground, July 4. The species was common along the valley of the Kern, July 3-13; at Walker Basin, July 13-16; and at Bakersfield in the San Joaquin Valley, July 17-20.

Record of specimens collected of Passerina amœna.

Collector's No.	Sex.	Locality.	Date.	Collector.	Remarks.
256	♂	Coso, Coso Mountains, Calif.	May 25, 1891	A. K. Fisher	
301	♂	Owens Valley, Calif	June 6, 1891	...do	Lone Pine.
241	♀	Death Valley, Calif	June 19, 1891	...do	Furnace Creek.

Calamospiza melanocorys. Lark Bunting.

A few miles north of Pilot Knob on the Mohave Desert, California, a lark bunting was killed by Mr. F. W. Koch April 6, and two others were seen by Dr. Merriam. One was shot in Pahrump Valley, Nevada, April 29, by Mr. Bailey. No others were observed by any members of the expedition.

Piranga ludoviciana. Western Tanager.

The western tanager was found commonly in many places during migration, and sparingly during the breeding season. The first individual observed was secured by Dr. Merriam in Surprise Cañon in the Panamint Mountains, California, April 23. When first seen it was in hot pursuit of a large beetle, which it failed to capture. At Maturango Spring in the Argus Range, a large flight of these tanagers occurred on May 4, where as many as a dozen males were seen at one time. From this date until the time of leaving, the middle of May, it was common among the willows in the vicinity of the spring. In the Coso Mountains a pair was seen near the top of the ridge, where they were evidently hunting for a nesting site, May 23. Mr. Nelson found it a rather common breeding species among the piñons on Willow Creek in the Panamint Mountains, and also in Mill Creek and Cottonwood cañons, though in smaller numbers, during the last of May. He saw none in the Grapevine Mountains.

Dr. Merriam saw two males of this species and one hepatic tanager in a tall cottonwood at the point where Beaverdam Creek joins the Virgin

River, in northwestern Arizona, May 9. He saw many males in the Lower Santa Clara Valley, Utah, May 11-14; six males in the Juniper Mountains, Nevada, May 18, and several in Pahranagat Valley, May 22-26.

At Keeler, early in June, an individual alighted for a few moments on the wagon during a gale. In the same valley a few were seen and two secured at Lone Pine, June 6-8; Mr. Stephens reported it a rather common migrant at Olancha May 16-23; not common at Bishop August 4-10, and rather common at Menache Meadows May 24-26. Mr. Nelson found it at the head of Owens River the latter part of July; several were seen among the hills above Walker Basin July 14, and several were observed in the Sequoia National Park during the first week of August. Mr. Palmer saw one in Tejon Pass July 12.

Record of specimens collected of Piranga ludoviciana.

Collector's No.	Sex.	Locality.	Date.	Collector.	Remarks.
105	♂	Panamint Mountains, Calif.	Apr. 23, 1891	C. Hart Merriam	Surprise Cañon.
220	♂	Argus Range, Calif.	May 4, 1891	A. K. Fisher	Matarango Spring.
221	♂	...do	May 10, 1891	...do	Do.
222	♂	...do	...do	...do	Do.
250	♂	...do	...do	...do	Do.
306	♀	Coso Mountains, Calif.	May 23, 1891	...do	
315	♂	Owens Valley, Calif.	June 6, 1891	...do	Lone Pine.
71	♂	...do	June 8, 1891	...do	
145	♂	...do	June 1, 1891	F. Stephens	Owens Lake.
	♂	Sierra Nevada, Calif.	July 27, 1891	...do	

Piranga hepatica. Hepatic Tanager.

The only individual of this species observed during the entire season was seen by Dr. Merriam in a cottonwood at the point where Beaverdam Creek empties into the Virgin in northwestern Arizona, May 9. Two adult male western tanagers (*P. ludoviciana*) were in the same tree, and both species were probably migrating.

Progne subis hesperia. Western Martin.

A colony of martins was found breeding at Old Fort Tejon in the Cañada de las Uvas, California, June 28, 1891, by Dr. Merriam and Mr. Palmer. They were nesting in woodpeckers' holes in the large oaks in front of the old fort, where three were killed. Mr. Belding noted the species at Crocker's, 21 miles northwest of the Yosemite Valley, in May.

Record of specimens collected of Progne subis hesperia.

Collector's No.	Sex.	Locality.	Date.	Collector.	Remarks.
	♂ ad.	Old Fort Tejon, Calif.	June 28, 1891	C. Hart Merriam	
	♂ im.	...do	...do	...do	
	♂ im.	...do	...do	...do	

Petrochelidon lunifrons. Cliff Swallow.

This widely distributed species was found breeding in various localities visited by the expedition. In Nevada Dr. Merriam found a colony breeding in the cañon at the lower end of Vegas Wash, May 3, and saw several at the Bend of the Colorado, May 4; he found it common in Pahranagat Valley, May 22–26, and in Oasis Valley, June 1. In Utah he saw a colony which was breeding near St. George, in the Lower Santa Clara Valley, where many nests were found on the red sandstone cliffs a mile or two from the settlement.

The cliff swallow was common in Owens Valley, California. It was seen along the edge of the lake at Keeler, May 30–June 4; at the mouth of the cañon above Lone Pine, June 12; and Mr. Stephens found it common at Haway Meadows, May 12–14; abundant at Olancha, May 16–23; at Ash Creek, May 30 to June 3; breeding in the cañon at Benton, July 9–10; and not common at the Queen mine, Nevada, July 11–16. Mr. Nelson saw it on Willow Creek in the Panamint Mountains, the last of May, and found it at the head of Owens River, in the Sierra Nevada, up to 2,100 meters (7,000 feet) altitude. It was common in Kern Valley, July 3–13, and in Walker Basin, July 13–16. At the latter place a number of nests were found fastened against the ceiling and walls of the rooms in several of the deserted buildings. Dr. Merriam found it breeding commonly at Kernville, under the eaves and piazzas of houses, June 23, and in the Cañada de las Uvas, under the eaves of Old Fort Tejon, June 28–29.

At Twin Oaks, in western San Diego County, he was shown a large sycamore tree on the outside of which these swallows used to fasten their nests, and was told that after heavy rains the nests were frequently washed down in great numbers. The species was common at Bakersfield, in the San Joaquin Valley, July 17–20, and Mr. Stephens found it not uncommon at Reche Cañon, near San Bernardino, September 22–24.

Chelidon erythrogaster. Barn Swallow.

The barn swallow was found nowhere common except in Owens Valley, California. It was first seen at Ash Meadows, Nevada, where two were noted, March 19. In the same State, Dr. Merriam saw one at Mount Magruder, June 8; one in Oasis Valley, June 1; a number in Pahranagat Valley, May 22–26, where it was doubtless breeding, and several near Bunkerville, in the Virgin Valley, May 7–8. He saw a single bird near St. George, in the Lower Santa Clara Valley, Utah, about the middle of May.

Mr. Nelson saw it as a migrant on the divide between Panamint and Saline valleys, the last of May, and at the head of Willow Creek, in the Panamint Mountains, about the same time. He saw barn swallows at the head of Owens Valley in the White Mountains, at the head of Owens River, and also in the Yosemite Valley. Mr. Stephens found it common all through Salt Wells and Owens valleys, and the writer found it common in the latter valley at Keeler, near Owens Lake, and at Lone Pine, in June. At Keeler a male was noticed every day during our stay. He sat for hours on a wire in front of the signal station and produced a series of notes which were well worth the title of a song. The sounds were more or less disconnected, but the writer does not remember hearing so perfect a song from any swallow, and as Mr. Bicknell states (Auk, Vol. I, 1884, p. 325) the notes suggest those produced by the marsh wren.

Tachycineta bicolor. Tree Swallow.

White-bellied swallows were seen in a few places during migration. Several were seen at Ash Meadows, Nevada, March 12, and a number near the Colorado River, March 10–13. At Furnace Creek, Death Valley, it was common about the reservoir, March 23–24, and again the middle of April. A few were seen in Johnson Cañon in the Panamint Range, April 4, and Mr. Nelson observed stragglers at the head of Willow Creek in the same range, the last of May.

Tachycineta thalassina. Violet-green Swallow.

The violet-green swallow is a common summer resident among the mountains and was frequently seen in the neighboring valleys while searching for food. Two or three were seen near the upper end of Vegas Wash, Nevada, March 10, and many were observed in Death Valley, at Furnace Creek, April 10, and at Saratoga Springs, near the south end, April 26. In Nevada, Dr. Merriam found it common in Pahranagat Valley, May 22–26, saw it on Mount Magruder, June 8, and in Oasis Valley, June 1. In Utah it was common in the Lower Santa Clara Valley, May 11–15. Mr. Nelson found it a common species in the Panamint and Grapevine mountains, where it bred in the crevices of the lofty cliffs, from the summits down to the border of the surrounding valleys. In the former range violet-green swallows were common, and a specimen was secured on the summit of Telescope Peak, June 23. In the Argus Range it was common about the summit above Maturango Spring, May 12–14, and at Coso, four or five came about camp, May 28.

Mr. Nelson saw the species from the lower part of Saline Valley to the summit of the Inyo Mountains, in June; up to timber line in the White Mountains, in July, and at the heads of Owens and Merced rivers, in the Sierra Nevada, in July and August. In Owens Valley this swallow was common about the lake at Keeler and at Lone Pine during the first half of June. At the latter place it was seen flying about in company with the cliff swallows, white-throated and cloud swifts, at the mouth of the cañon, and with the barn swallows over the meadows and marshes. Mr. Stephens found it more or less common in other parts of the valley. It was common along the valley of Kern

River, July 3-13; in Walker Basin, July 13-16, and along the route to Bakersfield, July 16-20. Dr. Merriam and Mr. Palmer found it abundant at Old Fort Tejon, where it was breeding in the oaks and crevices of the adobe buildings; it was very common about the summit of Frazier Mountain, July 9, and at the summit of Tejon Pass, July 12. In the High Sierra it was common about the openings at Horse Corral Meadows, August 9-13; in Kings River Cañon, August 13-16; Big Cottonwood Meadows, August 25-26; at Soda Springs or Kern River Lakes, September 3, and above timber line at Mineral King, and along the route from that place to Three Rivers in the western foothills, September 10-13. Mr. Bailey found the species numerous at Monterey, September 28 to October 9, and Mr. Stephens saw several at Reche Cañon, September 22-24.

Record of specimens collected of Tachycineta thalassina.

Collector's No.	Sex.	Locality.	Date.	Collector.	Remarks.
269	♀	Coso, Coso Mountains, Calif.	May 28, 1891	A. K. Fisher	
272	♀	Keeler Inyo County, Calif.	June 1, 1891	do	
293	♂	do	do	do	
286	♂	do	June 2, 1891	do	
287	♀	do	do	do	
354	♂	Panamint Mountains, Calif.	June 23, 1891	do	Telescope Peak.

Clivicola riparia. Bank swallow.

Bank swallows were seen in two places only by members of the expedition. Mr. Nelson saw a few in company with rough-winged swallows at the Bend of the Colorado, in Nevada, about March 10. Mr. Stephens found it common at Alvord, in Owens Valley, where they were breeding in the banks along the sloughs, June 26-28.

Stelgidopteryx serripennis. Rough-winged Swallow.

The rough-winged swallow was tolerably common in a number of the desert valleys, where it was a summer resident. It was first seen at Ash Meadows, Nevada, March 10, and in Vegas Wash, near the Bend of the Colorado River, March 10-13. A specimen was secured at Hot Springs, in Panamint Valley, April 22, and Mr. Nelson observed a few migrants along Willow Creek, in the Panamint Mountains, the last of May. Dr. Merriam saw this swallow at Saratoga Springs in Death Valley, April 26; at the Bend of the Colorado River, May 4; in the Valley of the Virgin near Bunkerville, Nevada, May 8; and in Pahranagat Valley Nevada, where it was tolerably common and doubtless breeding, May 22-26. He found it common where Beaverdam Creek joins the Virgin in northwestern Arizona, May 9-10, and the commonest swallow in the Santa Clara Valley Utah, May 11-15. In Owens Valley a pair was seen about a pond at Lone Pine, June 8, and others were observed at Big Pine June 10. At Furnace Creek, Death Valley, several were secured about the reservoir June 19-21, and a number were seen in Kern River Valley June 22-23.

Record of specimens collected of Stelgidopteryx serripennis.

Collector's No.	Sex.	Locality.	Date.	Collector.	Remarks.
176	♂	Panamint Valley, Calif	Apr. 22, 1891	A. K. Fisher	Hot Springs.
340	♂ im.	Death Valley, Calif	June 19, 1891	...do	Furnace Creek.
	♀ im.	...do	...do	V. Bailey.	Do.

Ampelis cedrorum. Cedar Waxwing.

The only cedar birds observed during the entire trip were two seen at Lone Pine, in Owens Valley, June 14, and a flock of five, at Three Rivers, Tulare County, September 15. At the former place they were feeding on mulberries, which were cultivated along one of the irrigating ditches of a fruit ranch. This berry, when it can be obtained, seems to be their favorite food, and one which they will take in preference to any other. Among the Creoles of Louisiana the knowledge of this fact has given rise to the name of *mûrier* for the cedar bird in that locality.

At Three Rivers the specimens secured were gorged with a small wild grape (*Vitis californica*), which was ripening in abundance in the low thickets along the streams.

Phainopepla nitens. Phainopepla.

This species is a characteristic bird of the Lower Sonoran zone, where it remains throughout the year. Several were seen among the mesquite at Hot Springs in Panamint Valley, in January, and a fine male was secured at the mouth of Surprise Cañon, not far from the above place, April 23. Its stomach was filled with the berries of the mistletoe, which is a parasite on the mesquite. Several were seen at Resting Spring in the Amargosa Desert, about the middle of February, feeding on the same berries, which appear to be their principal food.

An adult male was seen at Maturango Spring in the Argus Range, May 10, and one or two were observed at Coso the latter part of May. Mr. Nelson found it rather common in the lower part of Vegas Valley and upper part of Vegas Wash and very abundant in the lower part of the Wash, near the Colorado River, in March. It was seen by Dr. Merriam at Mountain Spring in the Charleston Mountains, April 30, and was common in the Lower Santa Clara Valley, Utah, June 11-15, where several pairs were breeding in the village of St. George. An adult female was seen by Mr. Stephens at Morans, in Owens Valley, July 4-7, and Mr. Nelson found it rather common in the western foothills of the Sierra Nevada, between the San Joaquin and Merced rivers in August. One was seen in the chaparral above Kaweah, July 25, and another July 30.

At Kernville the species was abundant in cañons above the village July 11-13, where as many as a dozen were seen at once, some sitting on the tree tops, while others were busily engaged in capturing winged insects after the manner of the cedar bird.

Dr. Merriam met with unusual numbers among the live oaks and chaparral between Kernville and Havilah, June 23; saw many in Walker Basin June 24, and several in Tehachapi Pass June 25. He also noted it as common in the Sierra Liebre June 30, and in the Granite Range, in western San Diego County, July 1–10.

Mr. Palmer saw several in the San Francisquito Pass, north of Newhall, July 1, and Mr. Nelson found it common among the piñons a few miles west of the Cañada de las Uvas, the middle of October.

Mr. Bailey found a nest containing three fresh eggs in a mesquite, near Fort Mohave, Ariz., March 4, 1889, and one containing young, several days old, February 28.

Record of specimens collected of Phainopepla nitens.

Collector's No.	Sex.	Locality.	Date.	Collector.	Remarks.
109	♀	Resting Springs, Calif.	Feb. 12, 1891	A. K. Fisher	
183	♂	Panamint Mountains, Calif.	Apr. 23, 1891	....do	Surprise Cañon.

Lanius ludovicianus excubitorides. White-rumped Shrike.

The white-rumped shrike is very generally distributed over the greater part of the desert region of southern California and Nevada. From its habit of associating in pairs and not congregating in flocks, it is seldom common in the sense that other birds are, though a considerable number may be seen in the course of a day's ride through suitable localities. It is especially partial to the country covered by tree yuccas and seldom builds its nest in other growths where these abound. Many old as well as new nests were found which were so well protected by the strong, bayonet-like leaves of this plant that it was with difficulty they could be reached. The species was tolerably common at Hesperia in the Mohave Desert, January 4–5, and at Granite Wells, about the middle of January. At Furnace Creek and Saratoga Springs, in Death Valley, several were seen the last of January.

At Resting Springs, California, a number were seen each day during the first half of February, and at Ash Meadows, Nevada, in March. It was not uncommon in Vegas Valley, Nevada, where Mr. Nelson found a small *Perognathus* and lizard impaled on thorns by it. In Coso Valley, California, the writer observed a number of insects and lizards fastened on the sharp-pointed leaves of the yuccas. In the latter place several nests containing eggs were found in the tree yuccas during the first half of May, and one near Darwin, in the north end of the valley, June 17. In the Coso Mountains shrikes were in sight most of the time, and a nest containing four young was found May 27. Four other young, just able to fly, were seen on the same date.

In Nevada Dr. Merriam found a nest containing six eggs on the east slope of the Pahranagat Mountains, May 26. It was so placed in a fork of a tree yucca that although easily seen it could not be reached from any direction. He found the species at Mountain Spring in the Charleston Mountains, April 30; in Desert Valley, May 20; in the Juniper Mountains, May 18-19; and on Gold Mountain, among the yuccas on the south slope, June 3. On Mount Magruder several were seen in Tule Cañon, and thence up to an altitude of 2,450 meters (8,000 feet) in the nut pines, where it evidently was breeding, June 4-8. In Utah it was seen in the Santa Clara Valley near St. George, May 11-15; at Mountain Meadows, May 17; and among the tree yuccas on the south slope of the Beaverdam Mountains, May 10. Several were seen in the nut pines on the White and Inyo mountains, California.

In Owens Valley the species was quite common and numbers of young birds were seen about the orchards and roadsides in June. Mr. Nelson found it breeding in the Panamint, Grapevine, Inyo, and White mountains and the adjacent valleys, and Dr. Merriam saw several in the clumps of mesquite, in Death Valley and Mesquite Valley, April 8-18

It was common in Kern River Valley, Walker Pass, and Walker Basin, and in the San Joaquin Valley between Bakersfield and Visalia. It is a question whether the individuals seen by the writer at San Bernardino, December 27-30, 1890; by Dr. Merriam in the southern part of San Diego County, July 1-10, and by Mr. Nelson along the route from San Simeon to Carpenteria and Santa Paula should not be referred to the California shrike (*Lanius ludovicianus gambeli*).

Record of specimens collected of Lanius ludovicianus excubitorides.

Collector's No.	Sex.	Locality.	Date.	Collector.	Remarks.
37	♂	Hesperia, Calif.	Jan. 4, 1891	A. K. Fisher	Mohave Desert.
61	♂	Granite Wells, Calif.	Jan. 15, 1891	...do...	Do.
97	♀	Death Valley, Calif.	Feb. 3, 1891	...do...	Furnace Creek.
116	♀	Ash Meadows, Nev.	Mar. 4, 1891	...do...	
26	♀	Twelve-mile Spring, Calif.	Feb. 21, 1891	F. Stephens	North of Resting Springs.
262	♂ juv.	Coso Mountains, Calif.	May 27, 1891	A. K. Fisher	
263	♀ juv.	...do...	...do...	...do...	
264	♀ juv.	...do...	...do...	...do...	
296	♂ juv.	Owens Valley, Calif.	June 5, 1891	...do...	Lone Pine.
56	♀	...do...	May 13, 1891	F. Stephens	Haway Meadows.
57	♂ juv.	...do...	...do...	...do...	Do.
106	♀	...do...	June 19, 1891	...do...	Independence Creek

Vireo gilvus swainsoni. Western Warbling Vireo.

The warbling vireo was seen with very little regularity and was common in few localities visited by the expedition. In Owens Valley Mr. Stephens saw one among the willows at Haway Meadows, May 13; found it common and migrating at Olancha, May 16-23; common in the lower part of the cañon of Independence Creek, June 18-23; and heard several among the willows at the Queen mine in the White Mountains, Nevada, July 11-16. At Coso one was seen among the willows and rose bushes bordering a spring, May 23, and two were secured at the same place the following day. Dr. Merriam shot a specimen in worn breeding-plumage at Ash Meadows, Nevada, May 30, and saw a pair at Kernville, in Kern River Valley, June 23. It was not uncommon among the hills above Walker Basin, July 14, and Mr. Nelson noted a few at the head of Owens River the latter part of the month. Mr. Palmer found it common at Old Fort Tejon, where a nest containing four eggs, just ready to hatch, was discovered in a willow 10 or 12 feet from the ground, July 4.

Record of specimens collected of Vireo gilvus swainsoni.

Collector's No.	Sex.	Locality.	Date.	Collector.	Remarks.
252	♂	Coso, Coso Mountains, Calif	May 24, 1891	A. K. Fisher	
253	♂	......do..................	...do...	...do..........	

Vireo solitarius cassinii. Cassin's Vireo.

Cassin's vireo was observed in a number of places in the Sierra Nevada and sparingly in some of the other ranges. Dr. Merriam took a specimen in worn breeding-plumage, June 28, at Old Fort Tejon, in the Cañada de las Uvas, California, the type locality of the species. At Maturango Spring, in the Argus Range, a specimen was taken among the piñons, May 8. Mr. Nelson found it common at the head of Owens River and Dr. Merriam shot one among the junipers at Sheep Spring in the Juniper Mountains, Nevada, May 19. It was observed among the pines above Walker Basin, July 14; was common in the Sequoia National Park during the first week in August; was seen at Horse Corral Meadows, August 11; common at Kings River Cañon, August 13-16; and one was secured at Big Cottonwood Meadows, September 5.

Record of specimens collected of Vireo solitarius cassinii.

Collector's No.	Sex.	Locality.	Date.	Collector.	Remarks.
210	♂	Juniper Mountains, Nev	May 19, 1891	C. Hart Merriam	
	♀	Argus Range, Calif	May 8, 1891	A. K. Fisher	Maturango Spring.
	♂	Old Fort Tejon, Calif	June 28, 1891	T. S. Palmer	
393	♀	Walker Basin, Calif	July 14, 1891	A. K. Fisher	
157	♀ im.	Sierra Nevada, Calif	Aug. 22, 1891	F. Stephens	Olancha Peak.

Vireo solitarus plumbeus. Plumbeous Vireo.

The only specimen of this vireo taken on the expedition was a male secured by Dr. Merriam at Sheep Spring in the Juniper Mountains, Nevada, May 19, 1891. It was in full song and was shot in the same tree in which a Cassin's vireo was killed a few minutes before.

Vireo bellii pusillus. Least Vireo.

The least vireo is a tolerably common summer resident in Owens Valley, where at Lone Pine adult and young were secured in June; it was seen by Mr. Stephens at Olancha, May 16-23, and at Bishop Creek, August 4-10. A specimen was secured at Furnace Creek, Death Valley,

Vireo huttoni. A few seen at Monterey (McLellan Field Notes Feb 27 - Mch 1 1894).
Jamesburgh. One seen in the willows at the bottom of a canon (McLellan Field Notes, Mch 18

Mniotilta varia One was shot at Pasadena Calif Oct. 8, 1895 -
Horace A. Gaylord (Auk vol XIII, July 1896 p. 260).

June 20, and the species was not uncommon in the cañon above the ranch the following day. West of the Sierra Nevada, it was common at Bakersfield, in the San Joaquin Valley, July 17-20.

Record of specimens collected of Vireo bellii pusillus.

Collector's No.	Sex.	Locality.	Date.	Collector.	Remarks.
343	♂	Ash Meadows, Nev.	May 30, 1891	V. Bailey	
351	♂	Death Valley, Calif.	June 23, 1891	A. K. Fisher	Furnace Creek.
318	♂	do	June 24, 1891	do	Do.
328	♀ juv.	Owens Valley, Calif.	June 8, 1891	do	Lone Pine.
397	♂	do	June 11, 1891	do	Do.
		Bakersfield, Calif.	July 19, 1891	do	

Vireo vicinior. Gray Vireo.

Mr. Nelson found this vireo rather common in the Grapevine Mountains, Nevada, where he secured a specimen June 8. In Wood Cañon, he saw several among the piñons, and on June 10 observed one carrying material for its nest. This is the only locality at which the bird was found.

Helminthophila luciæ. Lucy's Warbler.

This rare warbler breeds in the Lower Santa Clara Valley in southwestern Utah, where two specimens were shot by Dr. Merriam, May 11 and 13, the former in cottonwoods along the Santa Clara River and the latter at a small pond near the village of St. George.

Record of specimens collected of Helminthophila luciæ.

Collector's No.	Sex.	Locality.	Date.	Collector.	Remarks.
	♂	Santa Clara, Utah	May 11, 1891	C. Hart Merriam	
	♀	St. George, Utah	May 16, 1891	do	

Helminthophila ruficapilla gutturalis. Calaveras Warbler.

The Calaveras warbler, with the exception of a pair seen in Shepherd Cañon in the Argus Range, California, April 29, was seen only in the Sierra Nevada. It was common in the Sequoia National Park during the first week of August, and a few were seen at Round Valley, 12 miles south of Mount Whitney, August 28. Mr. Nelson found it common at the head of Owens River and also on the western slope in the Yosemite Valley, in July and August.

Record of specimens collected of Helminthophila ruficapilla gutturalis.

Collector's No.	Sex.	Locality.	Date.	Collector.	Remarks.
194	♀	Argus Range, Calif.	April 29, 1891	A. K. Fisher	Shepherd Cañon.
405		Sierra Nevada, Calif.	Aug. 4, 1891	do	Sequoia National Park.

Helminthophila celata lutescens. Lutescent Warbler.

This active little warbler was found to be abundant in a few places during migration. At San Bernardino one was seen on the border of a stream, December 29, 1890. In the Panamint Mountains it was seen in Johnson Cañon, April 12; by Mr. Nelson among the willows at the heads of Willow and Mill creeks, the last of May; and by Mr. Bailey and the writer near the 'charcoal kilns' at the head of Wild Rose Cañon, June 23. In the Argus Range, it was common both in Shepherd Cañon and at Maturango Spring the first half of May. Mr. Stephens saw a few migrating by Little Owens Lake, May 6-11; and at Haway Meadows, May 12-14.

It was common along the South Fork of the Kern, July 3-10. In the High Sierra it was abundant in the Sequoia National Park, the first week in August; common at Horse Corral Meadows, August 9-13; at Round Valley, 12 miles south of Mt. Whitney, August 28; and at Mineral King, September 10-11. Mr. Nelson found it common at the head of Owens River and in the Yosemite Valley in July and August.

Record of specimens collected of Helminthophila celata lutescens.

Collector's No.	Sex.	Locality.	Date.	Collector.	Remarks.
215	♀	Argus Range, Calif	May 8, 1891	A. K. Fisher	Maturango Spring.
216	♂	do	May 9, 1891	do	Do.
217	♂	do	do	do	Do.
	♂ im	Panamint Mountains, Calif.	June 24, 1891	V. Bailey	Coal kilns.
	♂ im	Sierra Nevada, Calif.	Aug. 3, 1891	E. W. Nelson	South Fork Merced River.
159	♀ im	do	Aug. 22, 1891	F. Stephens	Olancha Peak.

Dendroica æstiva. Yellow Warbler.

The yellow warbler was tolerably common in a number of localities visited by members of the expedition. Mr. Nelson found it a rather common breeding species among the willows along Willow Creek, Mill Creek, and Cottonwood Creek cañons in the Panamint Mountains, and noted a few in Wood Cañon in the Grapevine Mountains. The same observer found it common at the head of Owens Valley at the base of the White Mountains and up to 2,600 meters (8,500 feet) altitude at the head of Owens River, in the Sierra Nevada. The writer first observed the species at Coso, where an adult male was seen busily engaged catching insects among some willows and rose bushes on the evening of May 24 and the following morning.

At Lone Pine, in Owens Valley, yellow warblers were common among the orchards and shade trees, June 4-15. In the same valley, Mr. Stephens found it common at Independence Creek, June 18-24; not common at Benton, July 9-10, and the Queen mill, Nevada, July 11-16, and saw two or three individuals in the cottonwoods at Morans, July 4-7.

In Nevada, Dr. Merriam shot a male in Pahrump Valley, on a solitary mesquite bush at a small spring six miles south of Yount's ranch,

April 29. He saw others at Upper Cottonwood Springs, at the east base of the Charleston Mountains, April 30; at Vegas ranch, May 1; at the Bend of the Colorado River, May 4; in the valley of the Virgin and Lower Muddy, May 6 and 8, and on Mount Magruder, June 4-8. In Pahranagat Valley it was breeding commonly, May 22-26, this being the only locality in Nevada at which he observed it in any numbers. He found it common where Beaverdam Creek joins the Virgin in northwestern Arizona, May 10, and breeding plentifully in the Lower Santa Clara Valley, Utah, near St. George, May 11-15. Mr. Palmer found it very common at Old Fort Tejon the first of July. All through Kern Valley, Walker Basin, and at Bakersfield, in the San Joaquin Valley, this warbler was common in the willows along the streams during the first three weeks of July, and sparingly in the latter valley as late as October.

Record of specimens collected of Dendroica æstiva.

Collector's No.	Sex.	Locality.	Date.	Collector.	Remarks.
203	♂	Owens Valley, Calif	June 5, 1891	A. K. Fisher	Lone Pine.
94	♂	do	June 12, 1891	F. Stephens	Olancha.
128	♀	do	July 9, 1891	do	Benton.
129	♂ juv	do	do	do	Do.

Dendroica auduboni. Audubon's Warbler.

The western yellow-rumped warbler was common as a migrant in various localities and not uncommon as a breeder in some of the mountain ranges. At San Bernardino a flock was seen in a clump of willows, and a number associated with chipping sparrows were seen gleaning insects from a field of early cabbage, December 28, 1890. A few were found among the willows bordering the reservoir at Furnace Creek, Death Valley, California, during the latter part of January, and again on April 10, and a single one was seen at Ash Meadows, Nevada, March 21. It was not uncommon at Hot Springs in Panamint Valley, April 20-23, and at Maturango Spring, in the Argus range, the first half of May.

In Nevada Audubon's warbler was seen by Mr. Nelson at Pahrump and Vegas ranches in February and March; and by Dr. Merriam in Pahrump Valley at Yount's Ranch, April 28-29; at Mountain Spring in the Charleston Mountains, and at Upper Cottonwood Springs at the east base of these mountains, April 30. In Utah a few were observed still lingering in the Santa Clara Valley, May 11-15, though the bulk of the species had gone into the mountains before this date.

In California Mr. Nelson saw a few migrants the last of May among the piñons at the head of Willow Creek in the Panamint Mountains, though none were seen later by him in these or in the Grapevine Mountains. The same observer saw a few in the Inyo Mountains from the upper edge of the piñon belt to the summit of the range, June 24 to July 4, and sparingly in the White Mountains a little later. It was common at the head of Owens River, from 2,500 to 2,900 meters (8,200 to 9,500 feet) altitude, and also on the west slope in the Yosemite Valley and on the head of the Merced River. In Owens Valley it was observed at Lone Pine in December, 1890, and at Little Owens Lake, May 6-11.

Along the east slope of the Sierra Nevada it was seen at Independence Creek, where it was probably breeding, June 18-21; at Bishop Creek August 4-10; at Menache Meadows May 24-26; and at Big Cottonwood Meadows during the summer and early fall.

It was common at Horse Corral Meadows August 10, and along the Kaweah River, where it was breeding, from 2,130 meters (7,000 feet) altitude up to timber line during the first part of August. Mr. Palmer found it rather common on the summit of Frazier Mountain, near Old Fort Tejon, on July 9. Mr. Nelson found it common at San Luis Obispo, Santa Paula, Carpenteria, and in the San Joaquin Valley in November and December, 1891.

Record of specimens collected of Dendroica auduboni.

Collector's No.	Sex	Locality	Date	Collector	Remarks
2	♀ im.	San Bernardino, Calif	Dec. 28, 1890	A. K. Fisher	
96	♂	Death Valley, Calif	Feb. 1, 1891	...do...	Furnace Creek.
2	♂	Sierra Nevada, Calif	June 19, 1891	B. H. Dutcher	Big Cottonwood Meadows.
3	♂	...do...	...do...	...do...	...do...
12	♀	...do...	July 7, 1891	...do...	...do...
142	♂	...do...	July 26, 1891	F. Stephens	

Dendroica nigrescens. Black-throated Gray Warbler.

The black-throated gray warbler was first observed among the piñons above Maturango Spring, in the Argus Range, California, where a female was secured May 8, containing a large egg in the oviduct, and on the following day one was seen carrying nesting material in its beak. Mr. Nelson saw a few in the Panamint Mountains among the piñons on Willow Creek the last of May, and found them breeding among the same trees in the Grapevine Mountains. Above the 'charcoal kilns' in Wild Rose Cañon in the Panamint Mountains, males were heard singing by Mr. Bailey and the writer June 25. This warbler was found breeding in the Inyo and White Mountains and in the Sierra Nevada, at the head of Owens River. Dr. Merriam shot one at Sheep Spring in the Juniper Mountains, Nevada, May 19, and two in the nut pines on Mt. Magruder, June 5. Mr. Bailey saw a few among the pines on the Kaweah River the last of July, and the writer saw one on the Hockett trail near Little Cottonwood Creek, August 23, and secured a specimen at Three Rivers, September 14.

Mr. Nelson reported a few as seen along the coast from San Simeon to Carpenteria, Calif., November 4 to December 18.

Record of specimens collected of Dendroica nigrescens.

Collector's No.	Sex.	Locality.	Date.	Collector.	Remarks.
211	♂	Argus Range, Calif.	May 9, 1891	T. S. Palmer	Maturango Spring.
212	♂	......do......	......do......	......do......	Do.
238	♂	......do......	May 8, 1891	A. K. Fisher	Do.
239	♂	......do......	......do......	......do......	Do.
435	♂	......do......	May 13, 1891	......do......	Do.
132	♀	Three Rivers, Calif.	Sept. 14, 1891	......do......	Do.
	♂	Queen mine, Nev	July 11, 18-1	F. Stephens	White Mountains.
	♂	Juniper Mountains, Nev	May 19, 1891	C. Hart Merriam	
	♂	Mount Magruder, Nev	June 5, 1891	V. Bailey	
	♀	......do......	......do......	C. Hart Merriam	

Dendroica townsendi. Townsend's Warbler.

Townsend's warbler was first noted on the ridge above Maturango Spring in the Argus Range, California, where a male in full song was secured, and others seen among the piñons May 6. From this date until the departure of the party, May 15, the species was not uncommon, though there was no evidence of its intention to remain and breed, as in the case of the black-throated gray warbler. One was seen at Coso on May 19, and Mr. Stephens saw a small flock migrating among the creosote bushes northeast of Little Owens Lake, the second week in May.

In the Sierra Nevada Mr. Nelson saw two or three on the South Fork of the Merced River August 9. They were in company with a large number of other small birds of several species, gleaning insects from among the lower branches as they passed from tree to tree. On the coast Mr. Bailey found it common at Monterey September 28 to October 9, and Mr. Nelson saw it, though very sparingly, at Morro Bay and southward.

Record of specimens collected of Dendroica townsendi.

Collector's No.	Sex.	Locality.	Date.	Collector.	Remarks.
200	♂	Argus Range, Calif.	May 6, 1891	A. K. Fisher	Maturango Spring.
219	♂	......do......	May 9, 1891	......do......	Do.
226	♂	......do......	May 11, 1891	......do......	Do.
	♂	Monterey, Calif.	Oct. 5, 1891	V. Bailey	
	♀	Morro	Nov. 8, 1891	E. W. Nelson	

Dendroica occidentalis. Hermit Warbler.

This rare warbler was first seen among the piñons in the Argus Range, above Maturango Spring, where a pair was observed and a female secured May 6. The following day another was seen. Mr. Nelson saw a few among a migrating flock on the South Fork of the Merced, near Wawona, August 9. Mr. Palmer saw one in a mixed flock of warblers at Halsted Meadows, in the Sequoia National Park, August 7, and the writer secured a specimen at Horse Corral Meadows August 13. Mr. Belding saw migrants at Crocker's, 21 miles northwest of Yosemite Valley, in May.

Record of specimens collected of Dendroica occidentalis.

Collector's No.	Sex.	Locality.	Date.	Collector.	Remarks.
109	♀	Argus Range, Calif	May 6, 1891	A. K. Fisher	Maturango Spring.
415	♀ im.	Sierra Nevada, Calif	Aug. 13, 1891	....do	Horse Corral Meadows.

Seiurus noveboracensis notabilis. Grinnell's Water-Thrush.

The only individual of this species obtained by the expedition was an adult male secured by Dr. Merriam and Mr. Bailey at the eastern edge of the Santa Clara settlement, in the Lower Santa Clara Valley, Utah, May 11, 1891.

Geothlypis macgillivrayi. Macgillivray's Warbler.

This warbler was first observed in Shepherd Cañon in the Argus Range, California, April 27, and afterwards at Maturango Spring, where it was common among the willow thickets. At Coso, the species was common in the shrubbery about the springs and along the cañons to the summit of the range, the latter part of May. Mr. Nelson found it a rather common migrant along the upper part of Willow and Mill Creeks in the Panamint Mountains during the last week of May. After this date comparatively few were seen, and these only within the sage belt along the willow-grown banks of springs and streams. A few were seen also in Wood Cañon in the Grapevine Mountains. In the Sierra Nevada, Mr. Nelson found it at the head of Owens River, though not common. Mr. Stephens saw a female accompanied by young at Bishop Creek, August 4-10; Mr. Dutcher secured specimens at Big Cottonwood Meadows, where the writer saw it August 26; and several were seen in the Sequoia National Park during the first week in August.

In Nevada Dr. Merriam found Macgillivray's Warbler common in Pahranagat Valley, May 22-26, immediately after a severe snowstorm, and thought it did not breed in the valley. He saw a single individual on Mount Magruder, Nevada, June 8, and Mr. Nelson found a few at the heads of streams on the east slope of the White Mountains.

Record of specimens collected of Geothlypis macgillivrayi.

Collector's No.	Sex.	Locality.	Date.	Collector.	Remarks.
218	♀	Argus Mountains, Calif	May 9, 1891	A. K. Fisher	Maturango Spring.
254	♂	Coso, Coso Mountains, Calif	May 21, 1891	....do	
255	♂	......do	May 25, 1891	....do	
267	♀	......do	May 28, 1891	....do	

Geothlypis trichas occidentalis. Western Yellow-throat.

The western yellow-throat was common in only a few localities visited by the expedition. At San Bernardino, Calif., it was tolerably common along the streams and in the thickets, December 28-29, 1890. It was seen in Surprise Cañon in the Panamint Mountains, April 16, and was not uncommon at Hot Springs in Panamint Valley, April 20-25. Mr. Nelson found a few during the latter part of May in the willows on Mill and Willow creeks in the Panamint Mountains, but observed none in the Grapevine Mountains. He saw a few at Hunter Cañon on the east slope of the Inyo Mountains, and also among some willows in Saline Valley. In Owens Valley it was a tolerably common summer resident from Little Owens Lake up to the head of the valley at the base of the White Mountains. In Death Valley the species was not uncommon in Furnace Creek Cañon and at Bennett Wells, June 19-21.

In Nevada, Dr. Merriam found it tolerably common and breeding in Pahranagat Valley, and saw it at Vegas Ranch, May 1, and along the Lower Santa Clara in Utah, May 11-15.

It was common along the South Fork of the Kern River, California, July 3-10; at Kernville, July 11-13; in Walker Basin, July 13-16, and at Bakersfield in the San Joaquin Valley, July 17-20.

On the coast of California Mr. Nelson found it, though in limited numbers, at the head of Morro Bay, and thence southward.

Record of specimens collected of Geothlypis trichas occidentalis.

Collector's No.	Sex.	Locality.	Date.	Collector.	Remarks.
8	♀ im.	San Bernardino, Calif	Dec. 28, 1890	A. K. Fisher	
174	♂	Panamint Valley, Calif	Apr. 21, 1891	....do	Hot Springs.
350	♂	Death Valley, Calif	June 21, 1891	....do	Furnace Creek.
78	♂	Owens Valley, Calif	June 9, 1891	F. Stephens	Olancha.
82	♀	......do	June 10, 1891	....do	

Icteria virens longicauda. Long-tailed Chat.

Owing to the lack of suitable localities for nesting the yellow-breasted chat was found sparingly in most of the region traversed by the expedition. It was moderately common in Owens Valley, at Lone Pine, June 4-15, and Mr. Stephens found it in the same valley, though not commonly, at Olancha, May 16-23; at Ash Creek, May 30-June 3; at Independence Creek, June 18-23, and at Morans, July 4-7. Mr. Nelson saw and heard one, which sang in the evening and the greater part of the night of May 22, near his camp on Willow Creek in the Panamint Mountains, and observed others in the Inyo Mountains, from Hunter's arastra down to the bottom of Saline Valley, during the latter part of June. At Furnace Creek, Death Valley, chats were tolerably common at the ranch and in the cañon above it, June 19-21. At Kernville, Calif., and along Kern Valley, chats were common June 22-23, and

July 11-13; in Walker Basin, July 13-16, and several were seen in the Cañada de las Uvas June 28, 29. At Bakersfield, in the San Joaquin Valley, it was seen or heard every day from July 17-20.

In Nevada, Dr. Merriam found it in the lower part of Vegas Wash, May 3; at the Bend of the Colorado, May 4; in the valleys of the Virgin and Muddy, May 6-8; and in Pahranagat Valley, as a common breeder, May 22-26. In the Santa Clara Valley, Utah, it was a tolerably common breeder, May 11-15.

Record of specimens collected of Icteria virens longicauda.

Collector's No.	Sex.	Locality.	Date.	Collector.	Remarks.
294	♂	Owens Valley, Calif	June 5, 1891	A. K. Fisher	Lone Pine.
349	♂	Death Valley, Calif	June 21, 1891	....do	Furnace Creek.

Sylvania pusilla pileolata. Pileolated Warbler.

The black-capped warbler was first seen in Surprise Cañon in the Panamint Mountains, April 17, and Mr. Nelson found it rather common among the willows at the head of Willow, Mill, and Cottonwood creeks in the same mountains the last of May, after which time he did not see it there. A few were seen in the Argus Range in Shepherd Cañon, April 27, and the species was common about Maturango Spring, in the willows and rosebushes during the first half of May. It was seen in the Coso Mountains in the bottom of the cañons among the shrubbery, the last of May, and at the head of the streams in the White Mountains, in July. Mr. Stephens found it migrating in Salt Wells Valley, May 1-5; at Little Owens Lake, May 6-11; at Olancha, May 16-23; and in Reche Cañon, September 22-24. In the High Sierra it was seen in the Sequoia National Park the first week in August; at Horse Corral Meadows, August 9-13; at the head of Owens River and on the western slope opposite, in July and August; at Big Cottonwood Meadows, during the summer; at Round Valley, 12 miles south of Mount Whitney, the last of August; and north of Mineral King, September 10-11.

In Nevada, Dr. Merriam saw it at a large spring in Pahrump Valley, April 29; at Mountain Spring in the Charleston Mountains, April 30; at Upper Cottonwood Springs at the east base of these mountains, the same day; at Vegas ranch, May 1; at the Bend of the Colorado, May 4; and in the Valley of the Virgin and Lower Muddy, May 6.

Record of specimens collected of Sylvania pusilla pileolata.

Collector's No.	Sex.	Locality.	Date.	Collector.	Remarks.
190	♂	Argus Range, Calif	Apr. 27, 1891	A. K. Fisher	Shepherd Cañon.
223	♀	....do	May 10, 1891	....do	Maturango Springs.
13	♂	Sierra Nevada, Calif	July 7, 1891	B. H. Dutcher	Big Cottonwood Meadows.

Cinclus. "Several pairs were found on the creek [at Sur]. It is said that they meet at the numerous waterfalls. They were singing (McLellan, Field Notes nch. 2-6, 1894). See also Auk XI, 1894, 258.

Anthus pensilvanicus. Titlark.

The titlark was found as a winter resident in suitable localities in southern California and Nevada.

In California Mr. Nelson saw a few at Lone Pine, and found it very common along the shore of Owens Lake in December, 1890; he also saw a few at Hot Springs, Panamint Valley, in the early part of January, where the writer secured a specimen, April 22, 1891. At San Bernardino several flocks were seen in a wet meadow bordering a stream, on December 28, 1890. In Death Valley a flock of twenty or more was always to be found in the alfalfa fields at Furnace Creek, and a few were observed at Saratoga Springs during the latter part of January. Dr. Merriam saw two in the Mohave Desert on the sand beach bordering the Mohave River at Victor, March 30. At various places in the San Joaquin Valley Mr. Nelson found it congregated in small flocks in October, and common in fields and along the coast from San Simeon to Carpenteria, in November and December.

In Nevada the species was common at Ash Meadows in flocks on the wet marshes and plowed fields during the first three weeks of March, and Mr. Nelson found it not uncommon about wet ground in both Vegas and Pahrump valleys, and near the upper end of Vegas Wash about the same time.

Record of specimens collected of Anthus pensilvanicus.

Collector's No.	Sex.	Locality.	Date.	Collector.	Remarks.
6	♂	San Bernardino, Calif	Dec. 28, 1890	A. K. Fisher	
89	♀	Death Valley, Calif	Jan. 30, 1891	....do	Furnace Creek.
90	♀	....do	....do	....do	Do.
182	♀	Panamint Valley, Calif	Apr. 22, 1891	....do	Hot Springs.

Cinclus mexicanus. Water Ousel.

The dipper or water ousel was seen only along the streams of the Sierra Nevada, in California. In December, 1890, Mr. Nelson saw one on Owens River at the mouth of Lone Pine Creek. The writer first observed the species on the South Fork of Kern River, where a specimen was secured July 7 as it was flying from boulder to boulder in a rapid portion of the stream. It was seen at Horse Corral Meadows August 9-13, and was common in Kings River Cañon August 13-16. At the latter place an old nest was discovered in the eroded end of a drift log which hung out over a waterfall. The dipper was met with by Mr. Nelson at the head of Owens River and in the Yosemite Valley, and by Mr. Stephens at Bishop Creek. It was common in the high mountains along the streams in Big Cottonwood and Whitney Meadows, where specimens were secured. Mr. Palmer observed one at an altitude of about 3,500 meters (11,600 feet) in Langley Meadow September 10.

Record of specimens collected of Cinclus mexicanus.

Collector's No.	Sex.	Locality.	Date.	Collector.	Remarks.
381	im.	Kern River, Calif	July 7, 1891	A. K. Fisher	South Fork
433	♂	Whitney Meadows, Calif	Aug. 31, 1891	do	
15	♂	Sierra Nevada, Calif	July 8, 1891	B. H. Dutcher	Big Cottonwood Meadows.
24	♂	do	Aug. 2, 1891	do	Do.
416	♂	Kings River Cañon, Calif	Aug. 14, 1891	A. K. Fisher	

Oroscoptes montanus. Sage Thrasher.

The sage thrasher is a characteristic inhabitant of the sage plains, occurring in company with the sage sparrow (*Amphispiza belli nevadensis*), Brewer's sparrow (*Spizella breweri*), and the lark sparrow (*Chondestes grammacus strigatus*). It was not found in the lower valleys except as a winter resident. A flock of six or eight was seen at Hesperia in the Mohave Desert, January 4, and about an equal number at Granite Wells, January 13-15. One was observed at Mesquite Well in Death Valley, January 20. Mr. Nelson saw about half a dozen in the sage brush on the divide between Willow and Cottonwood creeks in the Panamint Mountains, where they seemed to be breeding during the last of May. Dr. Merriam found the species common among the sage brush north of Telescope Peak April 15. A pair was observed in Coso Valley, below Maturango Spring, May 11, and Mr. Nelson reported the species common in the same place in January.

In Nevada a few were noted at Ash Meadows in March, and Mr. Nelson found them in both Pahrump and Vegas valleys. Dr. Merriam found them common in the sage brush on the rolling plateau of the Juniper Mountains, May 18; in the valley between Gold Mountain and Mount Magruder, June 4; and on Mount Magruder plateau, June 5-8, where a nest containing two fresh eggs was found in a sage bush, June 8. In the Santa Clara Valley in southwestern Utah, they were not found near St. George, but were seen first on May 15, about 8 miles northwest of that place where the sage brush begins. A few miles further north, at the upper Santa Clara Crossing, they were one of the most abundant birds, May 17; and at Mountain Meadows, Utah, where they were common, he shot an adult male sitting on a nest containing four fresh eggs, May 17. Mr. Nelson found them sparingly among the piñons in the Inyo Mountains, California, the latter part of June; saw a few on the White Mountains and found them rather common about the head of Owens Valley, in July. He reported them as common up to 2,450 meters (8,000 feet), at the head of Owens River. Mr. Stephens saw several at Morans, July 4-7; found them common at Benton, July 9-10; and at Queen mine, in the White Mountains, Nevada, where a few were heard singing, July 11-16.

Record of specimens collected of Oroscoptes montanus.

Collector's No.	Sex.	Locality.	Date.	Collector.	Remarks.
34	♂	Hesperia, Calif	Jan. 4, 1891	A. K. Fisher	
51	♂	Granite Wells, Calif	Jan. 14, 1891	do	
60	♂	......do......	......do......	......do......	
45	♂	Coso Valley, Calif	May 12, 1891	T. S. Palmer	
130	♂	Panamint Mountains, Calif	Apr. 15, 1891	F. Stephens	
30	♂	Owens Valley, Calif	July 9, 1891	do	Benton.
	♂	Ash Meadows, Nev	Mar. 11, 1891	do	
	♂	St. George, Utah	May 16, 1891	V. Bailey	3,800 feet altitude.
	♂	Mountain Meadows, Utah	May 17, 1891	C. Hart Merriam	Nest and eggs.

Mimus polyglottos. Mocking Bird.

The mocking bird was found sparingly in the desert regions of California, and was more or less common in similar localities in Nevada, Utah, and Arizona. It was common about San Bernardino, Calif., and in Cajon Pass the first of January and the latter part of March. In Death Valley, one was seen at Saratoga Springs in the latter part of January, and others in various other parts of the valley proper and in the northwest arm (Mesquite Valley), April 8–13, but was not seen anywhere in the valley during the trip of June 19–21. It was found at Hot Springs in Panamint Valley, April 20–24, and was tolerably common among the yuccas in Coso Valley and Mountains, throughout May. Mr. Nelson found it through the north end of the Panamint Mountains from the divide between Cottonwood and Willow creeks down to the bottom of Mesquite and Saline valleys. In the Grapevine Mountains it ranged up to the base of the main summits, at an altitude of 2,450 meters (8,000 feet). The same observer found it common as high as the lower edge of the piñons in the Inyo Mountains, to 2,370 meters (7,800 feet) at the head of Owens River in the Sierra, and a few from the head of Owens Valley up to 2,430 meters (8,000 feet) in the White Mountains.

In Nevada, Dr. Merriam found Mocking Birds in Tule Cañon, at the extreme northern end of the northwest arm of Death Valley, June 4; on the southern slope of Gold Mountain, among the tree yuccas, June 3; in Oasis Valley, June 1; in the Timpahute Mountains, May 26 (among the tree yuccas); in Pahranagat Valley, May 22–26 (common and breeding); at Pahroc Spring, May 20–22; in Meadow Creek Valley, May 19; in the valleys of the Muddy and Virgin, May 6–8 (common); at the Bend of the Colorado May 4; in Vegas Valley and Wash, April 30–May 3; and in Pahrump Valley, April 28–29 (several in the tree yuccas on east side of valley). In Utah, he found them common in the Lower Santa Clara Valley, May 11–15, and abundant on both sides of the Beaverdam Mountains, May 10–11.

They were tolerably common in Owens Valley, Calif., where they were seen at Little Owens Lake, Keeler, and Lone Pine. A pair was seen on the eastern slope of Walker Pass, July 1, and another at Walker Basin,

July 15; they were common at Bakersfield, July 17-20; in Tehachapi Pass, June 25, and a few were observed around Visalia in July. Several were seen in Reche Cañon, by Mr Stephens, September 22-24; and a male by Mr. Nelson at Santa Paula, during the last of December.

Harporhynchus redivivus. California Thrasher.

The California thrasher is a bird of the chaparral and was not found in the desert regions east of the Sierra Nevada. At San Bernardino the writer saw one December 29, 1890, and Mr. Stephens reported the species rather common in Reche Cañon near the same place, September 22-24, 1891. A pair was seen at Cane Brake ranch on the western slope of Walker Pass, July 3, and several at Kernville, where two were secured July 12. A number were seen in Walker Basin, July 13-16, and Dr. Merriam found the species common between that place and Caliente June 24; in the Cañada de las Uvas June 28-29; and in the Sierra Liebre June 30. In the latter range it passes over the divide and occurs in the chaparral on the north slope, close to the edge of the Mohave Desert. Several were seen at Bakersfield, in the San Joaquin Valley, July 17-20. Mr. Bailey saw a pair in the oak brush just below the edge of the conifers on the Kaweah River, and others at Boulder Creek; and Mr. Nelson found them common along the coast, from Morro to Santa Paula, during November and December.

Record of specimens collected of Harporhynchus redivivus.

Collector's No.	Sex.	Locality.	Date.	Collector.	Remarks.
386	♀ im.	Kernville, Calif	July 11, 1891	A. K. Fisher	
	♀	do	do	V. Bailey	
165	♂	Hesperia, Calif	Sept. 15, 1891	F. Stephens	

Harporhynchus lecontei. LeConte's Thrasher.

Le Conte's thrasher is a characteristic bird of the deserts of southeastern California and southern Nevada and Arizona, where it was found in all the Lower Sonoran valleys east of the Sierra visited by the expedition. It is not a migratory species and probably remains in the vicinity of its summer home the entire year. This statement is strengthened by the fact that in most places where the species was found old nests were also observed. These were placed in arborescent cactuses, mesquite, or other thorny shrubs.

This thrasher was first seen by us not far from Victor, in the Mohave Desert, California, January 7, and a number were noticed between Daggett and Granite Wells, January 8-13 and April 4-6. In Death Valley, a pair was seen at Bennett Wells January 21, others about the middle of April, and a pair with five young on June 21; at Furnace Creek one was seen the last of January. At Resting Springs the spe-

On Dec. 10, 1893 R.W. Hawling saw and Scolonti's staircase at Onyx, just above the junction of the north and south forks of Kiowa River (Zoe, IV, Oct. 1893 pp 223-224).

LeConte Thrasher / Dr C Hart Merriam
Auk, XII, 1895 54-60 —

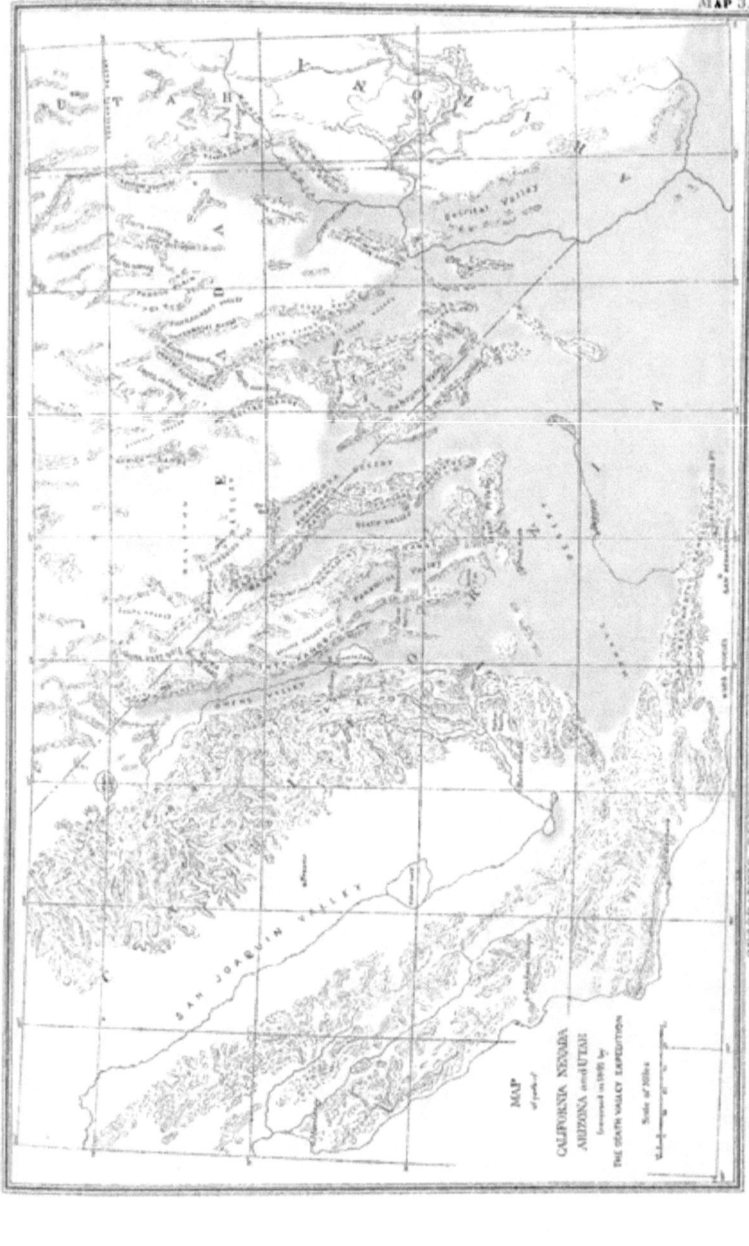

GEOGRAPHIC DISTRIBUTION OF LeCONTE'S THRASHER (*HARPORHYNCHUS LECONTEI*).

cies was very common among the mesquite, where the males were frequently heard singing from their perches on the uppermost branches, February 6-17.

In Nevada it was common at Ash Meadows in March, and Mr. Nelson found it in Pahrump Valley, at the western base of the Charleston Mountains. East of Pahrump Valley Dr. Merriam saw several April 29, and a full-grown young was shot among the yuccas. He killed one in Vegas Valley May 1, and found the species tolerably common in the valley of the Virgin and Lower Muddy. A nest was found in a branching cactus (*Opuntia echinocarpa*) on the mesa between these rivers, and, although the parent bird was on the nest, no eggs had been laid. In southwestern Utah it was found on the west side of the Beaverdam Mountains almost to the summit of the range, keeping in the tree yuccas and arborescent cactuses with the cactus wren.

At Hot Springs, in Panamint Valley, California, it was seen the last of April, and in Coso Valley and Mountains through May. It is common in Owens Valley, from Little Owens Lake, where Mr. Stephens found a nest and three eggs and a brood of nearly grown young, to Benton, where both he and Mr. Nelson saw it. Mr. Stephens found it common in Salt Wells Valley, where nests and young were observed. In Walker Pass it was common among the tree yuccas on the east side, and Dr. Merriam saw several on the west slope, about 4 miles from the summit, June 22-23. He found it common throughout the western tongue of the Mohave Desert, where a nest containing two half-grown young was found in a branching cactus (*Opuntia echinocarpa*) June 27.

In the San Joaquin Valley Mr. Nelson found it common about the southern and western sides of Buena Vista Lake, and thence west and northwest for 15 to 18 miles toward the base of the Temploa Mountains. This was the actual range in which he noted the species, though it undoubtedly occupied much more territory in the vicinity, where the low growth of desert bushes and sandy arroyos near the lake formed a congenial home.

LeConte's thrasher is a sly, skulking species, quite difficult to collect, and when running about among the desert shrubbery closely resembles the road-runner in form and actions.

The song of this species like that of the other members of the genus is sweet and variable, and in many respects rivals that of the mockingbird in musical elegance. In many places throughout its range the young (just before they leave the nest) are regularly hunted by both whites and Indians for the purpose of making cage birds of them.

At Keeler, in Owens Valley, Mr. H. E. Wilkinson, meteorological observer, had one which was allowed the freedom of the house. It was very tame and would allow itself to be caught and placed in the cage for the night. One of its favorite amusements was to sit on the window sill and catch the flies which were moving on the panes.

Record of specimens collected of Harporhynchus lecontei.

Collector's No.	Sex.	Locality.	Date.	Collector.	Remarks.
19	♂	Resting Springs, Calif	Feb. 14, 1891	F. Stephens	
20	♂	...do...	...do...	...do...	
23	♂	Twelve-mile Spring, Calif	Feb. 20, 1891	...do...	North of Resting Springs.
	♂	Ash Meadows, Nev	Mar. 19, 1891	E. W. Nelson	
121	♂	...do...	Mar. 16, 1891	A. K. Fisher	
133	♂	...do...	Mar. 19, 1891	...do...	
	♂	Pahrump Valley, Nev	Feb. 11, 1891	E. W. Nelson	
	♀	...do...	...do...	...do...	
	♂ juv.	...do...	Apr. 29, 1891	C. Hart Merriam	
	♀ im.	Vegas Valley, Nev	May 1, 1891	...do...	
	♂	Beaverdam Mountains, Utah.	May 10, 1891	...do...	
29	♂	Table Mountain, Nev	May 6, 1891	F. Stephens	Amargosa Desert.
	♂	Buena Vista Lake, Calif	Oct. 26, 1891	E. W. Nelson	San Joaquin Valley.
164	♀	Hesperia, Calif	Sept. 15, 1891	F. Stephens	
53	♂	Salt Wells Valley, Calif	May 4, 1891	...do...	
284	♂ im.	Owens Valley, Calif	June 2, 1891	A. K. Fisher	Keeler.
		...do...	Dec. 27, 1890	E. W. Nelson	Lone Pine.
126	♂ im.	...do...	July 3, 1891	F. Stephens	22 miles north of Bishop.
	♀	Coso Mountains	Dec. 31, 1890	E. W. Nelson	
	♂	...do...	...do...	V. Bailey	
	♂	Panamint Valley, Calif	Jan. 10, 1891	...do...	
44	♂	Daggett, Calif	Jan. 7, 1891	A. K. Fisher	
	♂ juv.	Mohave Desert, Calif	June 27, 1891	T. S. Palmer	Willow Spring.
	♀ juv.	...do...	...do...	...do...	Do.
	♀ im.	Death Valley, Calif	June 21, 1891	V. Bailey	Bennett Wells.
	♂	...do...	Jan. 30, 1891	E. W. Nelson	Saratoga Springs.
17	♀	Garlick Springs, Calif	Feb. 10, 1891	F. Stephens	
18	♀	...do...	...do...	...do...	
59	♀	Resting Springs, Calif	Feb. 7, 1891	A. K. Fisher	
100	♂	...do...	...do...	...do...	
104	♀	...do...	...do...	...do...	
107	♀	...do...	Feb. 11, 1891	...do...	

Harporhynchus crissalis. Crissal Thrasher.

The crissal thrasher was not found in the Mohave or Amargosa deserts, nor in Death, Panamint, or other valleys west of the Charleston Mountains, where LeConte's thrasher is so common. Dr. Merriam found it from Vegas Valley, Nevada, eastward. He observed it in the valley of the Virgin, near St. Joe, Nev., May 7, and near Bunkerville, May 8; and found it a common breeder in the Lower Santa Clara Valley, Utah, where a nest containing two fresh eggs was discovered in a bush of *Atriplex torreyi*, about 3 feet above the ground, May 16. Mr. Nelson also found a nest containing three eggs, at Cottonwood Spring, at the east base of the Charleston Mountains, March 8. The bird was shot from the nest, which was placed partly on one of the large branches of a desert willow (*Chilopsis saligna*) and partly on top of an *Atriplex canescens* bush growing under it. The structure was formed externally of coarse twigs, a few inches long, and lined with hemp-like strips of bark from a plant growing in the vicinity.

Heleodytes brunneicapillus. Cactus Wren.

The cactus wren is an abundant and characteristic bird of the Lower Sonoran Zone, breeding wherever there are suitable forests of tree yuccas or arborescent cactuses, and sometimes in other forms of spiny vegetation, as the desert acacia (*Acacia greggii*). It was first seen in the Mohave Desert, at Hesperia, a few miles from the summit of Cajon Pass, where the males were singing from the tops of the tree yuccas, January 4-5. Mr. Stephens found a nest containing four fresh eggs in a 'cholla' (cactus) in Salt Wells Valley, about 8 miles north of Indian Wells, the 1st of May, and saw the species sparingly in Owens Valley, a few miles north of Little Owens Lake. In the Coso Valley, and at Coso in the mountains of the same name, Mr. Palmer and the writer found this species among the tree yuccas, and the former observer found a number of old nests during the first half of May. In the early part of July, the species was very common in Walker Pass, where as many as half a dozen were seen in one yucca, and at the South Fork of the Kern River it was found to be common wherever yuccas occurred. Mr. Nelson found it rather common about the ranch in Vegas Valley, Nevada, and still more numerous among the mesquite in Vegas Wash near the Colorado River, where the birds were in full song, March 10.

Dr. Merriam furnished the following notes on this species: "In the Mohave Desert, California, many nests were found in tree yuccas between Cajon Pass and Pilot Knob, the first week in April, but none of them contained eggs. The species reaches the extreme western end of the desert (Antelope Valley), and a few were seen in yuccas and sage-brush in a wash leading south from Gorman ranch toward Peru Creek, June 30.

"From the Mohave Desert the cactus wren extends up the wash leading to Tehachapi Basin, where it was tolerably common in the yuccas and 'chollas' below Cameron. In Walker Pass, it ranges from the east or Mohave Desert side completely across the Sierra to the valley of Kern River, where it is abundant in groves of tree yuccas and in 'chollas' down to 820 meters (2,700 feet) altitude, and where dozens of their large nests were seen in the cactuses, June 22. In Nevada two nests were found in *Acacia greggii* at Bitter Springs in the Muddy Mountains, May 5; both had been used the present season, and one contained an addled egg. The species was common on the high mesa between the Muddy and Virgin rivers, May 7, where nearly every branching cactus contained the remnants of a nest, but all the young had hatched and flown away. In the Beaverdam Mountains, in southwestern Utah, they were common in yuccas and cactuses up to 1,150 meters (3,800 feet) on the west slope. In the Lower Santa Clara Valley, Utah, near St. George, they were common, breeding in the arborescent cactus, May 11-15. This valley is the extreme northeastern limit of distribution of the species. In Southern California, on the coast slope, it is abundant on the San Bernardino Plain, and thence southward. Many were seen in the Santa Clara Valley at its junction with Castac Creek, June 30, where its nests were conspicuous in the tall cactus (*Opuntia bernardina*)."

Record of specimens collected of Heleodytes brunneicapillus.

Collector's No.	Sex.	Locality.	Date.	Collector.	Remarks.
32	♂	Hesperia, Calif	Jan. 4, 1891	A. K. Fisher	
33	♂	....do....	....do....	....do....	
389	♂	Kern River, Calif	July 6, 1891	....do....	South Fork.

Salpinctes obsoletus. Rock Wren.

The rock wren was seen wherever there were bare rocks suited to its wants, from the lowest valleys to above timber line on the highest mountains. It was seen at Granite Well in the Mohave Desert, January 13; at Lone Willow Spring, January 17; at Mesquite Well, in Death Valley, January 20; and in Furnace Creek Cañon, in the Funeral Mountains, February 5. In the Panamint Mountains, it was common in Johnson, Surprise, and Emigrant cañons in April, and Mr. Nelson found it common and widely distributed along Cottonwood Cañon, where young, following their parents, were seen during the last of May. In the latter part of June several were seen in Death Valley Cañon, a few hundred feet above the valley, and thence to the summit of Telescope Peak, where a family of six or eight were seen among the loose rocks.

In Nevada this wren was not uncommon at Ash Meadows, in Oasis Valley, and in the Grapevine Mountains in March, and in the latter mountains was breeding commonly in May. Mr. Nelson found it sparingly at various places in Pahrump Valley and along the route to the Bend of the Colorado in March. Dr. Merriam found it common in Tule Cañon, and thence up to the summit of Mount Magruder, in rocky places, June 4–9; on Gold Mountain, June 3; in Pahranagat Valley, May 22–26; and in the Pahroc Mountains, near Pahroc Spring, May 21–22. In Utah, he reported it common along the cliffs of the Santa Clara Valley, May 11–15; at the Upper Santa Clara Crossing, May 16; and saw two pairs in the junipers in the Beaverdam Mountains, May 11.

In Shepherd Cañon and at Maturango Spring, in the Argus Range, California, it was common during the first half of May, and in the cañons in the Coso Mountains during the latter part of the month. Mr. Nelson found it ranging from the bottoms of the valley to the summit of Inyo and White mountains and to timber line at the head of Owens River. In the former range, at Cerro Gordo, Mr. Palmer found young just out of the nest, May 31. The species was common and well distributed in Owens Valley from the lower end of Owens Lake to the upper part, at the base of the White Mountains. It was common along the western slope of Walker Pass, along Kern River Valley and below Old Fort Tejon, in the Cañada de las Uvas. In the High Sierra it was common at Big Cottonwood Meadows during the summer, and one was seen at Round Valley, 12 miles south of Mount Whitney, above timber line, August 28, and one at Whitney Meadows about the same time.

Record of specimens collected of Salpinctes obsoletus.

Collector's No.	Sex.	Locality.	Date.	Collector.	Remarks.
9	♂	Daggett, Calif.	Feb. 7, 1891	F. Stephens	Mohave Desert.
64	♂	Lone Willow Spring, Calif.	Jan. 17, 1891	A. K. Fisher	
275	♂ juv.	Owens Valley, Calif.	June 1, 1891	do	Keeler.
330	♀	do	June 11, 1891	do	Lone Pine.
42	♂	Grapevine Spring, Calif.	April 2, 1891	F. Stephens	

Catherpes mexicanus conspersus. Cañon Wren.

The cañon wren was found in a number of the mountain ranges visited by the expedition in California and Nevada. In a few places in the Panamint Mountains it was common, but in no other of the desert ranges was it found in any numbers. We first observed it in Furnace Creek Cañon in the Funeral Mountains, on our way to the Amargosa Desert early in February, and again on the return trip in the latter part of March. Mr. Bailey saw one at Saratoga Springs in the southern end of Death Valley, in February. In Johnson and Surprise cañons, in the Panamint Range, it was common, and males were heard singing at all times of day during the first half of April. A few were seen by Mr. Nelson on the east or Saline Valley side of the Inyo Mountains in the latter part of the same month. In the Argus Range it was seen in Shepherd Cañon in January and April, and at Lookout in the latter part of June. Dr. Merriam found it among the cliffs in the juniper belt on both sides of the Beaverdam Mountains, in southwestern Utah, May 10-11. He also found it breeding along the cliffs in the Lower Santa Clara Valley, Utah, May 11-15, and at the Upper Santa Clara crossing, May 16. Two were seen in the Pahroc Mountains, near Pahroc Spring, Nevada, May 22. In the northern part of the range, and in the Grapevine Mountains, Nevada, Mr. Nelson did not find it common during May and early June.

The following notes may refer wholly or in part to the present race of the cañon wren, or to the California coast form (*punctulatus*), as no specimens were preserved for identification. Several were seen along the South Fork of Kern River, and near Kernville, Calif., in early July. Dr. Merriam saw several in the Cañada de las Uvas, and heard it in the cañon of Peru Creek below Alamo ranch, in the Sierra Liebre, June 30. A few were seen at Three Rivers, Tulare County, in the western foothills of the Sierra, July 25-29, and September 17, and in the Sequoia National Park, at Halsted Meadows, August 6. Several were seen by Mr. Palmer at Michigan Bluff, Placer County, the last week in September.

Record of specimens collected of *Catherpes mexicanus conspersus*.

Collector's No.	Sex.	Locality.	Date.	Collector.	Remarks.
	♀	Panamint, Calif	Jan. 10, 1891	V. Bailey	
	♂	Panamint Mountains, Calif	Mar. 30, 1891	E. W. Nelson	Johnson Cañon.
145	♂	....do....	Mar. 28, 1891	....do....	Do.
156	♂	....do....	do	A. K. Fisher	Do.
157	♂	....do....	Apr. 13, 1891	....do....	Surprise Cañon.
165	♂	....do....	do	....do....	Do.
	♂	....do....	Apr. 18, 1891	....do....	Do.

Thryothorus bewickii spilurus. Vigors's Wren.

A specimen taken at San Bernardino, December 29, 1890, although not typical of this race, resembles it more closely than it does any other. The bird which Mr. Bailey saw commonly at Monterey was undoubtedly this subspecies. Mr. Nelson found a form of Bewick's wren which probably belongs to this race common at San Luis Obispo, the last of October, in the Tejon and Tamploa mountains about the same time, and along the route from San Simon to Carpenteria and Santa Paula during November and December.

Thryothorus bewickii bairdi. Baird's Wren.

The white-throated wren was more or less common in various places visited by the expedition. One was seen among the tree yuccas at Hesperia, in the Mohave Desert, January 4. In Death Valley a specimen was secured at Furnace Creek January 31, and a few individuals were seen among the mesquite thickets at Bennett Wells, and between that place and Saratoga Springs, about the same time. A few were seen at Resting Springs in the Amargosa Desert, in February.

In the Panamint Mountains it was seen in Johnson Cañon, early in April; by Dr. Merriam in Emigrant Cañon, April 14–15; on the north side of Telescope Peak, April 17–19, and by Mr. Nelson in Surprise Cañon, in January. In the Argus Range a few were seen in Shepherd Cañon in January, and a specimen was secured at Maturango Spring May 13. In the Coso Mountains a family in which the young were full grown and able to fly was seen in one of the cañons, May 23. Dr. Merriam saw many on the summit of the White Mountains, between Deep Spring and Owens valleys, where young were following their parents about among the piñon and juniper, June 9. Mr. Nelson found it common at Lone Pine in December, 1890, and two or three were seen in Walker Pass, July 2–3. The species was common along the South Fork of Kern River to Kernville, July 3–13, and Mr. Palmer saw one in Kings River Cañon in August. Mr. Stephens saw it at the Queen mine in the White Mountains, Nevada, July 11–16.

In Nevada, several were seen at Ash Meadows, Pahrump and Vegas valleys, and in the Grapevine Mountains, in March. In the Santa Clara Valley, Utah, one was shot and several others seen, May 11–16, and an old nest was found in a hole in a cottonwood, about 3 feet above the ground.

"Troglodytes hiemalis pacificus"
Queen Charlotte Isd.   Nov. 24, 1893.   See Auk, XI, 1894, April, p.18

"Several written names have now come — the simplest being the record at Surf Inlet..." Field Mus. 1894

Record of specimens collected of *Thryothorus bewickii bairdi*.

Collector's No.	Sex.	Locality.	Date.	Collector.	Remarks.
12	♀	San Bernardino, Calif.	Dec. 20, 1890	A. K. Fisher	Resembling closely *spilurus*.
94	♂	Death Valley, Calif.	Jan. 31, 1891	...do	Furnace Creek.
236	♂	Argus Range, Calif.	May 13, 1891	...do	Maturango Spring.
21	♂	Resting Springs, Calif.	Feb. 17, 1891	F. Stephens	
	♂	White Mountains, Calif.	June 9, 1891	V. Bailey	
	♀ juv.	...do	...do	...do	
	♂	Santa Clara, Utah	May 11, 1891	C. Hart Merriam	

Troglodytes aëdon aztecus. Western House Wren.

The western house wren was not seen in many localities, though when found it was not an uncommon species. A few were seen at Ash Meadows, Nev., about March 20. Specimens taken at San Bernardino, Calif., in the latter part of December, 1890, were intermediate between this race and Parkman's wren of the northwest coast region. In the Panamint Mountains it was first observed in Johnson Cañon, April 12, in Suprise Cañon a little later, and in Emigrant Cañon April 14-15. A few were seen in an alfalfa field at Grapevine Spring, on the western slope of the Grapevine Mountains, the first week in April, and in Shepherd Cañon, in the Argus Range, the last week of the month. Mr. Stephens found it rather common at Searl's garden, near the south end of the same range, April 23-26; at Bishop Creek, in Owens Valley, August 4-10, and among the brush on the side of Reche Cañon, September 22-24. Several were seen along the South Fork of Kern River, July 3-10, and among the oaks above Walker Basin, July 14. Mr. Palmer found the house wren abundant at Old Fort Tejon early in July, and Mr. Nelson saw several in the Cañada de las Uvas and along San Emigdio Creek about the middle of October. In the High Sierra, Mr. Nelson saw it at the head of Owens River, and on the west slope down into the Yosemite Valley. It was common in the Sequoia National Park during the first week in August; at Horse Corral Meadows, August 9-13; near timber line in Round Valley, 12 miles south of Mount Whitney, August 28; Mineral King, September 9-10; and at Three Rivers, in the western foothills of the Sierra, September 14.

Record of specimens collected of *Troglodytes aëdon aztecus*.

Collector's No.	Sex.	Locality.	Date.	Collector.	Remarks.
3	♂	San Bernardino, Calif.	Dec. 23, 1890	A. K. Fisher	Inclining toward *parkmanii*.
4	♀	...do	...do	...do	Do.
	♂	Panamint Mountains, Calif.	Apr. 11, 1891	E. W. Nelson	Johnson Cañon.
	♂	Kern River, Calif.	July 4, 1891	V. Bailey	South Fork.
	♂	Sierra Nevada, Calif.	July 30, 1891	E. W. Nelson	San Joaquin River.
139	♂ im	...do	July 22, 1891	F. Stephens	
155	♀ im	...do	Aug. 21, 1891	...do	Olancha Peak.
424	♀	...do	Aug. 27, 1891	A. K. Fisher	Round Valley, 12 miles south Mount Whitney.

Cistothorus palustris paludicola. Tule Wren.

The long-billed marsh wren was common in a number of places where tules and other rank vegetation occurred along the streams, lakes, or marshes. In Death Valley a few were seen at Furnace Creek and Bennett Wells, and a considerable number at Saratoga Springs during the latter part of January. Dr. Merriam found it common at the latter place among the reeds April 26. In Owens Valley Mr. Nelson found it at Keeler and Lone Pine in December, 1890, and Mr. Stephens reported it common at Little Owens Lake May 6–11. In Nevada it was common in Pahrump, Vegas, and Oasis valleys, and not uncommon at Ash Meadows in March. Dr. Merriam also found it common in the valley of the Muddy May 6, in Pahranagat Valley May 23, breeding in the tules, and Mr. Stephens saw several at Grapevine spring April 1–4.

Record of specimens collected of Cistothorus palustris paludicola.

Collector's No.	Sex.	Locality.	Date.	Collector.	Remarks.
93	♂	Death Valley, Calif.	Jan. 31, 1891	A. K. Fisher	Furnace Creek.
132	♀	Ash Meadows, Nev.	Mch. 18, 1891	do	

Certhia familiaris occidentalis. California Creeper.

The tree creeper was seen nowhere except in the High Sierra. Mr. Palmer and the writer saw it at the deserted Kaweah sawmill in the Sequoia National Park, and at other places in the same general region, the first week in August, and at Horse Corral Meadows a week later. Mr. Nelson found it at the head of Owens River and in the Yosemite Valley, and Mr. Dutcher at Big Cottonwood Meadows. The writer saw it at the latter place and also at Whitney Meadows and Soda Springs about the 1st of September. Mr. Nelson observed a few at Mount Piños in October.

Sitta carolinensis aculeata. Slender-billed Nuthatch.

In California the slender-billed nuthatch was seen among the pines on several of the mountain ranges and in the oaks west of the Sierra Nevada. In the Panamint Mountains it was not uncommon in Johnson and Surprise cañons among the piñons, where a pair was seen hunting for a nesting site April 20. Dr. Merriam saw several among the junipers on the north side of Telescope Peak April 17–19, and Mr. Bailey and the writer heard and saw it near the same place June 23–24. A pair was seen among the piñons above Maturango Spring May 13; Mr. Nelson found it at the head of Owens River, and on the western slope opposite, in July and August; and Mr. Stephens heard it near Queen station, Nev., July 11–16. Dr. Merriam saw one among the live oaks between Havilah and Walker Basin, June 24, one in Tehachapi Pass June 25, and Mr. Palmer reported the species as common at Old

Fort Tejon the first week in July. The writer found it rather common in the Sequoia National Park during the first week in August, at Horse Corral Meadows August 9–13, in Kings River Cañon August 13–16, and in Round Valley, 12 miles south of Mount Whitney, and Whitney Meadows the last of the month. At Three Rivers, in the western foothills of the Sierra, it was common among the oaks July 25–30; Mr. Bailey saw it along the Kaweah River up to timber line in August; Mr. Dutcher found it a common summer resident at Big Cottonwood Meadows, and Mr. Stephens reported it as rather common at Menache Meadows May 24–26. Mr. Nelson saw it from the Cañada de las Uvas to the head of San Emigdio Cañon the last of October, and in the mountains near San Simeon in November.

Record of specimens collected of Sitta carolinensis aculeata.

Collector's No.	Sex.	Locality.	Date.	Collector.	Remarks.
352	♂	Panamint Mountains, Calif.	June 25, 1891	A. K. Fisher	Telescope Peak.
427	♀	Sierra Nevada, Calif.	Aug. 27, 1891	...do	Round Valley, 12 miles south Mount Whitney.
20	♂	......do......	July 30, 1891	B. H. Dutcher	Big Cottonwood Meadows.

Sitta canadensis. Red-bellied Nuthatch.

The red-bellied nuthatch was not seen in the mountain ranges east of the Sierra Nevada in California. It was common in the Sequoia National Park and Horse Corral Meadows, where it was often heard or seen during the first half of August. Mr. Nelson saw a few on the western slope of the mountains opposite the head of Owens River, and the writer found it common among the flocks of migrants in Round Valley, 12 miles south of Mount Whitney, August 27–28, and at timber line above Mineral King September 9–11. On the coast Mr. Bailey reported the red-bellied nuthatch as common at Monterey September 28 to October 9.

Record of specimens collected of Sitta canadensis.

Collector's No.	Sex.	Locality.	Date.	Collector.	Remarks.
406	♀	Sierra Nevada, Calif.	Aug. 4, 1891	A. K. Fisher	Sequoia National Park.
431	♀	......do......	Aug. 28, 1891	...do	Round Valley, 12 miles south Mount Whitney.

Sitta pygmæa. Pygmy Nuthatch.

The only locality east of the Sierra Nevada where this nuthatch was met with was the Charleston Mountains, Nevada, where Mr. Palmer and Mr. Nelson found it common in February high up among the fox-tail pine (*Pinus aristata*). Mr. Stephens found it not uncommon nearly up to timber line at Menache Meadows, Calif., May 24-26, and a few at Bishop Creek August 4-10. Mr. Palmer reported it common among the pines at the summit of Frazier Mountain July 9; near the summit of Tejon Pass July 12; and Mr. Dutcher saw it frequently at Big Cottonwood Meadows during the summer. The pygmy nuthatch was not uncommon among the pines on the ridge above Walker Basin July 14, among the sequoias on the Kaweah River the first of August, at the Sequoia National Park about the same date, and at Big Cottonwood Meadows and Round Valley the last of the month.

Record of specimens collected of Sitta pygmæa.

Collector's No.	Sex.	Locality.	Date.	Collector.	Remarks.
10	♂	Sierra Nevada, Calif	July 1, 1891	B. H. Dutcher	Big Cottonwood Meadows.
32	♂	......do......	Aug. 11, 1891	....do......	Do.
35		......do......	Aug. 24, 1891	....do......	Do.
152	♀	......do......	Aug. 9, 1891	F. Stephens	Bishop Creek.
391	♀ im.	Walker Basin, Calif	July 14, 1891	A. K. Fisher	
425	♂	Sierra Nevada, Calif	Aug. 27, 1891	....do......	Round Valley, 12 miles south of Mount Whitney.
426	♂	......do......	...do......	....do......	Do.

Parus inornatus. Plain Titmouse.

The plain titmouse was first met with in the Sierra Nevada in California. It was not uncommon on the western slope of Walker Pass, where a specimen was taken July 3, and the birds seen elsewhere in the Sierra Nevada may probably be correctly referred to this species. It was common along the valley of the Kern July 3-13; in Walker Basin, July 13-16; and at Three Rivers in the western foothills of the Sierra, July 25-30, and September 13-15. Dr. Merriam saw the species in the Tejon Mountains, where it was common in the Cañada de las Uvas, June 28-29, and Mr. Nelson saw it at Mount Piños the last of October, in the hills along the route from La Panza to San Luis Obispo, and sparingly from the sea to the summit of the hills between San Simeon and Carpenteria, in November and December.

A specimen taken by the writer in Cajon Pass January 2, although not typical *inornatus*, was nearer it than *griseus*.

Record of specimens collected of Parus inornatus.

Collector's No.	Sex.	Locality.	Date.	Collector.	Remarks.
25	♂	Cajon Pass, Calif	Jan. 2, 1892	A. K. Fisher	Not typical.
367	♀ im.	Walker Pass, Calif	July 3, 1891	....do......	Western slope.

Parus inornatus griseus. Gray Titmouse.

The gray titmouse was seen in most of the desert ranges. In the Charleston Mountains, Nevada, it was common among the junipers in

March. In the Panamint Mountains, California, it was seen in Johnson and Surprise cañons among the piñons and junipers in April, and Dr. Merriam found it common north of Telescope Peak, where a female, containing eggs nearly ready to be deposited, was killed, April 17-19. The writer saw a few at the same place June 22. Mr. Nelson noted it sparingly among the piñons on the Panamint, Grapevine, Inyo, and White mountains during the breeding season. Along the eastern slope of the Sierra Nevada a few were seen at the head of Owens River, and at Benton, in July.

Record of specimens collected of Parus inornatus griseus.

Collector's No.	Sex.	Locality.	Date.	Collector.	Remarks.
47	♀	Panamint Mountains, Calif.	Apr. 18, 1891	F. Stephens	Johnson Cañon.
145	♂	do	Mar. 28, 1891	A. K. Fisher	Do.
146	♀	do	do	do	Surprise Cañon.
168	♂	do	Apr. 19, 1891	do	
	♂	Charleston Mountains, Nev	Mar. 7, 1891	V. Bailey	

Parus gambeli. Mountain Chickadee.

The mountain chickadee was seen on all the mountains which support a growth of pines. In Nevada Mr. Palmer reported it common about the camp in the Charleston Mountains in February, and Mr. Stephens found a few in the Grapevine Mountains in March. Dr. Merriam found it breeding on Mount Magruder, high up among the nut pines, June 5-11, and Mr. Stephens saw several at the Queen mine in the White Mountains, July 11-16.

In the Panamint Mountains, California, it was tolerably common in Johnson and Surprise cañons in April. Dr. Merriam found it common near Telescope Peak about the middle of the month, though Mr. Nelson reported it as apparently rare among the piñons in the northern end of the range as well as in the Grapevine Mountains in June. At the 'charcoal kilns' near the head of Wild Rose Cañon, the writer noted it as quite common and found a nest with young June 24.

It was not uncommon in the Argus Range, where a nest containing eight fresh eggs was found in a piñon on the ridge above Maturango Spring, May 14. The nest, which was composed of fine grass and hair, was placed in an eroded cavity behind the end of one of the lower limbs which had been partially torn and twisted from the trunk by heavy snow or violent wind. It was perfectly concealed and would never have been discovered had the bird remained quiet when the writer accidentally struck the drooping branch. Mr. Nelson reported it as breeding sparingly from the lower edge of the piñons up to the summit in the Inyo Mountains and to timber line in the White Mountains. This chickadee was common at the head of Owens River, and Mr. Stephens noted it as rather common at Independence Creek, June 18-23; at Menache Meadows, May 24-26; several at Bishop Creek, August 4-10. Mr.

Palmer found it common on Frazier Mountain July 9, sparingly at Tejon Pass, July 12; and Mr. Nelson reported it common on Mount Piños the last of October. In the High Sierra it was common in the Sequoia National Park the first week in August; at Horse Corral Meadows, August 9–13; at Round Valley, 12 miles south of Mount Whitney, August 27–28; Big Cottonwood Meadows during the summer; and at Whitney Meadows and Mineral King the last of August and first of September. Mr. Palmer saw one at an altitude of 3,900 meters (13,000 feet) near the head waters of the Kern River, September 1.

Record of specimens collected of Parus gambeli.

Collector's No.	Sex.	Locality.	Date.	Collector.	Remarks.
40	♂	Grapevine Mountains, Nev.	Mar. 24, 1891	F. Stephens	Johnson Cañon.
142	♂	Panamint Mountains, Calif.	Mar. 28, 1891	A. K. Fisher	Do.
151		do	April 6, 1891	do	Do.
152	♂	do	April 9, 1891	do	Do.
	♂	Argus Range, Calif	May 7, 1891	T. S. Palmer	Maturango Peak.
	♂	White Mountains, Calif	July 12, 1891	E. W. Nelson	

Parus rufescens neglectus. California Chickadee.

Mr. Bailey found the California chickadee common at Boulder Creek, California (north of Monterey Bay), where he secured a specimen October 14, 1891.

Chamæa fasciata henshawi. Pallid Wren-Tit.

This interesting little bird was first met with by Mr. Bailey and the writer at Kernville, Calif., on July 11, where specimens were secured. It was common there, as it was the following week in Walker Basin. Mr. Nelson saw a few in the foothills between the Merced and San Joaquin rivers; Mr. Palmer heard a number among the chamisal in the San Francisquito Pass, July 1, and Mr. Stephens heard several in Reche Cañon, near San Bernardino, September 22–24. Mr. Bailey reported it common along the Kaweah River in the thick chapparal below the pines. Mr. Nelson found the ground-tit common in the thickets on the sand dunes along the coast between San Simeon and Carpenteria, and on the bushy hillsides between the latter place and Santa Paula, in November and December. Dr. Merriam reported it as a common breeder in the coast ranges of San Diego County, where he found it in March and again in July.

Record of specimens collected of Chamæa fasciata henshawi.

Collector's No.	Sex.	Locality.	Date.	Collector.	Remarks.
385	♂	Kernville, Calif	July 11, 1891	A. K. Fisher	
	♀	do	do	V. Bailey	
167	♂	San Bernardino, Calif	Sept. 23, 1891	F. Stephens	Reche Cañon.
		Morro, Calif	Nov. 8, 1891	E. W. Nelson	

Psaltriparus minimus californicus. California Bush-Tit.

The California bush-tit is common in the coast region, on the western slope of the Sierra Nevada, and sparingly on the eastern slope of the same range. Mr. Stephens found it tolerably common in the lower part of the cañon at Independence Creek, where a nest containing young was found, June 16-23; and saw a small flock at Bishop Creek, August 4-10. Individuals were seen on the western slope of Walker Pass, July 2-3, and Dr. Merriam found it common in the chaparral from Kernville to Havilah, and thence to Walker Basin and Caliente, June 23-24, and in the Cañada de las Uvas, June 28-29. It was common at Three Rivers in the western foothills, in flocks of 25 or more, July 25-30, and Mr. Bailey reported it common along the Kaweah River up to the conifers, about the same time. The latter observer found a species of bush-tit common at Monterey, the first of October; Mr. Stephens saw two flocks at Reche Cañon, September 22-24; and Dr. Merriam noticed it near the coast in San Diego County in July. Mr. Nelson reported it common along the coast in small flocks in thickets and on bushy hillsides, from San Simeon to Carpenteria, in November and December.

Record of specimens collected of Psaltriparus minimus californicus.

Collector's No.	Sex.	Locality.	Date.	Collector.	Remarks.
76	♀	Owens Valley, Calif.	June 8, 1891	F. Stephens	Olancha.
369		Walker Pass, Calif.	July 3, 1891	A. K. Fisher	Western Slope.

Psaltriparus plumbeus. Lead-colored Bush-Tit.

The lead-colored bush-tit is common in a number of the desert ranges visited. In Nevada Mr. Stephens found it rather common in the Grapevine Mountains in March, and saw one flock at the Queen mine in the White Mountains in July. Dr. Merriam found it high up on Mount Magruder in the nut pines, June 5-9, among the junipers in the Juniper Mountains May 19, and common in the Beaverdam Mountains, Utah, May 11. A few were seen by Mr. Stephens at Twelve Mile Spring, near Resting Springs, Calif., in February. In the Panamint Mountains it was observed daily in Johnson and Surprise Cañons in April, in small flocks on the north side of Telescope Peak April 17-19, and among the sage in the northern part of the range, as well as in the Grapevine Mountains May 4 to June 15. Mr. Nelson found a few among the piñons near Waucoba Peak in the Inyo Mountains the last of June, and a few on the eastern slope of the White Mountains among the same kind of trees in July.

Record of specimens collected of Psaltriparus plumbeus.

Collector's No.	Sex.	Locality.	Date.	Collector.	Remarks.
38	♂	Juniper Mountains, Nev	May 19, 1891	C. Hart Merriam	
	♀	Mount Magruder, Nev	June 5, 1891	V. Bailey	
21	♀	Grapevine Mountains, Nev	Mar. 24, 1891	F. Stephens	
25	♀	Resting Springs, Calif	Feb. 21, 1891	do	
		do	do	do	
144	♀	Panamint Mountains, Calif	Mar. 28, 1891	A. K. Fisher	Johnson Cañon.
153		do	Apr. 9, 1891	do	Do.
169		do	Apr. 19, 1891	do	Surprise Cañon.
131	♀ im.	Owens Valley, Nev	July 14, 1891	F. Stephens	Queen station.

Auriparus flaviceps. Yellow-headed Tit.

The verdin is a characteristic bird of a large part of the Lower Sonoran zone. The most western locality at which it was observed by the expedition was Resting Springs, near the Amargosa River, Calif., where a male was shot by Mr. Stephens February 13, 1891. Here the yellow-headed tit was common in February, and it was seen every day among the mesquit thickets, and its nests were frequently found. As is the case with several other members of the family, the old nests, after being relined with feathers and hair, are used for winter homes. East of this point it was found wherever suitable thickets exist, all the way to Utah. Many nests were found in bushes of *Pluchea borealis* at the Great Bend of the Colorado, Nev., by Dr. Merriam. These nests were usually about five feet above the ground, and, with the exception of one containing three eggs nearly ready to hatch, were still empty. Other nests were observed along the Virgin River and the lower part of the Muddy May 7-10, and at Beaverdam Creek, Ariz., May 9-10; and a single nest was discovered near the junction of the Santa Clara with the Virgin in southwestern Utah May 14.

Regulus calendula. Ruby-crowned Kinglet.

The ruby-crowned kinglet was a common migrant or winter resident in the valleys visited, and occurred sparingly as a summer resident in the higher mountains. In Nevada a few were seen at Ash Meadows in March; in Pahrump Valley Mr. Nelson found it common among the willows at the ranch in February; Mr. Stephens observed it in full song in Oasis Valley in March; not uncommon in the Grapevine Mountains in the same month, and Dr. Merriam shot one at Mountain Spring, in the Charleston Mountains, April 30.

At San Bernardino, Calif., it was numerous in the bushes along the streams December 28-29, 1890, and on the slopes in Cajon Pass January 2. A few were seen at Furnace Creek, Death Valley, about the first of February and again April 9-12. In the Panamint Mountains this kinglet was common in Johnson and Surprise cañons, and tolerably so in Emigrant Cañon in April. It was common at Hot Springs, in Panamint Valley, April 20-25, and was observed in Shepherd Cañon, in the Argus Range, later in the month. Mr. Nelson saw a few at the heads of streams on the eastern slope of the White Mountains, and reported it common at the head of Owens River and on the western slope of the Sierra Nevada. It was common at timber line at Round Valley, 12 miles south of Mount Whitney, August 28; in the San Joaquin Valley in October; and along the route from San Simeon to Carpenteria and Santa Paula in November and December.

Regulus satrapa olivaceus. Western Golden-crowned Kinglet.

The only record of this kinglet made by the expedition was of one seen by Mr. Nelson near San Luis Obispo about the first of November. Mr. Belding reports it as rare at Crocker's, 21 miles northwest of the Yosemite Valley.

Polioptila cærulea obscura. Western Gnatcatcher

Blue-gray gnatcatchers were common in a number of scattered localities. At San Bernardino, a small flock associated with other birds was seen December 28, and again on the following day. Several were seen at Daggett, January 8-10, and one was secured at Furnace Creek, Death Valley, January 24. The species was common in the Panamint Mountains, in both Johnson and Surprise cañons, in April, and at Hot Springs in Panamint Valley, among the mesquite, April 20-25. Mr. Nelson found it breeding in both the Panamint and Grapevine mountains. At Willow Creek, in the former range, he found a nest containing five eggs, May 19, and another containing three eggs, May 24. Both nests were placed within 3 feet of the ground, and were neat, compactly built structures, with deep cup-shaped depressions, more or less contracted at the rims. A few individuals were seen in the Argus Range, at Maturango Spring, the first half of May, and in the Coso Mountains during the latter part of the same month. Mr. Nelson saw a single bird in a mesquite clump in Saline Valley, a few in the sage near Waucoba Peak, in the Inyo Range, the last of June, and in the White Mountains in July. He saw a few in the western foothills of the Sierra Nevada in August, and on the east slope Mr. Stephens found it uncommon in the lower part of the cañon of Independence Creek, in June. One was seen on the western slope of Walker Pass, July 3; it was common in the hills above Walker Basin, July 14; along the Kaweah, below the conifers, in August and September; and Mr. Palmer saw one in Kings River Cañon, August 13. On Mount Magruder, Nevada, Dr. Merriam shot a pair June 7, and reported the species as tolerably common in the lower part of the piñons. He found it breeding commonly in the Santa Clara Valley, Utah, May 11-15, and in the junipers on the Beaverdam Mountains, May 10-11. Mr. Nelson found it common in the thickets along the coast from Morro, Calif., to Carpenteria, November 4 to December 18, and rather common from Carpenteria to Santa Paula, the last of the year.

Record of specimens collected of Polioptila cærulea obscura.

Collector's No.	Sex.	Locality.	Date.	Collector.	Remarks.
9	♂	San Bernardino, Calif	Dec. 28, 1890	A. K. Fisher	
10	♂	....do......	....do......	....do......	
11	....	....do......	Dec. 29, 1890	....do......	
50	♂	Daggett, Calif	Jan. 10, 1891	....do......	Mohave Desert.
70	....	Death Valley, Calif	Jan. 24, 1891	....do......	Furnace Creek.
164	♂	Panamint Valley, Calif	Apr. 16, 1891	....do......	Hot Springs.
214	♂	Argus Range, Calif	May 8, 1891	....do......	Maturango Spring.
	♂	Panamint Valley, Calif	Apr. 22, 1891	E. W. Nelson	Hot Springs.
	♀	Mission Santa Ynez, Calif	Dec. 6, 1891	....do......	
	♂	St. George, Utah	May 16, 1891	V. Bailey	

Polioptila plumbea. Plumbeous Gnatcatcher.

This gnatcatcher was common at Resting Springs, near the Amargosa River, California, in February, where a number of specimens were secured. In Vegas Valley, Nevada, Mr. Nelson and Mr. Bailey saw several and secured one, March 13. At Bunkerville, Nev., Mr. Bailey secured an adult male, May 9. The species may have been seen in other places, but was not distinguished from the blue-gray gnatcatcher. In March, 1889, Mr. Bailey found it common at Fort Mohave, Ariz.

Record of specimens collected of Polioptila plumbea.

Collector's No.	Sex.	Locality.	Date.	Collector.	Remarks.
103	♀	Resting Springs, Calif	Feb. 8, 1891	A. K. Fisher	
	♀	....do......	Feb. 12, 1891	V. Bailey	
	♀	....do......	....do......	....do......	
	♀	Vegas Valley, Nev	Mar. 13, 1891	....do......	
	♂	Bunkerville, Nev	May 9, 1891	....do......	

Polioptila californica. Black-tailed Gnatcatcher.

The only place where the Californian gnatcatcher was observed was Reche Cañon, near San Bernardino, where Mr. Stephens found it common, September 22-24.

Myadestes townsendii. Townsend's Solitaire.

Townsend's solitaire was found nowhere common by the expedition. In Cajon Pass, California, several were observed and two secured, January 2. One was shot at Lone Pine, in Owens Valley, in December, 1890, and others were seen at Hot Springs, Panamint Valley, in January.

In the Panamint Mountains, a few were seen in Johnson and Surprise cañons, in April. Mr. Nelson found a few among the piñons about the head of Willow Creek, the 1st of May, and the writer saw a family in Death Valley Cañon, June 22. In the Sierra Nevada, Mr. Nelson found it sparingly on the western slope opposite the head of Owens River; Mr. Stephens secured the young at Bishop Creek, the 1st of August; Mr. Bailey saw one among the sequoias and another among the *Pinus monticola* on the Kaweah River; a few were seen in the Giant forest, August 3; and several at Trout Meadows, September 7. Mr. Belding found a nest and four eggs, June 4, near Crocker's, on the Big Oak Flat and Yosemite Valley stage road. It was placed in a nearly perpendicular bank of a gold mine, within a short distance of the hoisting works, which were in constant use.

In Nevada Townsend's solitaire was not uncommon among the cedars on the Charleston Mountains in March, and a specimen was secured in Oasis Valley, March 15, the only one seen there.

Record of specimens collected of Myadestes townsendii.

Collector's No.	Sex.	Locality.	Date.	Collector.	Remarks.
23	♀	Cajon Pass, Calif	Jan. 2, 1891	A. K. Fisher	
24	♀	...do...	...do...	...do...	
148	♂	Panamint Mountains, Calif	Mar. 31, 1891	...do...	Johnson Cañon.
32	♂	Oasis Valley, Nev	Mar. 15, 1891	F. Stephens	
149	♂ im.	Sierra Nevada, Calif	Aug. 8, 1891	...do...	Bishop Creek; altitude, 9,000 feet.

Turdus ustulatus. Russet-backed Thrush.

A female russet-backed thrush was shot by the writer at Maturango Springs, California, in the Argus Range, May 15, 1891, the only one observed there, and Mr. Stephens saw one at Olancha, in Owens Valley, about the same time.

Turdus ustulatus swainsonii. Olive-backed Thrush.

Mr. Belding reported this thrush as common in the Yosemite Valley, California, in June, and Mr. Nelson secured a female on the northern end of the Panamint Mountains, May 18.

Turdus aonalaschkæ. Dwarf Hermit Thrush.

The dwarf thrush was seen only during migration. Several were seen in Johnson Cañon, in the Panamint Range, California, where a specimen was secured March 28. In the Argus Range, it was not uncommon in Shepherd Cañon the last week in April, and at Maturango Spring one was secured May 8. Mr. Dutcher shot another at Big Cottonwood Meadows September 11, which was probably a migrant, as the summer resident was *auduboni*, or at least what the committee on nomenclature of the American Ornithologists' Union consider Audubon's thrush.

Mr. Bailey found the dwarf thrush common at Monterey the first of October, and Mr. Nelson observed it commonly in the vicinity of San Luis Obispo the last of the month, and along the route from San Simeon to Carpenteria and Santa Paula in November and December.

Record of specimens collected of Turdus aonalaschkæ.

Collector's No.	Sex.	Locality.	Date.	Collector.	Remarks.
26	♂	Panamint Mountains, Calif.	Mar. 28, 1891	E. W. Nelson	Johnson Cañon.
		Sierra Nevada, Calif.	Sept. 11, 1891	B. H. Dutcher	Big Cottonwood Meadows.
	♀ ?	Monterey, Calif.	Oct. 6, 1891	V. Bailey	
	♂	Morro, Calif.	Nov. 10, 1891	E. W. Nelson	
	♀	....do........	....do.......	....do.......	

Turdus aonalaschkæ auduboni. Audubon's Hermit Thrush.

A race of the dwarf thrush, named *Turdus sequoiensis* by Mr. Belding, but which the committee on nomenclature of the American Ornithologists' Union decided to be not different from *auduboni* of the Rocky Mountain region, is a summer resident in the Sierra Nevada, and probably in some of the desert ranges, though this is not certain, as specimens were not taken in the latter in summer. This applies to the records of individuals seen at Willow Creek in the Panamint Mountains, during the latter part of May, and on the east side of Waucoba Peak, in the Inyo Mountains, in June. In the Sierra Nevada Mr. Dutcher found the species common during the summer at Big Cottonwood Meadows, and Mr. Nelson reported it as abundant at the head of Owens River and on the San Joaquin River. Mr. Stephens heard a thrush above the Queen mine in the White Mountains, Nevada, July 11–16; saw the species at Bishop Creek August 4–10, and about the lakes on Independence Creek June 18–23. Mr. Belding found it in the Yosemite Valley in June.

Record of specimens collected of Turdus aonalaschkæ auduboni.

Collector's No.	Sex.	Locality.	Date.	Collector.	Remarks.
9		Sierra Nevada, Calif.	June 23, 1891	B. H. Dutcher	Big Cottonwood Meadows.
16	♂	....do........	July 11, 1891	....do........	
	♀	White Mountains, Calif.	July 10, 1891	E. W. Nelson	
	♂	Sierra Nevada, Calif.	July 23, 1891	....do........	

Merula migratoria propinqua. Western Robin.

The robin is a rather rare bird in the desert regions, even during migration and in winter. In Nevada several were seen at Ash Meadows in March. Mr. Palmer found it rather common from the valley up to the piñons on the west side of the Charleston Mountains in February, and Mr. Nelson saw it about the ranches in Pahrump and Vegas valleys, and in Vegas Wash, in March. Dr. Merriam saw it on Mount Magruder June 8, and in Utah, at Mountain Meadows, May 17. In California a few were seen at Furnace Creek, Death Valley, the latter part of January, and again on April 10. Several were observed at Resting Springs, in the Amargosa Desert, the first half of February. A few robins were seen about a spring in Johnson Cañon, in the Panamint

Range, in April. Dr. Merriam saw several in the junipers in the same mountains April 16–19, and Mr. Nelson a few at the head of Willow Creek early in May, after which time none were seen. Several were seeen in the Argus Range, above Maturango Spring, the first half of May. Mr. Nelson found it in the Inyo Mountains among *Pinus flexilis* and *P. aristata*, and in the White Mountains from the piñons up to 10,000 feet. In the Sierra Nevada robins were common in many places. Mr. Nelson found them common at the head of Owens River, on the east slope, and in the Yosemite Valley, on the west slope of the Sierra, in July and August. Mr. Stephens found them common at Independence Creek, where a nest and four young was found at the edge of the creek June 18–23; at Bishop Creek, where they were feeding on a red berry locally known as buffalo berry, August 4–10, and at Menache Meadow, nearly to timber line, May 24–26. They were common also at Big Cottonwood and Whitney meadows; among the pines above Walker Basin July 14, in the Sequoia National Park, among the pines and firs, and in the meadows, the first week in August; at Horse Corral Meadows, August 9–13; in Kings River Cañon, August 13–16, and near Mineral King September 9–12. In the western foothills of the Sierra they were seen as early as July 30 at Three Rivers, and Mr. Nelson found a few in the San Joaquin Valley October 5–27; reported them as common about San Luis Obispo October 28 to November 4, and found them generally distributed along the route from San Simeon to Carpenteria and Santa Paula in November and December.

Record of specimens collected of Merula migratoria propinqua.

Collector's No.	Sex.	Locality.	Date.	Collector.	Remarks.
85	♂	Death Valley, Calif.	Jan. 29, 1891	A. K. Fisher	Furnace Creek.
108	♂	Resting Springs, Calif.	Feb. 11, 1891	....do........	
	♂	Panamint Mountains, Calif.	Mar. 28, 1891	E. W. Nelson	Johnson Cañon.
107	♀ juv.	Owens Valley, Calif.	June 19, 1891	F. Stephens	Independence Creek

Hesperocichla nævia. Varied Thrush.

Mr. Bailey saw several varied thrushes and secured a specimen at Monterey, Calif., the first week in October; he also found it common at Boulder Creek, Santa Cruz County, and at Auburn, Placer County, during the latter part of the month. Mr. Nelson observed a few in the lowlands about San Simeon, and found it common from Santa Maria south to Carpenteria and Santa Paula, where it was particularly numerous among the trees along the streams and in the cañon.

Record of specimens collected of Hesperocichla nævia.

Collector's No.	Sex.	Locality.	Date.	Collector.	Remarks.
	♀	Monterey, Calif.	Oct. 5, 1891	V. Bailey	
	♂	Boulder Creek, Calif.	Oct. 12, 1891	....do........	

Sialia mexicana. Western Bluebird.

The western bluebird was common in a number of places. At San Bernardino a flock of twenty or more was seen December 29, 1890; in Cajon Pass, March 30; in the cottonwoods bordering the Mohave River at Victor, the same day, and at Granite Wells January 13. Mr. Nelson found the species common near Hot Springs, in Panamint Valley, California, in January, and a few at Pahrump and Vegas ranches in Nevada, in February and March. Dr. Merriam saw several small flocks on the north side of Telescope Peak, in the Panamint Mountains, April 17–19, and Mr. Nelson found it on the western slope of the Sierra Nevada in August. It was very common along the South Fork of the Kern River, July 3–10; in Walker Basin, from the valley to the summit of the ridge, July 13–16, and in the Cañada de las Uvas, June 28–29. In the High Sierra it was not uncommon at Sequoia National Park during the first week of August; was common in Horse Corral Meadows and Kings River Cañon August 9–16, and was observed at Big Cottonwood Meadows and at the head of the Kaweah River later in the season. In the western foothills of the Sierra, at Three Rivers, it was common July 25–30 and September 12–16; and at Monterey, September 28–October 9. Mr. Nelson saw a few in various parts of the San Joaquin Valley in October, and found it common along the route from San Simeon to Carpenteria and Santa Paula in November and December.

Record of specimens collected of Sialia mexicana.

Collector's No.	Sex.	Locality.	Date.	Collector.	Remarks.
13	♀	San Bernardino, Calif	Dec. 29, 1890	A. K. Fisher	
14	♂	......do......	...do...	...do...	
15	♂	......do......	...do...	...do...	
	♂	Charleston Mountains, Nev	Feb. 13, 1891	E. W. Nelson	
370	♀ juv.	Kern River, Calif	July 4, 1891	A. K. Fisher	South Fork.
39	♂	Sierra Nevada, Calif	Sept. 14, 1891	B. H. Dutcher	Mount Whitney.

Sialia arctica. Mountain Bluebird.

The mountain bluebird is more or less common in the desert valleys during the winter, and breeds in the higher ranges among the pines.

At Granite Wells, in the Mohave Desert, a number were seen January 13–14. Unlike the western bluebird, this species was wary and difficult of approach. It is not evident what causes this shyness, unless, perhaps, contact with the Indian, that ruthless and inveterate enemy to animal life, who attacks every bird throughout the year, no matter how small or in what condition, killing the mother of a dependent brood with as much eagerness as a fattened buck in season.

In Death Valley a flock was seen at Mesquite Well, January 21. It was common at Bennett Wells and Saratoga Springs, and at Furnace Creek, associated with titlarks and savanna sparrows in the alfalfa fields, the last of January. Several were seen at Resting Springs, in the Amargosa Desert, in February. Dr. Merriam saw a pair at Mountain Meadows, Utah, May 17. In Nevada he found several in the juniper forest on the Juniper Mountains, May 18; on the Pahroc Mountains, May 21-22, and on Mount Magruder, June 4-8. In the latter locality this bluebird was breeding among the nut pines, where it was tolerably common. Several were seen at Ash Meadows, and among the cedars on the Charleston Mountains, in March, and in Pahrump Valley, near the ranch, in February. Mr. Stephens found it not common in the Grapevine Mountains in March, and Mr. Nelson saw a few pairs about the summit of the peak and among the piñons, where they were apparently breeding, June 10-11. In the Panamint Mountains, California, Dr. Merriam saw several pairs at the north base of Telescope Peak, April 17-19, and Mr. Bailey and the writer found a number among the pines (*Pinus aristata* and *P. flexilis*), near the summit of the same peak, June 23. It was not uncommon in the Argus Range above Maturango Spring during the first half of May, and a pair was seen on the summit of the Coso Mountains, May 23. Mr. Nelson found it not uncommon in the Inyo Range above the piñons in June; a few among the upper piñons in the White Mountains in July, and at the latter place Dr. Merriam saw a number of males June 9—the females evidently were sitting. In Owens Valley, according to Mr. Nelson, it was common in winter, and Mr. Stephens found it more or less common above this valley along the eastern slope of the Sierra Nevada up to timber line at Menache Meadows, May 24-26; at the lakes on Independence Creek, June 23; among the piñons at Benton, July 9-10, and at the lake on Bishop Creek, August 4-10. Mr. Nelson reported it generally distributed up to timber line at the head of Owens River the last of July, but nowhere common, and Mr. Stephens found it common at the Queen mine in the White Mountains, Nevada, July 11-16. Mr. Bailey saw a few on the western slope of Walker Pass, July 3, found it common at timber line near the head of the Kaweah River, in August, and at Whitney Meadows in September. Mr. Dutcher found it a common summer resident at Big Cottonwood Meadows and vicinity, and Mr. Nelson saw a few on the high ridge near San Luis Obispo, and in the mountains along the coast from San Simeon to Carpenteria in November and December.

Record of specimens collected of Sialia arctica.

Collector's No.	Sex.	Locality.	Date.	Collector.	Remarks.
50	♂	Granite Wells, Calif	Jan. 14, 1891	A. K. Fisher	
	♂	Death Valley, Calif	Jan. 20, 1891	E. W. Nelson	Bennett Wells.
87	♂	do	Jan. 30, 1891	A. K. Fisher	Furnace Creek.
88	♂	do	do	do	Do.
14	♂	Garlick Spring, Calif	Feb. 10, 1891	F. Stephens	
15	♀	do	do	do	
125	♂	Ash Meadows, Nev	Mar. 15, 1891	A. K. Fisher	
37	♀	Grapevine Mountains, Nev	Mar. 21, 1891	F. Stephens	
255	♂	Argus Range, Calif	May 13, 1891	A. K. Fisher	Maturango Spring.

LIST OF BIRDS OBSERVED IN DEATH VALLEY, CALIFORNIA.

1. *Colymbus nigricollis californicus.* Eared Grebe.
    A specimen was secured at Furnace Creek April 10.
2. *Anas boschas.* Mallard.
    One was secured at Furnace Creek in January.
3. *Anas americana.* Baldpate.
    The species was secured at Saratoga Springs and Furnace Creek in January.
4. *Anas carolinensis.* Green-winged Teal.
    Common at Furnace Creek and Saratoga Springs in January.
5. *Anas cyanoptera.* Cinnamon Teal.
    At Furnace Creek flocks were seen in March, and one female secured June 19.
6. *Spatula clypeata.* Shoveller.
    A small flock seen at Furnace Creek in January.
7. *Dafila acuta.* Pintail.
    Seen and secured at Saratoga Springs in February.
8. *Erismatura rubida.* Ruddy Duck.
    A small flock was seen at Furnace Creek March 22.
9. *Anser albifrons gambeli.* White-fronted Goose.
    One was seen with the following subspecies.
10. *Branta canadensis* (subspecies?)
    Four were seen at Furnace Creek in the latter part of March.
11. *Plegadis guarauna.* White-faced Glossy Ibis.
    The remains of one were seen at the ranch at Furnace Creek.
12. *Nycticorax nycticorax nævius.* Night Heron.
    An immature specimen was secured at Furnace Creek June 19.
13. *Rallus virginianus.* Virginia Rail.
    Common at Saratoga Springs in February.
14. *Fulica americana.* Coot.
    Common at Saratoga Springs in February and April.
15. *Phalaropus tricolor.* Wilson's Phalarope.
    One specimen was secured at Furnace Creek June 19.
16. *Gallinago delicata.* Wilson's Snipe.
    One seen at Furnace Creek April 11.
17. *Ægialitis vocifera.* Killdeer.
    Not uncommon; found at Furnace Creek in January, April, and June; breeds.
18. *Callipepla gambeli.* Gambel's Quail.
    Common at Furnace Creek ranch. Introduced.
19. *Zenaidura macroura.* Mourning Dove.
    Not uncommon; breeds.
20. *Cathartes aura.* Turkey Buzzard.
    Not uncommon; seen in March, April, and June.
21. *Circus hudsonius.* Marsh Hawk.
    One was secured at Furnace Creek in January.
22. *Accipiter velox.* Sharp-shinned Hawk.
    Seen at Furnace Creek and Bennett Wells in January and April.
23. *Accipiter cooperi.* Cooper's Hawk.
    Seen at Furnace Creek in January.
24. *Buteo borealis calurus.* Western Red tail.
    Seen at Furnace Creek and Bennett Wells in January, and at the latter place in June.
25. *Falco mexicanus.* Prairie Falcon.
    Seen at Furnace Creek in January and June.
26. *Falco columbarius.* Pigeon Hawk.
    Remains of one found at Furnace Creek.

27. *Falco sparverius deserticolus.* Desert Sparrow Hawk.
    Seen at Mesquite Wells, Bennett Wells, and Furnace Creek in January, March, and April.
28. *Pandion haliaëtus carolinensis.* Osprey.
    One was seen at Furnace Creek April 10.
29. *Speotyto cunicularia hypogæa.* Burrowing Owl.
    A pair was seen at Bennett Wells June 21.
30. *Geococcyx californianus.* Road-runner.
    Common resident.
31. *Coccyzus americanus occidentalis.* California Cuckoo.
    One secured at Furnace Creek June 20.
32. *Ceryle alcyon.* Kingfisher.
    One seen at Furnace Creek April 15.
33. *Colaptes cafer.* Red-shafted Flicker.
    One was seen at Furnace Creek, April 10.
34. *Phalænoptilus nuttalli.* Poor-will.
    Secured at Bennett Wells January 28, at Saratoga Springs February 4, and seen at Furnace Creek April 10.
35. *Chordeiles virginianus henryi.* Western Nighthawk.
    A specimen was secured at Furnace Creek June 19.
36. *Chordeiles texensis* Texas Nighthawk.
    Seen at Saratoga Springs April 26.
37. *Aëronautes melanoleucus.* White-throated Swift.
    Common at Furnace Creek in April and June.
38. *Calypte costæ.* Costa's Hummingbird.
    Seen at Furnace Creek April 12 and again June 19.
39. *Myiarchus cinerascens.* Ash-throated Flycatcher.
    A pair was seen in Furnace Creek Cañon June 21.
40. *Sayornis saya.* Say's Phœbe.
    Not uncommon resident.
41. *Sayornis nigricans.* Black Phœbe.
    It was seen at Furnace Creek April 12.
42. *Empidonax wrightii.* Wright's Flycatcher.
    A specimen was taken at Furnace Creek February 1.
43. *Corvus corax sinuatus.* Raven.
    Resident.
44. *Molothrus ater.* Cowbird.
    One was secured at Furnace Creek June 20.
45. *Xanthocephalus xanthocephalus.* Yellow-headed Blackbird.
    One was secured at Bennett Wells April 1.
46. *Agelaius phœniceus.* Red-winged Blackbird.
    A flock was seen at Furnace Creek the latter part of January.
47. *Sturnella magna neglecta.* Western Meadowlark.
    A not uncommon resident.
48. *Icterus bullocki.* Bullock's Oriole.
    One was observed at Furnace Creek about the middle of April.
49. *Scolecophagus cyanocephalus.* Brewer's Blackbird.
    A few were seen at Furnace Creek in January.
50. *Carpodacus mexicanus frontalis.* House Finch.
    Not uncommon resident.
51. *Ammodramus sandwichensis alaudinus.* Western Savanna Sparrow.
    Not uncommon at Furnace Creek in January and April.
52. *Zonotrichia leucophrys intermedia.* Intermediate Sparrow.
    Common at Furnace Creek in January and April.

53. *Spizella breweri.* Brewer's Sparrow.
    One was seen in Mesquite Valley April 13.
54. *Amphispiza bilineata.* Black-throated Sparrow.
    Seen on June 22 in the Panamint Mountains just above the valley.
55. *Amphispiza belli nevadensis.* Sage Sparrow.
    Common winter resident.
56. *Melospiza fasciata montana.* Mountain Song Sparrow.
    Common winter resident at Furnace Creek and Saratoga Springs.
57. *Guiraca cærulea eurhyncha.* Western Blue Grosbeak.
    One was secured at Furnace Creek, June 19.
58. *Passerina amœna.* Lazuli Bunting.
    A female was secured at Furnace Creek, June 19.
59. *Tachycineta bicolor.* Tree Swallow.
    Common at Furnace Creek in March and April.
60. *Tachycineta thalassina.* Violet Green Swallow.
    Observed at Furnace Creek and Saratoga Springs in April.
61. *Stelgidopteryx serripennis.* Rough-winged Swallow.
    A not uncommon summer resident.
62. *Lanius ludovicianus excubitorides.* White-rumped Shrike.
    Seen at Furnace Creek and Saratoga Springs in January.
63. *Vireo belli pusillus.* Least Vireo.
    A not uncommon summer resident.
64. *Dendroica auduboni.* Audubon's Warbler.
    Seen at Furnace Creek in January and April.
65. *Geothlypis trichas occidentalis.* Western Yellow-throat.
    A not uncommon summer resident.
66. *Icteria virens longicauda.* Long-tailed Chat.
    A not uncommon summer resident.
67. *Anthus pensilvanicus.* Titlark.
    Winter resident.
68. *Oroscoptes montanus.* Sage Thrasher.
    One seen at Mesquite Well in January.
69. *Mimus polyglottos.* Mockingbird.
    Observed in January and April.
70. *Harporhynchus lecontei.* Le Conte's Thrasher.
    An uncommon resident; seen at Saratoga Springs, Bennett Wells, Furnace Creek, and in the northwest arm or Mesquite Valley.
71. *Salpinctes obsoletus.* Rock Wren.
    One was seen at Mesquite Wells in January; breeds in the mountains just above the valley.
72. *Catherpes mexicanus conspersus.* Cañon Wren.
    One was seen at Saratoga Springs in February.
73. *Thryothorus bewickii bairdi.* Baird's Wren.
    Seen at Furnace Creek, Bennett Wells, and Saratoga Springs in January.
74. *Cistothorus palustris paludicola.* Tule Wren.
    Seen at Furnace Creek, Bennett Wells, and Saratoga Springs in January.
75. *Regulus calendula.* Ruby-crowned Kinglet.
    Seen at Furnace Creek in February and April.
76. *Polioptila cærulea obscura.* Western Gnatcatcher.
    One secured at Furnace Creek, January 24.
77. *Merula migratoria propinqua.* Western Robin.
    A few were seen at Furnace Creek in January.
78. *Sialia arctica.* Mountain Bluebird.
    A common winter resident.

LIST OF BIRDS FOUND IN OWENS VALLEY, CALIFORNIA.

1. *Colymbus nigricollis californicus.* Eared Grebe.
    Abundant on Owens Lake; breeds at the smaller lakes.
2. *Larus californicus.* California Gull.
    Seen in December, 1890.
3. *Larus delawarensis.* Ring-billed Gull.
    Seen at Lone Pine and Owens Lake in December, 1890.
4. *Larus philadelphia.* Bonaparte's Gull.
    One seen at Lone Pine, about the same time as the other gulls.
5. *Pelecanus erythrorhynchos.* White Pelican.
    A flock was seen at Haway Meadows in May and an individual at Lone Pine in August.
6. *Merganser serrator.* Red-breasted Merganser.
    Seen at Lone Pine and Owens Lake in winter.
7. *Anas boschas.* Mallard.
    Not uncommon; probably breeds.
8. *Anas discors.* Blue-winged Teal.
    Seen at Little Owens Lake in May.
9. *Anas cyanoptera.* Cinnamon Teal.
    Seen at Little Owens Lake; breeds.
10. *Spatula clypeata.* Shoveller.
    Common during migrations.
11. *Aythya americana.* Redhead.
    One was seen at Little Owens Lake in May.
12. *Glaucionetta clangula americana.* Golden-eye.
    Seen at Lone Pine, in December, 1890.
13. *Charitonetta albeola.* Buffle-head.
    Seen at Lone Pine in December, 1890.
14. *Branta canadensis* (subspecies?).
    A flock heard at Lone Pine in December, 1890.
15. *Dendrocygna fulva.* Fulvous Tree Duck.
    Breeds at Little Owens Lake.
16. *Plegadis guarauna.* White-faced Glossy Ibis.
    Seen at Little Owens Lake in May.
17. *Botaurus lentiginosus.* Bittern.
    Seen at Lone Pine in winter, and at Alvord and Bishop in summer.
18. *Ardea herodias.* Great Blue Heron.
    Seen at Lone Pine, and at Little Owens Lake in June.
19. *Ardea virescens.* Green Heron.
    Seen at Little Owens Lake in May.
20. *Nycticorax nycticorax nævius.* Night Heron.
    Not uncommon in the valley.
21. *Rallus virginianus.* Virginia Rail.
    Breeds at Lone Pine.
22. *Porzana carolina.* Sora.
    Seen at Little Owens Lake early in May.
23. *Fulica americana.* Coot.
    Common; breeds.
24. *Phalaropus tricolor.* Wilson's Phalarope.
    Two specimens were secured at Alvord, June 27.
25. *Recurvirostra americana.* Avocet.
    Seen at Little Owens Lake in May, 1891, at Owens Lake in June, at the north end of the valley in July, and Lone Pine in December, 1890.

26. *Gallinago delicata.* Wilson's Snipe.
   Seen at Lone Pine in winter.
27. *Tringa minutilla.* Least Sandpiper.
   Common at Owens Lake in December, 1890.
28. *Ereunetes occidentalis.* Western Sandpiper.
   Secured at Owens Lake in June.
29. *Totanus melanoleucus.* Greater Yellow-legs.
   Seen at Lone Pine in December.
30. *Numenius longirostris.* Long-billed Curlew.
   Seen at Owens Lake in December and June.
31. *Ægialitis vocifera.* Killdeer.
   Common; breeds.
32. *Ægialitis nivosa.* Snowy Plover.
   Not uncommon at Owens Lake, where it is a resident.
33. *Oreortyx pictus plumiferus.* Plumed Quail.
   Common along the eastern slope of the Sierra Nevada.
34. *Callipepla californica vallicola.* Valley Quail.
   Common resident.
35. *Zenaidura macroura.* Mourning Dove.
   Abundant breeder.
36. *Cathartes aura.* Turkey Buzzard.
   Seen all through the valley.
37. *Circus hudsonius.* Marsh Hawk.
   Not uncommon; breeds.
38. *Accipiter velox.* Sharp-shinned Hawk.
   Seen at Olancha and Bishop Creek in the latter part of May and first part of August.
39. *Accipiter cooperi.* Cooper's Hawk.
   Seen at Bishop Creek in August.
40. *Accipiter atricapillus striatulus.* Goshawk.
   A hawk thought to be this species was seen at Lone Pine in December, 1890.
41. *Buteo borealis calurus.* Western Red-tail.
   Resident; more or less common.
42. *Aquila chrysaëtos.* Golden Eagle.
   A pair was seen in June.
43. *Falco mexicanus.* Prairie Falcon.
   Not uncommon; undoubtedly breeds in the neighboring mountains.
44. *Falco columbarius.* Pigeon Hawk.
   Seen at Little Owens Lake.
45. *Falco sparverius deserticolus.* Desert Sparrow Hawk.
   A more or less common resident throughout the valley.
46. *Strix pratincola.* Barn Owl.
   The remains of one were found at Alvord.
47. *Speotyto cunicularia hypogæa.* Burrowing Owl.
   A not uncommon resident.
48. *Geococcyx californianus.* Road-runner.
   A common resident.
49. *Coccyzus americanus occidentalis.* California Cuckoo.
   One seen at Bishop, August 11.
50. *Ceryle alcyon.* Kingfisher.
   Not uncommon; breeds.
51. *Dryobates villosus hyloscopus.* Cabanis's Woodpecker.
   Seen at Bishop Creek in August.
52. *Melanerpes torquatus.* Lewis's Woodpecker.
   One seen at the head of the valley in July.

53. *Colaptes cafer.* Red-shafted Flicker.
   A not uncommon resident.
54. *Phalænoptilus nuttalli.* Poor-will.
   Not uncommon; breeding throughout the valley.
55. *Chordeiles texensis.* Texas Nighthawk.
   A common summer resident.
56. *Cypseloides niger.* Black Swift.
   Common; breeds in the mountains on each side of the valley.
57. *Chætura vauxii.* Vaux's Swift.
   Seen at Olancha about the middle of May.
58. *Aëronautes melanoleucus.* White-throated Swift.
   A common summer resident.
59. *Trochilus alexandri.* Black-chinned Humming Bird.
   A common summer resident.
60. *Calypte costæ.* Costa's Humming Bird.
   A common summer resident.
61. *Tyrannus verticalis.* Arkansas Kingbird.
   A common summer resident.
62. *Tyrannus tyrannus.* Kingbird.
   One was seen at Olancha, June 29.
63. *Myiarchus cinerascens.* Ash-throated Flycatcher.
   A not uncommon summer resident.
64. *Sayornis saya.* Say's Phœbe.
   A not uncommon breeding species.
65. *Sayornis nigricans.* Black Phœbe.
   Seen and apparently breeding at Little Owens Lake and Bishop Creek.
66. *Contopus richardsoni.* Western Wood Pewee.
   A common summer resident.
67. *Empidonax pusillus.* Little Flycatcher.
   Seen at Olancha in May, and at Lone Pine June 11.
68. *Empidonax wrightii.* Wright's Flycatcher.
   Found at Olancha in May, and at Bishop Creek in August.
69. *Otocoris alpestris arenicola.* Desert Horned Lark.
   A common summer resident.
70. *Otocoris alpestris chrysolæma.* Mexican Horned Lark.
   Found at Owens Lake in December, 1890.
71. *Cyanocitta stelleri frontalis.* Blue-fronted Jay.
   Seen at Bishop Creek in August.
72. *Aphelocoma californica.* California Jay.
   Found on the east slope of the Sierra Nevada.
73. *Corvus corax sinuatus.* Raven.
   Resident.
74. *Picicorvus columbianus.* Clarke's Nutcracker.
   Observed at the head of the valley and Bishop Creek.
75. *Cyanocephalus cyanocephalus.* Piñon Jay.
   Seen at Benton and Bishop Creek.
76. *Xanthocephalus xanthocephalus.* Yellow-headed Blackbird.
   A not uncommon resident.
77. *Agelaius phœniceus.* Red-winged Blackbird.
   A common resident.
78. *Agelaius gubernator.* Bicolored Blackbird.
   A specimen was secured at Olancha, June 11.
79. *Sturnella magna neglecta.* Western Meadowlark.
   A common resident.

80. *Icterus bullocki.* Bullock's Oriole.
    A common summer resident.
81. *Scolecophagus cyanocephalus.* Brewer's Blackbird.
    A common summer resident. It may be a resident.
82. *Carpodacus mexicanus frontalis.* House Finch.
    A common resident.
83. *Spinus psaltria.* Arkansas Goldfinch.
    A common summer resident.
84. *Poocætes gramineus confinis.* Western Vesper Sparrow.
    Not uncommon at the head of the valley.
85. *Ammodramus sandwichensis alaudinus.* Western Savanna Sparrow.
    A not uncommon resident.
86. *Chondestes grammacus strigatus.* Western Lark Sparrow.
    A common summer resident.
87. *Zonotrichia leucophrys.* White-crowned Sparrow.
    Observed along the east slope of the Sierra Nevada, where it breeds higher up.
88. *Spizella breweri.* Brewer's Sparrow.
    A common summer resident.
89. *Spizella atrigularis.* Black-chinned Sparrow.
    Secured at Independence Creek on the east slope of the Sierra Nevada.
90. *Junco hyemalis thurberi.* Thurber's Junco.
    Winter visitant in the valley; breeds on the east slope of the Sierra Nevada.
91. *Amphispiza bilineata.* Black-throated Sparrow.
    A common summer resident.
92. *Amphispiza belli nevadensis.* Sage Sparrow.
    A not uncommon resident.
93. *Melospiza fasciata heermanni.* Heermann's Song Sparrow.
    Tolerably common resident.
94. *Melospiza lincolni.* Lincoln's Sparrow.
    Found breeding at Independence Creek, on the east slope of the Sierra Nevada.
95. *Passerella iliaca megarhyncha.* Thick-billed Sparrow.
    Found in the same place as the preceding species.
96. *Pipilo maculatus megalonyx.* Spurred Towhee.
    A not uncommon resident.
97. *Pipilo chlorurus.* Green-tailed Towhee.
    A common summer resident in the upper end of the valley.
98. *Habia melanocephala.* Black-headed Grosbeak.
    Seen at Olancha and Ash Creek in May, and Independence Creek in June.
99. *Guiraca cœrulea eurhyncha.* Western Blue Grosbeak.
    A common summer resident.
100. *Passerina amœna.* Lazuli Bunting.
    A common summer resident.
101. *Piranga ludoviciana.* Western Tanager.
    A not uncommon summer resident.
102. *Petrochelidon lunifrons.* Cliff Swallow.
    A common summer resident.
103. *Chelidon erythrogaster.* Barn Swallow.
    A common summer resident.
104. *Tachycineta thalassina.* Violet Green Swallow.
    A common summer resident.
105. *Clivicola riparia.* Bank Swallow.
    Common at Alvord the last of June, where it was breeding.
106. *Stelgidopteryx serripennis.* Rough-winged Swallow.
    A not uncommon summer resident.

107. *Ampelis cedrorum.* Cedar Bird.
  A pair was seen at Lone Pine June 14.
108. *Phainopepla nitens.* Phainopepla.
  One was seen at Morans in July.
109. *Lanius ludovicianus excubitorides.* White-rumped Shrike.
  A common resident.
110. *Vireo gilvus swainsoni.* Western Warbling Vireo.
  A not uncommon summer resident.
111. *Vireo belli pusillus.* Least Vireo.
  A not uncommon summer resident.
112. *Helminthophila celata lutescens.* Lutescent Warbler.
  A few migrants were seen at Little Owens Lake in May.
113. *Dendroica æstiva.* Yellow Warbler.
  A common summer resident.
114. *Dendroica auduboni.* Audubon's Warbler.
  Occurs in winter, and probably breeds on Independence and Bishop creeks.
115. *Dendroica townsendi.* Townsend's Warbler.
  Migrants were seen at Little Owens Lake.
116. *Geothlypis macgillivrayi.* Macgillivray's Warbler.
  Found with young at Bishop Creek in August.
117. *Geothlypis trichas occidentalis.* Western Yellow-throat.
  A common summer resident.
118. *Icteria virens longicauda.* Long-tailed Chat.
  A common summer resident.
119. *Sylvania pusilla pileolata.* Pileolated Warbler.
  A not uncommon migrant.
120. *Anthus pensilvanicus.* Titlark.
  A common winter resident.
121. *Cinclus mexicanus.* Water Ousel.
  Follows down the streams into the valley in winter.
122. *Oroscoptes montanus.* Sage Thrasher.
  Breeds commonly in the upper part of the valley.
123. *Mimus polyglottos.* Mockingbird.
  A not uncommon resident.
124. *Harporhynchus lecontei.* LeConte's Thrasher.
  A common resident.
125. *Heleodytes brunneicapillus.* Cactus Wren.
  Breeds in the southern end of the valley.
126. *Salpinctes obsoletus.* Rock Wren.
  A common resident.
127. *Thryothorus bewickii bairdi.* Baird's Wren.
  Common at Lone Pine in December, 1890.
128. *Troglodytes aëdon aztecus.* Western House Wren.
  Seen in migrations and probably breeds on the eastern slope of the Sierra Nevada.
129. *Cistothorus palustris paludicola.* Tule Wren.
  A not uncommon resident.
130. *Parus gambeli.* Mountain Chickadee.
  Rather common along the eastern slope of the Sierra Nevada.
131. *Psaltriparus minimus californicus.* California Bush-Tit.
  Seen on Independence and Bishop creeks.
132. *Polioptila cærulea obscura.* Western Gnatcatcher.
  Seen at Independence Creek in June.
133. *Myadestes townsendii.* Townsend's Solitaire.
  Seen at Lone Pine in December, 1890.

134. *Turdus ustulatus.* Russet-backed Thrush.
   One seen at Olancha about the middle of May.
135. *Turdus aonalaschkæ auduboni.* Audubon's Hermit Thrush.
   Breeds on Independence and Bishop creeks.
136. *Merula migratoria propinqua.* Western Robin.
   Common summer resident along the eastern slope of the Sierra Nevada.
137. *Sialia arctica.* Mountain Bluebird.
   Common along the eastern slope of the Sierra Nevada.

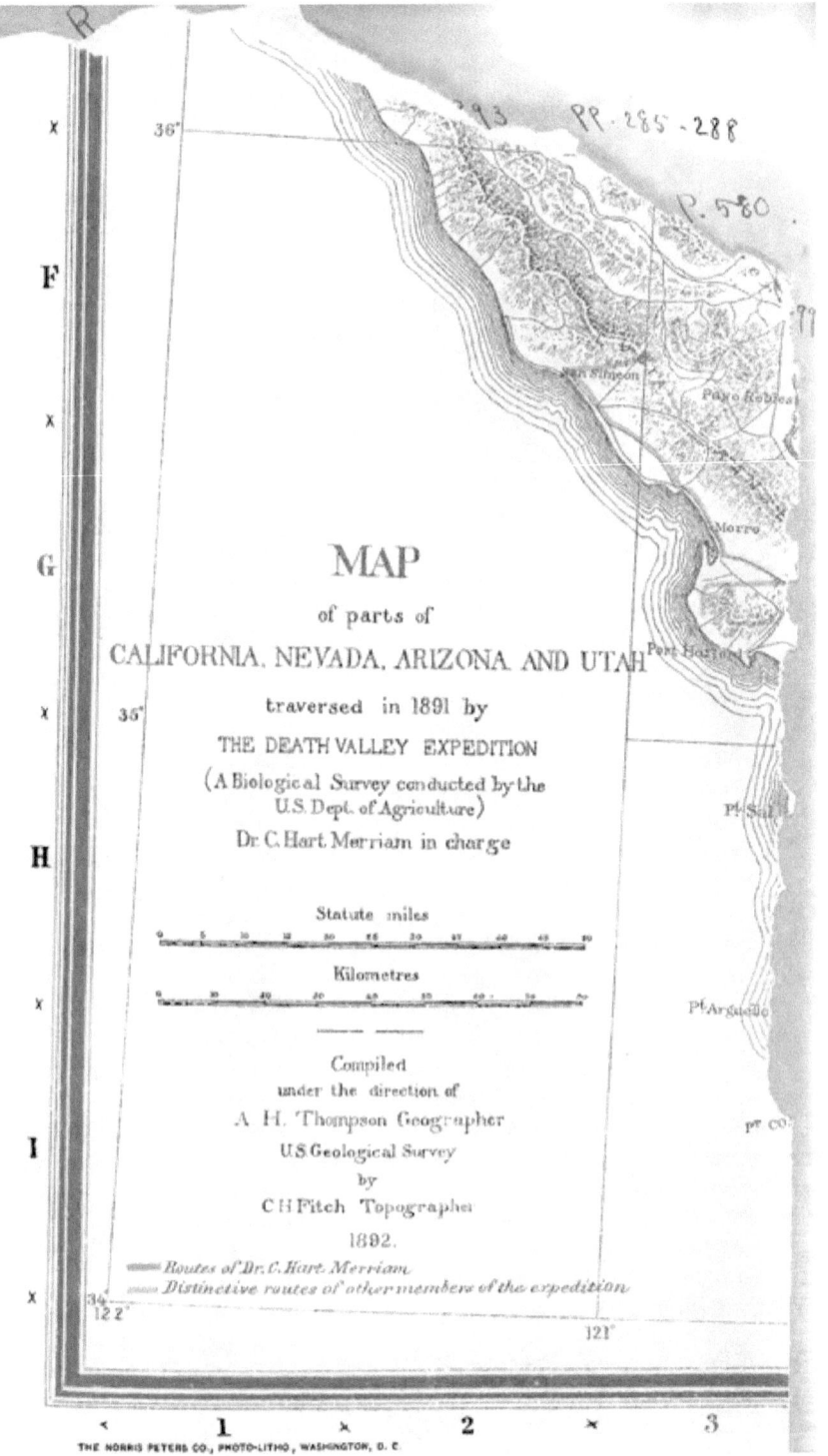